Good Housekeeping

The Complete Healthy Cookbook

Good Housekeeping

The Complete Healthy Cookbook

DELICIOUS AND NUTRITIOUS TRIPLE-TESTED RECIPES

COLLINS & BROWN

First published in the United Kingdom in 2013 by
Collins & Brown
10 Southcombe Street
London
W14 0RA

An imprint of Anova Books Company Ltd

This edition published in 2013 for WHSmith

The Good Housekeeping website is
www.allboutyou.com/goodhousekeeping

10 9 8 7 6 5 4 3 2 1

ISBN 978-1-908449-59-7

A catalogue record for this book is available from the British Library.

Repro by Dot Gradations Ltd, UK
Printed and bound by 1010 Printing International Ltd, China

This book can be ordered direct from the publisher at
www.anovabooks.com

Picture Credits:

Neil Barclay (pages 87, 90, 91, 115, 121 and 217); Steve Baxter (page 310); Martin Brigdale (pages 119, 170, 171, 188, 191, 223, 240, 271 and 303); Nicki Dowey (pages 26, 28, 29, 31, 32, 33, 34, 37, 39, 45, 46, 47, 49, 52, 53, 54, 58, 60, 61, 61, 63, 64, 65, 67, 69, 70, 71, 72, 73, 77, 78, 79, 84, 88, 89, 92, 93, 95, 98, 100, 101, 107, 109, 112, 113, 114, 116, 122, 123, 126, 127, 129, 131, 135, 138, 143, 144, 145, 146, 147, 148, 150, 151, 153, 154, 155, 157, 158, 159, 161, 166, 168, 176, 177, 180, 181, 183, 184, 185, 190, 193, 195, 197, 198, 201, 202, 203, 207, 210, 214, 215, 219, 220, 221, 224, 230, 231, 233, 235, 236, 237, 238, 239, 241, 242, 244, 248, 249, 250, 251, 252, 254, 260, 265, 266, 269, 272, 273, 274, 279, 280, 281, 287, 290, 291, 292, 293, 295, 296, 297, 298, 300, 306, 307, 309, 311, 312, 315, 318, 319, 320, 321, 322, 323, 324, 326, 327, 328, 329, 330, 332 and 333); Will Heap (pages 41, 96, 130, 136, 142, 163, 169, 212, 229, 253 and 270); Gareth Morgans (pages 57, 267, 275, 276, 282 and 288); Craig Robertson (pages 29, 30, 35, 38, 44, 48, 51, 56, 81, 86, 97, 04, 108, 110, 120, 137, 160, 162, 165, 174, 182, 186, 187, 194, 196, 204, 205, 213, 224, 227, 228, 234, 245, 255, 256, 257, 258, 259, 261, 286, 299, 304 and 314); Lucinda Symons (pages 50, 68, 82, 85, 117, 124, 132, 179, 200 and 264)
Home Economists: Anna Burges-Lumsden, Joanna Farrow, Emma Jane Frost, Teresa Goldfinch, Alice Hart, Lucy McKelvie, Kim Morphew, Bridget Sargeson, Sarah Tildesley, Jennifer White and Mari Mererid Williams
Stylists: Wei Tang, Sarah Tildesley, Helen Trent and Fanny Ward
Cover Photograph: Gareth Morgans

Notes

Both metric and imperial measures are given for the recipes. Follow either set of measures, not a mixture of both, as they are not interchangeable.
All spoon measures are level.
1 tsp = 5ml spoon; 1 tbsp = 15ml spoon.
Ovens and grills must be preheated to the specified temperature.
Medium eggs should be used except where otherwise specified.
Dietary guidelines
Note that certain recipes contain raw or lightly cooked eggs. The young, elderly, pregnant women and anyone with immune-deficiency disease should avoid these because of the slight risk of salmonella.
Note that some recipes contain alcohol. Check the ingredients list before serving to children.

Contents

Foreword

I know it's an old adage, but we are what we eat, and I feel fortunate that I was taught from an early age that you should feed your body with food that will make it run efficiently. It's similar to filling your car with the wrong fuel, which I imagine would allow it to run smoothly for a couple of miles, then splutter a little and eventually stop in indignation. The same is true of your body, there's only so much processed food it can take before the effects of eating badly become apparent.

With obesity and Type 2 diabetes rates still surging, it's high time that more of us learnt how to eat healthily – and this doesn't just mean a diet of brown rice and worthy lentils but rather fuelling your body with food that's full of the right sort of things, rather than salt, sugar, fat and more calories than we need (although a little of these in moderation is a good thing in my books). It comes down to a simple statement: we are eating too much and not moving enough. The virtues of physical activity are undeniable – muscles are strengthened and toned, calories are burnt and appetite is regulated. What's not to like about that?

It's important to realise that healthier cooking for you and your family can be quick, easy and enjoyable. This fantastic book is filled with nutritious recipes that are triple-tested in our dedicated kitchens so they are sure to succeed (and be full of flavour!). There's also plenty of useful information to aid you in munching your way to a happier, healthier you.

So turn the page and allow yourself be inspired to rustle up healthy family meals, which are sure to become firm favourites.

Enjoy!

Meike.

Meike Beck
Cookery Editor
Good Housekeeping

Basics

EAT WELL, STAY WELL

'We are what we eat' – nutritionists from around the world agree that the food we eat has an important effect on our health and vitality. From the moment of conception and throughout life, diet plays a crucial role in helping us stay fit and healthy. A healthy balanced diet can protect against serious illnesses such heart disease and cancer, increase resistance to colds and other infections, boost energy levels, help combat the stresses of modern living and also improve physical and mental performance. So, eating a diet that is healthy, varied and tasty should be everyone's aim.

Choose wisely

Our body needs over forty different nutrients to function and stay healthy. Some, such as carbohydrates, proteins and fats, are required in relatively large amounts; others, such as vitamins, minerals and trace elements, are required in minute amounts, but are nonetheless essential for health. No single food or food group provides all the nutrients we need, which is why we need to eat a variety of different foods. Making sure your body gets all the nutrients it needs is easy if you focus on foods that are nutrient rich and dump those highly refined and processed foods that provide lots of saturated fat, sugar and calories but not much else.

Nutrition labelling

The five key nutrients are calories, sugar, fat, saturated fat and salt. Two sets of guidelines that claim to help us select a healthy balanced diet are currently in use. The traffic light scheme developed by the Food Standards Agency provides information on fat, saturated fat, sugar and salt and uses a red, amber or green colour coding to indicate whether a food is high, medium or low in these nutrients. The other scheme is based on Guideline Daily Amounts (GDAs) and gives an indication of how many calories, fat, salt, sugar and fibre a food contains and what it contributes to the amount of that nutrient you should eat in a day. GDAs are guidelines for an average person of a healthy weight and average level of activity, and are just that – a guide, not a target. You should try to eat no more than the GDAs for sugars, fat, saturated fat and salt. The GDA values on the front of pack labels are based on the average requirements of an adult woman.

Fruit & Vegetables: Five a day

One of the easiest ways to stay healthy is to eat plenty of fruit and vegetables. We can probably all remember being told by our parents to eat our 'greens' because they were good for us, and all the major reports on healthy eating have endorsed this good advice. It's no coincidence that in Mediterranean countries, where people eat almost twice the amount of fruit and vegetables that we do in the UK, they live longer and healthier lives. Fruit and vegetables contain an arsenal of disease-fighting compounds – vitamins, minerals, fibre and phytochemicals, which is why nutrition experts believe that they are the cornerstone of a healthy diet. Eating a diet rich in fruit and vegetables can reduce the risk of a range of medical problems including heart disease, stroke, high blood pressure, certain types of cancer, cataracts and an eye condition called age-related macular degeneration, dementia and Alzheimer's disease.

Variety is key

Wherever we shop, most of us are lucky enough to have a wide range of different fruit and vegetables available to us, but do we really take advantage of the range? It's very easy to get stuck in a rut of buying the same things from one week to the next. Variety may be the spice of life, but it's also the key to a healthy diet and is particularly important when it comes to fruit and vegetables. Different coloured fruit and vegetables contain different vitamins, minerals and phytochemicals that help to keep you healthy in different ways, and so to make sure you get a good selection of all these nutrients you need to eat a variety of different produce. When you're buying fruit and vegetables don't just stick to your same old favourites – be adventurous and try something new. You'll find plenty of recipes to tempt you in this book.

Add colour to your meals

You probably already know that you should be eating at least five servings of fruit and vegetables a day, but did you know you should also be eating a rainbow? When you're planning meals, aim to fill your plate with colour – think of red, orange, yellow, green and purple fruit and vegetables and try to eat at least one serving from each of the colour bands every day.

Assessing nutrients

Another quick and easy way to assess if a food is high or low in a particular nutrient is to use the table below. Look at the amount of a particular nutrient per serving or per 100g (3½oz) for snacks or cooking ingredients and check the table below to find out if it's high or low.

	High	**Low**
Fat	more than 20g	less than 3g
Saturated fat	more than 5g	less than 1g
Sugar	more than 10g	less than 2g
Fibre	more than 3g	less than 0.5g
Sodium	more than 0.5g	less than 0.1g
Salt	more than 1.3g	less than 0.3g

GDAs

	Women	**Men**	**Children (5–10 years)**
Energy (calories)	2,000	2,500	1,800
Protein (g)	45	55	24
Carbohydrate (g)	230	300	220
Fat (g)	70	95	70
Saturated fat (g)	20	30	20
Total sugars (g)	90	120	85
Dietary fibre (g)	24	24	15
Sodium (g)	2.4	2.4	
Salt	6	6	4

Carbohydrates

Carbohydrates provide the body with the most readily accessible form of energy. Carbohydrates in the form of sugars are found in fruit, milk and sugar; starch carbohydrates are familiar in cereals, pasta, rice, potatoes, bread and pulses. In a healthy diet, starch carbohydrates supply a higher proportion of energy than fats or sugar carbohydrates.

With the recent craze for low-carbohydrate diets, you may be forgiven for thinking that carbohydrates are best avoided. In fact, this couldn't be further from the truth. Most nutritionists agree that foods in this group are an important part of a healthy balanced diet.

However, not all carbs are equal. Most of the vitamins and protective components in grains are concentrated in the bran and germ layers of the grain, but when grains are refined, as for instance in the production of white flour, the bran and germ are removed and most of the fibre and some of the nutrients are stripped away. This is why it is better to choose wholegrain carbohydrates such as brown rice and wholemeal bread over refined carbohydrates. Studies have shown that diets rich in wholegrain foods can reduce the risk of heart disease, stroke, certain types of cancer and Type 2 diabetes.

The Glycaemic Index

During the digestive process, carbohydrates need to be broken down into glucose – the simplest form of sugar – before they can be absorbed by your body. Recent research suggests the rate at which carbohydrates are broken down can also determine their healthiness. The Glycaemic Index (GI) is a system used for ranking carbohydrates according to how quickly they are broken down. Foods with a low GI (less than 55), such as lentils, apples and pears, are absorbed more slowly and steadily and generate a slow release of sugar into the bloodstream. Foods with a high GI (more than 70), such as cornflakes, bagels and soft drinks, are broken down into sugar quickly, which results in a sudden rush of sugar into the bloodstream. While this can be useful for athletes who need to replenish blood sugar after strenuous exercise, it is not necessary for the rest of us.

Diverse benefits

Although the GI diet was originally developed to help people with diabetes achieve better control of their blood sugar, the benefits are certainly not restricted to diabetics. Studies have shown that following a low-GI diet can help increase levels of 'good' cholesterol and reduce 'bad' cholesterol in the blood, which will help to reduce the risk of heart disease. Recent studies also show that people who ate a low-GI diet lost more weight than people who ate a higher GI diet. The GI is only one measurement of what makes a food healthy. Other factors, such as the vitamin content and the amount of fat a food contains, will affect its overall healthiness. Foods that have a low to medium GI and are also low in sugar and fat are the best choice.

LOW-GI SNACKS

Everyone needs to snack sometimes. Resist the temptation to reach for the biscuits or processed snacks and tuck into these healthy low-GI snacks instead.

Fresh fruit, nuts and seeds are ideal low-GI foods. Make sure you take some of each with you whenever you go out, or travel.

Dried apricots and prunes are delicious nutrient-packed low-GI snacks, and are the perfect handy snack instead of sweets.

Keep a dip and crudités in the fridge for emergency snacking. Good dips are mashed avocado (guacamole) and hummus. Mayonnaise blended with a little mustard and natural yogurt is excellent also.

An avocado is a light meal in itself, highly nutritious – a good source of EFAs (essential fatty acids) and vitamin E – and will keep hunger pangs at bay. Spoon a little extra virgin olive oil or your favourite health oil into the cavity and enjoy.

A couple of squares of dark plain chocolate (70% cocoa solids) is a permissible treat, and better than a sugary snack.

Bread

- White and brown processed breads in all forms have the highest GI ratings.
- Wholegrain, Granary, pumpernickel and seed breads, stoneground wholewheat and rye breads, sourdough breads.

Breakfast cereals

- Processed breakfast cereals such as Shredded Wheat, Rice Crispies, instant porridge oats, puffed grain cereals, cornflakes and those high in added sugar or honey such as crunchies and cereal bars.
- Porridge made with traditional rolled oats or stoneground oatmeal; sugar-free/low-sugar mueslis, All Bran.

Pasta

- As long as you eat smaller than normal portions and do not overcook it, pasta is generally OK. Rice noodles are medium-high GI and gluten-free pasta (which is often made from corn) is high GI.
- All kinds of durum wheat pasta; fresh pasta made with eggs; cellophane and glass noodles (which are made from pea and bean flours).

Rice

- Most varieties of white long-grain rice, including processed American long-grain, jasmine rice, and all short round varieties such as pudding, risotto and sticky glutinous rice.
- White and brown basmati, brown, red and wild rice.

Potatoes

- All potatoes: boiled, mashed, fried, instant, and so on.
- Boiled new potatoes (these are still high GI, but are significantly lower than maincrop potatoes); sweet potatoes and yams.

Sugar

Though it's sensible to use as little sugar as possible, the only form of sugar that is high GI is glucose. Table sugar (sucrose) and honey are medium GI; the sugar found in fresh fruit (fructose) is low GI. You can now buy low-GI fruit sugar to replace table sugar in tea and coffee and in baking. This is expensive, but you need one-third less. When baking with fruit sugar, reduce the cooking temperature by 25°C.

Chocolate

Generally, chocolates and bars tend to have medium-GI values. Because of their added sugar and fat, however, they are still indulgence foods. Dark plain chocolate, with a minimum of 70% cocoa solids, is low GI. Milk chocolate is also low GI, but is less healthy than dark chocolate because it contains more fat and sugar.

Dried fruits

These are low to medium GI. The one exception is dates, which are very high GI and have a GI value of 100.

FATS, FIBRE, SALT & PROTEIN

Fats – The Healthy & Not So Healthy

Of all the nutrients in our diet fat must be the most debated and the most misunderstood. Although, in terms of healthy eating, fat is often cast as the villain, it's worth remembering that it also plays a beneficial role. In the body, fat cushions and protects the vital organs, provides energy stores and helps insulate the body. In the diet, it is necessary for the absorption of fat-soluble vitamins (A, D, E and K) and to provide essential fatty acids that the body can't make itself. While some fat is essential, many of us are eating too much of the wrong types of fat and not enough of the right types. A high-fat diet, particularly one that contains a lot of saturated 'animal' fats, is known to increase the risk of problems such as heart disease, stroke and certain types of cancer. There are three types of fat: saturated, monounsaturated and polyunsaturated fatty acids, which occur in different proportions in foods. Saturated fatty acids are linked to higher blood cholesterol, which can then lead to heart disease.

Polyunsaturated fats

Omega-6 fats These are mostly found in vegetable oils and margarines such as sunflower oil, safflower oil, corn oil and soya bean oil. Omega-6 fats help lower the LDL 'bad' cholesterol in the blood, but if you eat too much they will also lower the 'good' HDL cholesterol.

Omega-3 fats These are found mainly in oil-rich fish such as salmon, fresh tuna, mackerel and sardines, in linseeds (flax) and rapeseed oil. They help to protect the heart by making the blood less sticky and likely to clot, by lowering blood pressure, and by encouraging the muscles lining the artery walls to relax, thus improving blood flow to the heart. It's important to have a balance of omega-3 and omega-6 fats in the diet. At the moment most of us have too much omega-6 fats and not enough omega-3 fats and recent research suggests that low levels of omega-3s in the blood may contribute to depression, antisocial behaviour and schizophrenia.

Monounsaturated fats

Monounsaturated fats are found mainly in olive oil, walnut oil and rapeseed oil, nuts and avocados. They can help reduce the risk of heart disease by lowering LDL 'bad' cholesterol.

Saturated fats

Saturated 'animal' fats are found in full-fat dairy products (cheese, yogurt, milk, cream), lard, fatty cuts of meat and meat products such as sausages and burgers, pastry, cakes, biscuits, and coconut and palm oil. A diet high in saturated fats can raise levels of LDL 'bad' cholesterol in the blood, which will cause narrowing of the arteries and increase the risk of heart attacks and stroke.

Trans fats

Trans fats occur naturally in small amounts in meat and dairy products, but they are also produced during the process of hydrogenation that is used to convert liquid vegetable oils into semi-solid fats in the manufacture of some types of margarine. Trans fats are most commonly found in biscuits, cakes, pastries, meat pies, sausages, crackers and takeaway foods. Although chemically trans fats are still unsaturated fat, studies show that in the body they behave like saturated fat, causing blood cholesterol levels to rise; in fact, some studies suggest that trans fats are worse than saturated fats.

Eating More Fibre

Despite the fact that it passes through the digestive tract largely undigested, fibre plays an important role in helping us stay fit and healthy. It helps keep our digestive tract in good working order and can also help reduce high blood cholesterol and keep blood sugar levels stable. If you start the day with a wholegrain cereal and eat plenty of fresh fruit and vegetables, you will easily have enough fibre in your diet. Fibre can be divided into two groups – insoluble and soluble; both groups help keep the body healthy in a different way.

Insoluble fibre

Insoluble fibre, which is found mainly in wholegrain cereals but also in fruit, vegetables and pulses, helps to prevent constipation and problems such as haemorrhoids (piles) and diverticular disease. It works by absorbing water, making the stools larger, softer and easier to pass. Sometimes referred to as 'nature's broom', insoluble fibre also speeds the passage of waste material through the body. The faster waste materials are excreted, the less time potentially harmful substances have to linger in the bowel.

Soluble fibre

Soluble fibre, found in oats and oat bran, beans and pulses and some fruit and vegetables, helps to lower high blood cholesterol levels, which in turn will help reduce the risk of heart disease. Soluble fibre also helps to slow the absorption of sugar into the bloodstream, which makes foods rich in soluble fibre a good choice for people with diabetes or anyone trying to balance blood sugar levels. The Guideline Daily Amount of fibre is 24g for adults and 15g for children aged between 5 and 10 years (see page 11); to reach this target, most of us need to increase our fibre intake by about 50%.

Cutting Down on Salt

Reducing the amount of salt in our diet is, say health experts, one of the most important steps we can take to reduce the risk of high blood pressure, a condition that affects one in three adults in the UK. Experts have calculated that reducing our salt intake to 6g a day would reduce the number of people suffering from stroke by 22% and from heart attacks by 16%, saving around 34,000 lives each year.

Hidden salt

You may think the easiest way to cut back on salt is not to sprinkle salt over your food when you're at the table, but unfortunately the answer isn't quite that simple – only around 15% of the salt we eat comes from salt added to our food during cooking and at the table. Three-quarters of all the salt we consume is hidden in processed foods – one small tin of chicken soup, for instance, can contain well over half the recommended daily intake of salt for an adult.

Re-educating our taste buds

Our taste for salt is something we learn to like the more we eat. But just in the same way that we can teach our taste buds to enjoy foods with less sugar, we can train them to enjoy foods with less salt (sodium chloride). If you gradually reduce the amount of salt you eat, the taste receptors on the tongue become more sensitive to salt. This process takes between two and three weeks. Use herbs and spices to enhance the natural flavours of foods and before long you'll be enjoying the real taste of food – not the flavour of salt.

Protein

Protein is made up of smaller units called amino acids, which are an important part of every cell in the body and therefore necessary for healthy skin, teeth, internal organs and other tissues. The body can manufacture some of these amino acids itself, but the 'essential amino acids' must be derived from food. Animal protein and soya protein contain almost all of these and are regarded as 'complete'. The best sources of protein are meat, poultry, fish, eggs, dairy products such as yogurt, milk and cheese, and soya products. Other vegetable proteins are lacking in one or more of the essential amino acids.

VITAMINS & MINERALS

Vitamins

Vitamins are vital for a variety of body processes and a deficiency will result in illness. Our bodies cannot make all the vitamins we need, so we have to get them from our food and drink. They are vital to good health and effective in very small amounts. The fat-soluble vitamins A, D, E and K – as their name suggests – are largely derived from foods that contain fat, though the body acquires most of its vitamin D from the action of sunlight on the skin. These vitamins are stored in the liver. Water-soluble vitamins B and C cannot be stored by the body so a regular intake through the diet is important.

Vitamin A – needed for growth and development, healthy eyesight and good skin. Yellow, orange and green fruit and vegetables are rich in the antioxidant betacarotene, which the body converts into vitamin A.

Vitamin B complex: B1 (thiamin), B2 (riboflavin), B3 (niacin), B6 (pyridoxine), B12 (cobalamin), biotin, pantothenic acid, folic acid – these vitamins work together to help digestion and aid resistance to infection. Whole grains are rich in these vitamins, as are sprouting seeds, green vegetables and citrus fruits.

Vitamin C – an antioxidant that protects the bones, joints, teeth, gums, nerves, glands and other tissues and aids the absorption of iron. Found in varying amounts in all fresh fruits and vegetables.

Vitamin E – an antioxidant held in cell membranes that is essential for normal metabolism, aids heart function and may protect against heart disease. it is found mainly in whole grains, seeds, nuts and green vegetables.

Minerals

These are needed in tiny quantities and are far more readily absorbed by the body than those from supplements. Some of the more important minerals are calcium (for healthy teeth and bones), iron (helps transport oxygen in the blood), magnesium, zinc, potassium, phosphorous, sulphur and selenium. A deficiency of iron will lead to anaemia. Meat and leafy green vegetables are good sources of iron, and the absorption of this mineral is greatly increased if some vitamin Crich food – even a glass of orange juice – is consumed at the same meal.

Antioxidants

Some vitamins and minerals are antioxidants: they can reduce the risk of many diseases by protecting cells against 'free radicals', which may be harmful.

Principles of healthy eating

1 **Water** Water is the elixir of life, and is nature's prime detoxifier.

Aim to drink at least 1 litre (1¾ pints) per day, preferably 1–2 litres (1¾–3½ pints).

Start the day with a glass of hot water and lemon.

Have a small bottle or a large glass of mineral or filtered water by your side always, and sip regularly.

Drinking water at room temperature is easier on the digestion than ice-cold water.

Bored with plain water? Flavour your water with a slice of lemon, lime or some peeled and chopped fresh ginger.

2 **Superfoods** For tiptop nutrition and long-term health, incorporate these foods into your regular eating plan:

- Avocado
- Broccoli
- Cabbage
- Carrots
- Garlic
- Ripe tomatoes
- Sprouted seeds: for example, alfalfa
- Watercress
- Winter squash (dense orange-fleshed varieties such as butternut)
- Apples
- Apricots
- Bananas
- Berries
- Kiwi fruit
- Lemons
- Pineapple
- Live, natural yogurt
- Miso
- Oats
- Sea vegetables (seaweed): for example, nori strips

3 **Good fats & oils** Fats are essential to all life processes, including the production of cholesterol, which is vital for nerve communication and an essential component of the brain, nerve fibres and sex hormones. For this reason, a low-fat diet is not a good idea for long-term health. The trick is to substitute bad (processed, hydrogenated and highly saturated) fats for omega-rich good fats and oils, found in oily fish, nuts and seeds, and to eat small amounts of other natural fats such as olive oil and butter.

Eat 1–2 tbsp extra virgin (cold pressed) oils every day. Olive oil, hemp, linseed and blends of omega oils are especially good. Do not heat. Use them to drizzle over salads, vegetables and fish, and in dips.

4 **Sensible eating** Eat plenty of foods rich in carbohydrates and fibre; whenever possible, choose wholegrain cereals. Keep sugary foods and drinks as a treat rather than something you consume every day. Avoid adding salt.

5 **Vegetables, salads & fruit** Vegetables, salads and fruit are star performers in all healthy eating plans. Eat at least 5 servings of fruit and/or vegetables each day. Not only do they contain a storehouse of vitamins and minerals, they also help to keep the body at its optimum pH, which is slightly alkaline.

6 **Eat regularly** Skipping meals leads to energy dips, stresses your system and is a sure-fire way to put on weight. Eating regularly keeps your body's physical and mental energy levels steady, avoiding hunger pangs and the need to snack.

Never skip breakfast – it's the most important meal of the day to set you up and it also sustains your energy levels through until lunchtime.
Eat slowly, and take your time – it takes 20 minutes for your body to register it is full and satiated.

7 **Enjoy a variety of food** Enjoy as wide a variety of foods as possible. This way you will ensure your diet contains all the health-giving micronutrients it needs for optimum health. It also helps to avoid developing intolerances to particular foods.

8 **Eat the right amount to be a healthy weight**

9 **Drink alcohol in moderation** If you drink alcohol, drink sensibly and stay within the safe guidelines, which are no more than 3 units of alcohol a day for women and no more than 4 units of alcohol a day for men, with at least one alcohol-free day a week.

10 **Exercise** Regular exercise is vital. It energises you, raises your metabolic rate, helps to maintain your correct weight, is a de-stressor, releases feel-good hormones, and helps you sleep better.

11 **Stress less** Stress is a major modern disease and comes in all shapes and sizes, be it pressure at work, from noise and traffic, or the constant barrage of environmental and electronic pollution. The body reacts to stress by going into red alert and your immune system is compromised. Learning to deal with stress, and removing stress from your life wherever you can, is essential for your health.

Build some form of relaxation into your daily life.
Learn simple deep breathing techniques.
Reduce the hours you watch TV or work/play on the computer. Listen to soothing music instead.

12 **Sleep** Sleep is Nature's happy pill, the ultimate physical and mental reviver, and the secret to staying young. Take care of your sleep and your body and your immune system will take care of you. Make getting enough sleep a top priority.

Make your bedroom a peaceful haven.
Avoid drinking coffee or too much alcohol in the evening.
Wind down before you go to bed.

13 **Positive outlook** How you feel has a critical impact on your health and overall wellbeing. Cultivate an optimistic outlook and do something that makes you happy every day. Laughter is great medicine, and is completely free.

SPECIAL DIETS: DAIRY FREE, WHEAT FREE & GLUTEN FREE

In recent years there has been a growing awareness that for some people food allergy or intolerance can cause a range of health problems, including eczema, asthma, skin rashes, migraine and irritable bowel syndrome (IBS). Any food can provoke an allergic reaction, although some are more likely than others. Wheat and dairy products are two of the most common causes of food intolerance.

Dairy-free Diets

Foods to avoid on a dairy-free diet:

- Milk
- Cheese
- Yogurt
- Butter
- Most margarines and low-fat spreads
- Milk chocolate
- Cream
- Ice cream
- Fromage frais
- Dairy desserts

Many processed foods contain lactose (milk sugar) or traces of cow's milk protein, and there is also a host of other names for ingredients derived from milk.

Avoid products that list any of the following words in the ingredients:

- Milk protein, milk, milk powder, skimmed milk powder
- Non-fat milk solids
- Animal fat
- Whey
- Casein or caseinate
- Hydrolysed casein or whey
- Lactose
- Lacalbumin
- Lactoglobulin
- Ghee

Non-dairy alternatives

Soya milk & yogurt

If you are allergic to dairy products or lactose-intolerant, drinking milk may cause a variety of symptoms, including skin rashes and eczema, asthma and irritable bowel syndrome. Soya milk and yogurt are useful alternatives – look for calcium-enriched products. Good non-dairy sources of calcium suitable for adding to smoothies include dark green leafy vegetables, such as watercress and spinach, and apricots.

Silken tofu

This protein-rich dairy-free product adds a creamy texture to salad dressings, sauces and desserts.

Calcium concern

Milk and dairy products are a major source of calcium in our diet. If you can't get enough calcium from your diet you may need to take a supplement. Check with a pharmacist that the supplement you choose does not contain lactose.

Good non-dairy sources of calcium include: canned fish such as pilchards and sardines, dark green leafy vegetables such as spinach and watercress, bread, apricots, canned, fresh and dried beans, including baked beans, and hard water.

Wheat- & Gluten-free Diets

Many people are discovering that their body reacts badly when they eat wheat. Symptoms include bloating, IBS, headaches and tiredness. Sometimes simply reducing your wheat intake can help; but some people may have to avoid wheat altogether. Coeliac disease is a more serious condition than wheat intolerance. It is caused by an intolerance to gluten, a protein found in wheat, rye, barley and oats. A gluten-free diet means cutting out wheat, oats, barley, rye and all products made using them. Products labelled as being wheat free are not necessarily gluten free because they may contain other gluten-containing grains. Equally, products labelled gluten free are not necessarily wheat free because they may contain wheat starch (gluten is a protein and people with a gluten intolerance don't have a problem with the starchy part of the grain).

Foods to avoid on a gluten-free diet include:

- Wheat, oats, barley, rye
- Wheat flour (white, wholemeal, self-raising)
- All foods made with wheat flour (bread, pasta, cakes, biscuits, crackers, pastry, batter, semolina, couscous)
- All products made with barley meal or flour
- All products made with rye meal or flour (rye bread or rye crispbread)
- All products containing oatmeal or oat flour
- Breakfast cereals containing wheat, bran, oats, barley
- Any dish that includes breadcrumbs
- Sausages, except 100% meat sausages and those labelled gluten free
- Sauces and gravies thickened with flour
- Many manufactured goods contain flour as a thickening agent or filler so it is essential to check the label on individual products.

Substitute:

- Rice, corn, polenta (cornmeal), buckwheat, quinoa
- Rice, potato, soya, corn (maize) or chickpea flour
- Arrowroot, cornflour, sago or tapioca
- Cornflakes, Rice Crispies
- Rice or buckwheat noodles, gluten-free pasta
- Gluten-free bread or bread mix, puffed rice cakes, rice crackers, taco shells

WATCHING YOUR WEIGHT

Food gives us energy – in the form of calories – which is burnt up naturally with everyday living, but if we consume more calories than the body can use, even with increased exercise, excess calories are stored in the body as fat and the result is weight gain. If you need to shed excess pounds and achieve a healthy weight, avoid high-calorie, low-nutrient, unhealthy foods and swap them for something healthier. Try:

- Swapping fatty, sugary snacks for fruit and vegetables
- Reducing portion sizes
- Drinking plenty of water
- Remember, small changes add up.

Breakfast Swap white toast with jam and butter, an orange juice and a cup of tea with milk and two sugars for a slice of lemon in hot water and enjoy some homemade porridge with semi-skimmed milk and a little honey. The porridge will provide a much slower release of energy that will keep you going until lunch.

Coffee break Swap a whole milk latte for a skimmed milk latte and you'll still get your caffeine boost, but with nearly half the calories.

Snacks Swap a bag of crisps for a handful of fruit or nuts. Swap a chocolate biscuit for a piece of fruit. Bananas are good if you're craving something sweet.

Lunch Swap a cheese, tomato and pesto panini for a jacket potato with cottage cheese and a salad. This will fill you up without giving you that mid-afternoon energy slump.

A drink after work Swap a bottle of beer for a glass of white wine, which has far fewer calories, or stick to water for zero calories and a much healthier night out.

Dinner Swap roast beef, roast potatoes and Yorkshire pudding for a warming beef casserole with mash and vegetables. You will save calories and it'll be just as satisfying.

Extra Boosts

There are many ingredients that you can add to your diet if you have specific nutritional requirements.

Acidophilus

A probiotic: 'friendly' bacteria that promotes good health. Acidophilus is most beneficial when taken if you are suffering from diarrhoea or after a course of antibiotics, or if you have digestive problems such as irritable bowel syndrome (IBS). Available from most chemists and health shops in capsule form, which usually need to be kept in the fridge. Probiotics are now included in some ready-made drinks and yogurt products.

Bee pollen

A natural antibiotic and a source of antioxidants, bee pollen is a good general tonic. It contains plenty of protein and essential amino acids. Available as loose powder, granules or in tablet or capsule form.

Warning: it can cause an allergic reaction in pollen-sensitive individuals.

Brewers' yeast

A by-product of beer brewing, brewers' yeast is exceptionally rich in B vitamins, with high levels of iron, zinc, magnesium and potassium. Highly concentrated and an excellent pick-me-up, but the flavour is strong and needs to be mixed with other ingredients. Available as pills or powder.

Warning: it is high in purines so should be avoided by gout sufferers.

Echinacea

Recommended by herbalists for many years, echinacea is a native plant of North America, taken to support a healthy immune system. A great all-rounder with anti-viral and anti-bacterial properties. Comes in capsules and in extracts taken in drops.

Warning: not recommended for use during pregnancy or when breastfeeding.

Eggs

High in protein, but eggs also contain cholesterol so you might need to limit your intake; ask your GP. Egg white powder is low in fat and can be added to smoothies for a protein boost. Be sure to always use the freshest eggs.

Warning: raw egg should not be eaten by the elderly, children, babies, pregnant women or those with an impaired immune system as there can be a risk of contracting salmonella.

Ginseng

Derived from the roots of a plant grown in Russia, Korea and China. The active constituents are ginsenosides, reputed to stimulate the hormones and increase energy. Available in dry root form for grinding or ready powdered.

Warning: should not be taken by those suffering from hypertension.

Nuts

Packed with nutrients, nuts are a concentrated form of protein and are rich in antioxidants, vitamins B1, B6 and E, and many minerals. Brazil nuts are one of the best sources of selenium in the diet. Nuts do have a high fat content, but this is mostly unsaturated fat. Walnuts are particularly high in omega-3, an essential fatty acid that is needed for healthy heart and brain function. Brazil, cashew, coconut, peanut and macadamia nuts contain more saturated fat, so should be used sparingly. Almonds are particularly easy to digest. Finely chop or grind the nuts just before using for maximum freshness.

Oats

Sold in the form of whole grain, rolled, flaked or ground (oatmeal), oats are high in protein, vitamin B complex, vitamin E, potassium, calcium, phosphorus, iron and zinc; they are easy to digest and can soothe the digestive tract. They are also a rich source of soluble fibre, which helps to lower high blood cholesterol levels, which in turn will help reduce the risk of heart disease. Toasted oatmeal has a nutty flavour and is ideal for smoothies.

Warning: oats should be avoided by those on a gluten-free diet.

Seeds

Highly nutritious, seeds contain a good supply of essential fatty acids (EFAs). Flaxseed (linseed) is particularly beneficial as it is one of the richest sources of omega-3 EFAs, with 57% more than oily fish. Seeds are best bought in small amounts, as their fat content makes them go rancid quickly, so store in airtight containers in the fridge. Grind them just before use for maximum benefit, or use the oils – these have to be stored in the fridge.

Sprouting seeds

These are simply seeds from a variety of plants – such as sunflower, chickpea and mung bean – which have been given a little water and warmth and have started to grow. Sprouts are full of vitamins, minerals, proteins and carbohydrates.

Wheat bran & germ

Wheat bran is the outside of the wheat grain removed during milling; it is very high in fibre and adds bulk to the diet. It is bland in taste but adds a crunchy texture. Wheat germ, from the centre of the grain, is very nutritious and easy to digest, with a mild flavour. Highly perishable, store in the fridge once the pack is opened.

Warning: keep your intake of bran to moderate levels; large amounts can prevent vitamins and minerals from being absorbed.

FOOD STORAGE & HYGIENE

Storing food properly and preparing it in a hygienic way is important to ensure that food remains as nutritious and flavourful as possible, and to reduce the risk of food poisoning.

Hygiene

When you are preparing food, always follow these important guidelines:

Wash your hands thoroughly before handling food and again between handling different types of food, such as raw and cooked meat and poultry. If you have any cuts or grazes on your hands, be sure to keep them covered with a waterproof plaster.

Wash down worksurfaces regularly with a mild detergent solution or multi-surface cleaner.

Use a dishwasher if available. Otherwise, wear rubber gloves for washing-up, so that the water temperature can be hotter than unprotected hands can bear. Change drying-up cloths and cleaning cloths regularly. Note that leaving dishes to drain is more hygienic than drying them with a teatowel.

Keep raw and cooked foods separate, especially meat, fish and poultry. Wash kitchen utensils in between preparing raw and cooked foods. Never put cooked or ready-to-eat foods directly on to a surface which has just had raw fish, meat or poultry on it.

Keep pets out of the kitchen if possible; or make sure they stay away from worksurfaces. Never allow animals on to worksurfaces.

Shopping

Always choose fresh ingredients in prime condition from stores and markets that have a regular turnover of stock to ensure that you buy the freshest produce possible.

Make sure items are within their 'best before' or 'use by' date. (Foods with a longer shelf life have a 'best before' date; more perishable items have a 'use by' date.)

Pack frozen and chilled items in an insulated cool bag at the check-out and put them into the freezer or fridge as soon as you get home.

During warm weather in particular, buy all your perishable foods just before you return home. When packing items at the check-out, sort them according to where you will store them when you get home – the fridge, freezer, storecupboard, vegetable rack, fruit bowl, etc. This will make unpacking much easier – and quicker.

The Storecupboard

Although storecupboard ingredients will generally last a long time, correct storage is important:

Always check the packaging for storage advice – even with familiar foods, because storage requirements may change if additives, sugar or salt have been reduced.

Check storecupboard foods for their 'best before' or 'use by' date and do not use them if the date has passed.

Keep all food cupboards scrupulously clean and make sure containers and packets are properly sealed.

Once opened, treat canned foods as though fresh. Always transfer the contents to a clean container, cover with a lid and keep in the fridge. Similarly, jars, sauce bottles and cartons should be kept chilled in the fridge after opening. (Always check the label for safe storage times after opening.)

Transfer dry goods such as sugar, rice and pasta to moisture-proof containers. When supplies are used up, wash the container well and thoroughly dry before refilling with new supplies.

Store oils in a dark cupboard away from any heat source as heat and light can make them turn rancid and affect their colour. For the same reason, buy olive oil in dark green bottles.

Store vinegars in a cool place; they can turn bad in a warm environment.

Store dried herbs, spices and flavourings in a cool, dark cupboard or in dark jars. Buy in small quantities as their flavour will not last indefinitely.

Store flours and sugars in airtight containers.

Fridge Storage

Fresh food needs to be stored in the cool temperature of the fridge to keep it in good condition and discourage the growth of harmful bacteria. Store day-to-day perishable items, such as opened jams and jellies, mayonnaise and bottled sauces, in the fridge along with eggs and dairy products, fruit juices, bacon, fresh and cooked meat (on separate shelves), and salads and vegetables (except potatoes, which don't suit being stored in the cold). A fridge should be kept at an operating temperature of 4–5°C. It is worth investing in a fridge thermometer to ensure that the correct temperature is maintained. To ensure your fridge is functioning effectively for safe food storage, follow these guidelines:

To avoid bacterial cross-contamination, store cooked and raw foods on separate shelves, putting cooked foods on the top shelf. Ensure that all items are well wrapped.

Never put hot food into the fridge, as this will cause the internal temperature of the fridge to rise.

Avoid overfilling the fridge, as this restricts the circulation of air and prevents the appliance from working properly.

It can take some time for the fridge to return to the correct operating temperature once the door has been opened, so don't leave it open any longer than is necessary.

Clean the fridge regularly, using a specially formulated germicidal fridge cleaner. Alternatively, use a weak solution of bicarbonate of soda: 1 tbsp to 1 litre (1¾ pints) water.

If your fridge doesn't have an automatic defrost facility, then defrost regularly.

Maximum fridge storage times

For pre-packed foods, always adhere to the 'use by' date on the packet. For other foods the following storage times should apply, providing the food is in prime condition when it goes into the fridge and that your fridge is in good working order

Vegetables & Fruit	
Green vegetables	3–4 days
Salad leaves	2–3 days
Hard & stone fruit	3–7 days
Soft fruit	1–2 days
Dairy Food	
Cheese, hard	1 week
Cheese, soft	2–3 days
Eggs	1 week
Milk	4–5 days
Fish	
Fish	1 day
Shellfish	1 day
Raw Meat	
Bacon	7 days
Game	2 days
Joints	3 days
Minced meat	1 day
Offal	1 day
Poultry	2 days
Raw sliced meat	2 days
Sausages	3 days
Cooked Meat	
Joints	3 days
Casseroles/stews	2 days
Pies	2 days
Sliced meat	2 days
Ham	2 days
Ham, vacuum-packed	1–2 weeks
(or according to the instructions on the packet)	

Start the Day

Serves 4

Toasted Oats with Berries

Preparation Time
10 minutes, plus cooling
Cooking Time
5–10 minutes

- 25g (1oz) hazelnuts, roughly chopped
- 125g (4oz) rolled oats
- 1 tbsp olive oil
- 125g (4oz) strawberries, sliced
- 250g (9oz) blueberries
- 200g (7oz) Greek yogurt
- 2 tbsp runny honey

NUTRITIONAL INFORMATION
Per Serving 327 calories, 15g fat (of which 3g saturates), 44g carbohydrate, 0.1g salt

1 Preheat the grill to medium. Put the hazelnuts into a bowl with the oats. Drizzle with the oil and mix well, then spread out on a baking sheet. Toast the oat mixture for 5–10 minutes until it starts to crisp up. Remove from the heat and set aside to cool.

2 Put the strawberries into a large bowl with the blueberries and yogurt. Stir in the oats and hazelnuts, drizzle with the honey and divide among four dishes. Serve immediately.

Healthy Tip

Oats are rich in soluble fibre which helps regulate blood sugar levels and lower blood cholesterol levels. They also supply vitamins, iron and magnesium. Blueberries provide anthocyanins, which helps protect against certain cancers and heart disease, while the strawberries provide a vitamin C boost.

Try Something Different

Use a mixture of raspberries, blackberries, or chopped nectarines or peaches instead of the strawberries and blueberries.

Granola

Preparation Time
5 minutes
Cooking Time
1 hour 5 minutes

- 300g (11oz) rolled oats
- 50g (2oz) each chopped Brazil nuts, flaked almonds, wheatgerm or rye flakes, and sunflower seeds
- 25g (1oz) sesame seeds
- 100ml (3½fl oz) sunflower oil
- 3 tbsp runny honey
- 100g (3½oz) each raisins and dried cranberries
- milk or yogurt to serve

NUTRITIONAL INFORMATION

Per Serving 254 calories, 14g fat (of which 2g saturates), 29g carbohydrate, 0g salt

Serves 15

Healthy Tip

Granola is a healthy breakfast option because it has a low GI (see page 12) – the oats provide a sustained rise in blood sugar, helping to keep hunger at bay longer. Brazil nuts used in this recipe are rich in selenium, a powerful antioxidant nutrient, while the almonds supply valuable amounts of bone-building calcium, protein and zinc.

1 Preheat the oven to 140°C (120°C fan oven) mark 1. Put the oats, nuts, wheatgerm or rye flakes, and all the seeds into a bowl. Gently heat the oil and honey in a pan. Pour over the oats and stir to combine. Spread on a shallow baking tray and bake in the oven for 1 hour or until golden, stirring once. Leave to cool.

2 Transfer to a large bowl and stir in the raisins and dried cranberries. Store in an airtight container – the granola will keep for up to a week. Serve with milk or yogurt.

Porridge with Dried Fruit

Preparation Time
5 minutes
Cooking Time
5 minutes

- 200g (7oz) porridge oats
- 400ml (14fl oz) milk, plus extra to serve
- 75g (3oz) mixture of chopped dried figs, apricots and raisins

NUTRITIONAL INFORMATION
Per Serving 279 calories, 6g fat (of which 1g saturates), 49g carbohydrate, 0.2g salt

Serves 4

1 Put the oats into a large pan and add the milk and 400ml (14fl oz) water. Stir in the figs, apricots and raisins and heat gently, stirring until the porridge thickens and the oats are cooked.

2 Divide among four bowls and serve with a splash of milk.

Energy-boosting Muesli

Preparation Time
5 minutes

- 500g (1lb 2oz) porridge oats
- 100g (3½oz) toasted almonds, chopped
- 2 tbsp pumpkin seeds
- 2 tbsp sunflower seeds
- 100g (3½oz) ready-to-eat dried apricots, chopped
- milk or yogurt to serve

NUTRITIONAL INFORMATION
Per Serving 208 calories, 9g fat (of which trace saturates), 28g carbohydrate, 0g salt

1 Mix the oats with the almonds, seeds and apricots. Store in a sealable container: it will keep for up to one month. Serve with milk or yogurt.

Cook's Tip

Oats contain gluten and, strictly speaking, are not suitable for coeliacs. However, because they contain a much smaller amount than wheat, rye or barley, research shows that most people with coeliac disease can safely eat moderate amounts. The oats must be from a source where there is no risk of contamination from wheat or wheat products during processing or packing. As individual tolerance to gluten varies, if you are a coeliac, seek expert advice before eating oats.

Makes 15 servings

Apple & Almond Yogurt

Preparation Time
5 minutes, plus overnight chilling

Serves 4

- 500g (1lb 2oz) natural yogurt
- 50g (2oz) each flaked almonds and sultanas
- 2 apples

NUTRITIONAL INFORMATION
Per Serving 193 calories, 8g fat (of which 1g saturates), 22g carbohydrate, 0.3g salt

Try Something Different

Use pears instead of apples.
Replace the sultanas with dried cranberries.

Healthy Tip

Natural yogurt contains lactobacillus bacteria, which aids digestion and promotes a healthy immune system. It is also a good source of protein, B vitamins and bone-strengthening calcium. The almonds add extra calcium while the apples provide useful amounts of fibre and the antioxidant quercetin.

1 Put the yogurt into a bowl and add the almonds and sultanas.

2 Grate the apples, add to the bowl and mix together. Chill in the fridge overnight. Use as a topping for breakfast cereal or serve as a snack.

Breakfast Bruschetta

Preparation Time
5 minutes
Cooking Time
5 minutes

- 1 ripe banana, peeled and sliced
- 250g (9oz) blueberries
- 200g (7oz) quark cheese
- 4 slices pumpernickel or wheat-free wholegrain bread
- 1 tbsp runny honey

NUTRITIONAL INFORMATION
Per Serving 145 calories, 1g fat (of which 0g saturates), 30g carbohydrate, 0.4g salt

Serves 4

Healthy Tip

This toasted treat is very low in fat. Pumpernickel bread is made from rye flour, which is rich in fibre, iron and zinc. It has a lower GI (see page 12) than bread made from wheat flour, which means it provides a sustained energy boost to see you through the morning. The blueberries are rich in anthocyanins, which help combat heart disease, certain cancers and stroke.

1 Put the banana into a bowl with the blueberries. Spoon in the quark cheese and mix well.

2 Toast the slices of bread on both sides, then spread with the blueberry mixture. Drizzle with the honey and serve immediately.

Serves 2

Apple Compôte

Preparation Time
10 minutes, plus chilling
Cooking Time
5 minutes

- 250g (9oz) cooking apples, peeled and chopped
- juice of ½ lemon
- 1 tbsp golden caster sugar
- ground cinnamon

TO SERVE

- 25g (1oz) raisins
- 25g (1oz) chopped almonds
- 1 tbsp natural yogurt

NUTRITIONAL INFORMATION
Per Serving 188 calories, 7g fat (of which 1g saturates), 29g carbohydrate, 0g salt

1 Put the cooking apples into a pan with the lemon juice, caster sugar and 2 tbsp cold water. Cook gently for 5 minutes or until soft. Transfer to a bowl.

2 Sprinkle a little ground cinnamon over the top, cool and chill. It will keep for up to three days.

3 Serve with the raisins, chopped almonds and yogurt.

Healthy Tip

Apples help promote healthy digestion, speeding the passage of waste products through the digestive tract and reducing the risk of constipation. Their high content of pectin also helps lower blood cholesterol levels. Apples are rich in quercetin, a powerful anti-cancer nutrient, as well as immunity boosting vitamin C.

Cook's Tip

To microwave, put the apples, lemon juice, sugar and water into a microwave-proof bowl, cover loosely with clingfilm and cook on full power in an 850W microwave oven for 4 minutes or until the apples are just soft.

Poached Eggs with Mushrooms

Preparation Time
15 minutes
Cooking Time
20 minutes

- 8 medium-sized flat or portabella mushrooms
- 25g (1oz) butter
- 8 medium eggs
- 225g (8oz) baby spinach leaves
- 4 level tsp (20g) fresh pesto

NUTRITIONAL INFORMATION
Per Serving 263 calories, 21g fat (of which 8g saturates), 1g carbohydrate, 0.7g salt,

1 Preheat the oven to 200°C (180°C fan oven) mark 6. Arrange the mushrooms in a single layer in a small roasting tin and dot with the butter. Roast for 15 minutes or until golden brown and soft.

2 Meanwhile, bring a wide shallow pan of water to the boil. When the mushrooms are half-cooked and the water is bubbling furiously, break the eggs into the pan, spaced well apart, then take the pan off the heat. The eggs will take about 6 minutes to cook.

3 When the mushrooms are tender, put them on a warmed plate, cover and return to the turned-off oven to keep warm.

4 Put the roasting tin over a medium heat on the hob and add the spinach. Cook, stirring, for about 30 seconds or until the spinach has just started to wilt.

5 The eggs should be set by now, so divide the mushrooms among four warmed plates and top with a little spinach, a poached egg and a teaspoonful of pesto.

Try Something Different

For a more substantial meal, serve on 100% rye bread or German pumpernickel.

Healthy Tip

Eggs once had a bad press with many people believing (wrongly) that they raised blood cholesterol levels. However, scientists have found that most people can safely eat up to two eggs a day without any effect on their cholesterol levels. Eggs are a good source of protein – 2 eggs supply roughly one-third of an adult's daily requirement – as well as vitamins A and D.

Serves 4

Mozzarella Mushrooms

Preparation Time
2–3 minutes
Cooking Time
15–20 minutes

Serves 4

- 8 large portabella mushrooms
- 8 slices marinated red pepper
- 8 fresh basil leaves
- 150g (5oz) mozzarella cheese, cut into 8 slices (see Cook's Tip, page 216)
- 4 English muffins, halved
- salt and ground black pepper
- green salad to serve

NUTRITIONAL INFORMATION

Per Serving 137 calories, 9g fat (of which 5g saturates), 5g carbohydrate, 0.4g salt

Healthy Tip

Mushrooms are an excellent source of potassium – a mineral that helps lower elevated blood pressure and reduces the risk of stroke. One medium portabella mushroom has even more potassium than a banana or a glass of orange juice. Mushrooms contain antioxidant nutrients that help inhibit the development cancers of the breast and prostate.

1 Preheat the oven to 200°C (180°C fan oven) mark 6. Lay the mushrooms side by side in a roasting tin and season with salt and pepper. Top each mushroom with a slice of red pepper and a basil leaf. Lay a slice of mozzarella on top of each mushroom and season again. Roast for 15–20 minutes or until the mushrooms are tender and the cheese has melted.

2 Meanwhile, toast the muffin halves until golden. Put a mozzarella mushroom on top of each muffin half. Serve immediately with a green salad.

Creamy Baked Eggs

Preparation Time
5 minutes
Cooking Time
15–18 minutes

- butter to grease
- 4 sun-dried tomatoes
- 4 medium eggs
- 4 tbsp double cream
- salt and ground black pepper
- Granary bread to serve (optional)

NUTRITIONAL INFORMATION
Per Serving 153 calories, 14g fat (of which 7g saturates), 1g carbohydrate, 0.2g salt

Serves 4

1 Preheat the oven to 180°C (160°C fan oven) mark 4. Grease four individual ramekins.

2 Put a tomato into each ramekin and season to taste with salt and pepper. Carefully break an egg on top of each tomato, then drizzle 1 tbsp cream over each egg.

3 Bake for 15–18 minutes – the eggs will continue to cook once they have been taken out of the oven.

4 Leave to stand for 2 minutes before serving. Serve with Granary bread, if you like.

Serves 4

Lemon & Blueberry Pancakes

Preparation Time
15 minutes
Cooking Time
10–15 minutes

- 125g (4oz) wholemeal plain flour
- 1 tsp baking powder
- ¼ tsp bicarbonate of soda
- 2 tbsp golden caster sugar
- finely grated zest of 1 lemon
- 125g (4oz) natural yogurt
- 2 tbsp milk
- 2 medium eggs
- 40g (1½oz) butter
- 100g (3½oz) blueberries
- 1 tsp sunflower oil
- natural yogurt and fruit compote to serve

NUTRITIONAL INFORMATION
Per Serving 290 calories, 13g fat (of which 6g saturates), 39g carbohydrate, 0.6g salt

1 Sift the flour, baking powder and bicarbonate of soda into a bowl, tipping in the contents left in the sieve. Add the sugar and lemon zest. Pour in the yogurt and milk. Break the eggs into the mixture and whisk together.

2 Melt 25g (1oz) butter in a pan, add to the bowl with the blueberries and stir everything together.

3 Heat a dot of butter with the oil in a frying pan over a medium heat until hot. Add four large spoonfuls of the mixture to the pan to make four pancakes. After about 2 minutes, flip them over and cook for 1–2 minutes. Repeat with the remaining mixture, adding a dot more butter each time.

4 Serve with natural yogurt and some fruit compote.

Try Something Different

Instead of blueberries and lemon, use 100g (3½oz) chopped ready-to-eat dried apricots and 2 tsp grated fresh root ginger.

Soups & Salads

Autumn Barley Soup

Preparation Time
10 minutes
Cooking Time
1 hour 5 minutes

- 25g (1oz) pot barley, washed and drained
- 1 litre (1¾ pints) hot vegetable stock
- 2 large carrots, diced
- 1 turnip, diced
- 2 leeks, trimmed and sliced
- 2 celery sticks, diced
- 1 small onion, finely chopped
- 1 bouquet garni
- 2 tbsp freshly chopped parsley
- salt and ground black pepper

NUTRITIONAL INFORMATION
Per Serving 83 calories, 1g fat (of which trace saturates), 16g carbohydrate, 0.6g salt

Serves 4

Healthy Tip

Pot barley is a highly nutritious addition to this soup. It is considered a whole grain as it contains the outer bran layer of the grain, which is rich in the soluble fibres beta glucan and pectin – the type that can help lower high blood cholesterol. It contains around 10g protein per 100g, as well as good amounts of folic acid, iron, phosphorus and zinc.

Try Something Different

Replace the barley with 75g (3oz) soup pasta: add for the last 10 minutes of cooking.

1 Put the barley and stock into a pan and bring to the boil. Reduce the heat and simmer for 45 minutes or until the barley is tender.

2 Add the vegetables to the pan with the bouquet garni and season to taste with salt and pepper. Bring to the boil, then reduce the heat and simmer for about 20 minutes or until the vegetables are tender.

3 Discard the bouquet garni. Add the parsley to the soup, stir well and serve immediately.

Spring Vegetable Broth

Preparation Time
20 minutes
Cooking Time
20 minutes

- 1 tbsp olive oil
- 4 shallots, chopped
- 1 fennel bulb, chopped
- 1 leek, trimmed and chopped
- 5 small carrots, chopped
- 1.1 litres (2 pints) hot vegetable stock
- 2 courgettes, chopped
- 1 bunch of asparagus, chopped
- 2 × 400g cans no-added-sugar-or-salt cannellini beans, drained and rinsed
- 50g (2oz) Gruyère or Parmesan cheese shavings to serve

NUTRITIONAL INFORMATION
Per Serving 228 calories, 8g fat (of which 3g saturates), 26g carbohydrate, 0.3g salt

Healthy Tip

This soup is a good source of potassium, which is important for regulating fluid balance and reducing blood pressure. Fennel contains betacarotene, folate and potassium as well as the phytonutrients anethole, anisic acid, fenchone and limonine, which produce the unique flavour of the vegetable.

Try Something Different

This broth is also good with a tablespoon of Pesto (see page 80) added to each bowl, and served with chunks of crusty bread.

1 Heat the oil in a large pan. Add the shallots, fennel, leek and carrots and fry for 5 minutes or until they start to soften.

2 Add the hot stock, cover and bring to the boil. Add the courgettes, asparagus and beans, then reduce the heat and simmer for 5–6 minutes until the vegetables are tender.

3 Ladle into warmed bowls, sprinkle with a little cheese and serve.

Full-of-goodness Broth

Preparation Time
10 minutes
Cooking Time
6–8 minutes

Serves 4

- 1–2 tbsp medium curry paste (see Cook's Tip)
- 200ml (7fl oz) reduced-fat coconut milk
- 600ml (1 pint) hot vegetable stock
- 200g (7oz) smoked tofu, cubed
- 2 pak choi, chopped
- a handful of sugarsnap peas
- 4 spring onions, chopped
- lime wedges to serve

NUTRITIONAL INFORMATION
Per Serving 107 calories, 4g fat (of which trace saturates), 9g carbohydrate, 1g salt,

Cook's Tip
Check the ingredients in the curry paste: some may not be suitable for vegetarians.

Try Something Different
Replace the smoked tofu with shredded leftover roast chicken and simmer for 2–3 minutes.

1 Heat the curry paste in a pan for 1–2 minutes. Add the coconut milk and hot stock and bring to the boil.

2 Add the smoked tofu, pak choi, sugarsnap peas and spring onions. Reduce the heat and simmer for 1–2 minutes.

3 Ladle the soup into warmed bowls and serve with a wedge of lime to squeeze over the broth.

Pepper & Lentil Soup

Preparation Time
15 minutes
Cooking Time
45 minutes

Serves 6

- 1 tbsp oil
- 1 medium onion, finely chopped
- 1 celery stick, chopped
- 1 leek, trimmed and chopped
- 1 carrot, chopped
- 2 red peppers, seeded and diced
- 225g (8oz) red lentils
- 400g can chopped tomatoes
- 1 litre (1¾ pints) hot light vegetable stock
- 25g pack flat-leafed parsley, chopped
- salt and ground black pepper
- toast to serve

NUTRITIONAL INFORMATION
Per Serving 165 calories, 3g fat (of which 1g saturates), 27g carbohydrate, 0.5g salt

Healthy Tip
Red lentils are a good source of protein, fibre, iron and B vitamins. They have a low GI (see page 12) thanks to their high content of soluble fibre, providing a sustained release of energy. The red peppers are rich in vitamin C and betacarotene, which are both powerful antioxidants that assist the immune system.

1 Heat the oil in a pan. Add the onion, celery, leek and carrot and cook for 10–15 minutes until soft.

2 Add the red peppers and cook for 5 minutes. Stir in the red lentils, add the chopped tomatoes and hot stock and season with salt and pepper.

3 Cover the pan and bring to the boil, then reduce the heat and cook, uncovered, for 25 minutes or until the lentils are soft and the vegetables are tender.

4 Stir in the parsley. Ladle into warmed bowls and serve with toast.

Leek & Potato Soup

Preparation Time
10 minutes
Cooking Time
45 minutes

- 25g (1oz) butter
- 1 onion, finely chopped
- 1 garlic clove, crushed
- 550g (1¼lb) leeks, trimmed and chopped
- 200g (7oz) floury potatoes, sliced
- 1.3 litres (2¼ pints) hot vegetable stock
- crème fraîche and chopped chives to garnish

NUTRITIONAL INFORMATION
Per Serving 117 calories, 6g fat (of which 4g saturates), 13g carbohydrate, 0.1g salt

Serves 4

Healthy Tip

Leeks are an excellent source of vitamin C as well as iron and fibre. They provide many of the health-giving benefits associated with garlic and onions, such as promoting the functioning of the blood and the heart.

1 Melt the butter in a pan over a gentle heat. Add the onion and cook for 10–15 minutes until soft. Add the garlic and cook for a further 1 minute. Add the leeks and cook for 5–10 minutes until softened. Add the potatoes and toss together with the leeks.

2 Pour in the hot stock and bring to the boil, then reduce the heat and simmer for 20 minutes or until the potatoes are tender.

3 Leave the soup to cool a little, then whiz in batches in a blender or food processor until smooth.

4 To serve, reheat the soup gently. Ladle into warmed bowls, drizzle the crème fraîche over it and garnish with chives.

Hot & Sour Soup

Preparation Time
20 minutes
Cooking Time
30–35 minutes

- 1 tbsp vegetable oil
- 2 turkey breasts, about 300g (11oz), or the same quantity of tofu, cut into strips
- 5cm (2in) piece fresh root ginger, peeled and grated
- 4 spring onions, finely sliced
- 1–2 tbsp Thai red curry paste
- 75g (3oz) long-grain wild rice
- 1.1 litres (2 pints) hot weak chicken or vegetable stock or boiling water
- 200g (7oz) mangetouts, sliced
- juice of 1 lime
- 4 tbsp freshly chopped coriander to garnish

NUTRITIONAL INFORMATION
Per Serving 255 calories, 10g fat (of which 1g saturates), 19g carbohydrate, 0.7g salt

Healthy Tip
This soup is a good source of protein, which comes from the turkey. It contains ginger, which is good for calming an upset stomach and providing relief from bloating and gas. Ginger is often recommended for alleviating and preventing nausea particularly in the form of seasickness, morning sickness and motion sickness.

1 Heat the oil in a deep pan. Add the turkey or tofu and cook over a medium heat for 5 minutes or until browned. Add the ginger and spring onions and cook for a further 2–3 minutes. Stir in the curry paste and cook for 1–2 minutes to warm the spices.

2 Add the rice and stir to coat in the curry paste. Pour the hot stock or boiling water into the pan, stir once and bring to the boil. Reduce the heat, cover and simmer for about 20 minutes.

3 Add the mangetouts and cook for a further 5 minutes or until the rice is cooked. Just before serving, squeeze in the lime juice and stir to mix.

4 To serve, ladle into warmed bowls and sprinkle with the coriander.

Carrot & Sweet Potato Soup

Preparation Time
15 minutes
Cooking Time
45 minutes

- 1 tbsp olive oil
- 1 large onion, chopped
- 1 tbsp coriander seeds
- 900g (2lb) carrots, roughly chopped
- 2 medium sweet potatoes, roughly chopped
- 2 litres (3½ pints) hot vegetable or chicken stock
- 2 tbsp white wine vinegar
- 2 tbsp freshly chopped coriander, plus extra coriander leaves to garnish
- 4 tbsp half-fat crème fraîche
- salt and ground black pepper

NUTRITIONAL INFORMATION
Per Serving 120 calories, 3g fat (of which 1g saturates), 22g carbohydrate, 0.7g salt

Freezing Tip
To freeze Freeze the soup at step 3 for up to one month. To use Thaw overnight in the fridge. Reheat gently and simmer for 5 minutes.

Serves 8

1 Heat the oil in a large pan. Add the onion and coriander seeds and cook over a medium heat for 5 minutes. Add the carrots and sweet potatoes and cook for a further 5 minutes.

2 Add the hot stock and bring to the boil, then reduce the heat and simmer for 25 minutes or until the vegetables are tender.

3 Leave the soup to cool a little, then whiz in batches in a blender or food processor until slightly chunky. Add the wine vinegar and season to taste with salt and pepper.

4 Pour the soup into a clean pan, stir in the chopped coriander and reheat gently.

5 Drizzle the crème fraîche over it and sprinkle with the coriander leaves. Serve in warmed bowls.

Mushroom, Spinach & Miso Soup

Preparation Time
5 minutes
Cooking Time
25 minutes

Serves 6

- 1 tbsp vegetable oil
- 1 onion, finely sliced
- 125g (4oz) shiitake mushrooms, finely sliced
- 225g (8oz) baby spinach leaves
- 1.1 litres (2 pints) fresh fish stock
- 4 tbsp mugi miso (see Cook's Tip)

NUTRITIONAL INFORMATION
Per Serving 55 calories, 2g fat (of which trace saturates), 6g carbohydrate, 1.3g salt

Healthy Tip
Although spinach contains high levels of iron and calcium, the presence of oxalic acid binds these minerals in a form that cannot be absorbed so readily by the body. But spinach is still very good for you – its high content of vitamins A and C and folic acid make this a versatile superfood.

Cook's Tip
Miso (fermented barley and soy beans) is a living food in the same way that yogurt is, and contains bacteria and enzymes that are destroyed by boiling. Miso is best added as a flavouring at the end of cooking. It's available from Asian shops and larger supermarkets.

1 Heat the oil in a large pan over a low heat. Add the onion and cook gently for 15 minutes until soft.

2 Add the mushrooms and cook for 5 minutes, then stir in the spinach and stock. Heat for 3 minutes, then stir in the miso – don't boil, as miso is a live culture. Ladle the soup into warmed bowls and serve hot.

Cauliflower Soup

Preparation Time
25 minutes
Cooking Time
40 minutes

Serves 6

- 2 × 400ml cans coconut milk
- 750ml (1¼ pints) vegetable stock
- 4 garlic cloves, finely chopped
- 5cm (2in) piece fresh root ginger, peeled and finely chopped
- 4 lemongrass stalks, roughly chopped
- 4 kaffir lime leaves, shredded (optional) or zest of 1 lime
- 4 red chillies
- 2 tbsp groundnut oil
- 2 tsp sesame oil
- 1 large onion, thinly sliced
- 2 tsp ground turmeric
- 2 tsp sugar
- 900g (2lb) cauliflower florets
- 2 tbsp lime juice
- 2 tbsp light soy sauce
- 4 spring onions, shredded
- 4 tbsp freshly chopped coriander
- salt and ground black pepper

NUTRITIONAL INFORMATION
Per Serving 113 calories, 5g fat (of which 1g saturates), 15g carbohydrate, 1.4g salt

1 Put the coconut milk and stock into a pan. Add the garlic and ginger with the lemongrass, lime leaves, if using, or lime zest and chillies. Bring to the boil, then reduce the heat, cover and simmer for 15 minutes. Strain the mixture and keep the liquid to one side.

2 Heat the oils together in a clean pan. Add the onion, turmeric and sugar and fry gently for 5 minutes. Add the cauliflower and stir-fry for about 5 minutes or until lightly golden.

3 Add the reserved liquid, the lime juice and soy sauce. Bring to the boil, then reduce the heat, cover and simmer for 10–15 minutes until the cauliflower is tender.

4 Season to taste with salt and pepper, then add the spring onions and coriander to the soup. Ladle into warmed bowls and serve.

Cock-a-Leekie Soup

Preparation Time
30–40 minutes
Cooking Time
1 hour 20 minutes

- 1 oven-ready chicken, about 1.4kg (3lb)
- 2 onions, roughly chopped
- 2 carrots, roughly chopped
- 2 celery sticks, roughly chopped
- 1 bay leaf
- 25g (1oz) butter
- 900g (2lb) leeks, trimmed and sliced
- 125g (4oz) ready-to-eat dried prunes, sliced
- salt and ground black pepper
- freshly chopped parsley to serve

FOR THE DUMPLINGS
- 125g (4oz) self-raising flour
- a pinch of salt
- 50g (2oz) shredded suet
- 2 tbsp freshly chopped parsley
- 2 tbsp freshly chopped thyme

NUTRITIONAL INFORMATION
Per Serving 280 calories, 4g fat (of which 1g saturates), 40g carbohydrate, 0.2g salt

Serves 8

1 Put the chicken into a pan in which it fits quite snugly, then add the chopped vegetables, bay leaf and chicken giblets (if available). Pour in 1.7 litres (3 pints) water and bring to the boil, then reduce the heat, cover and simmer gently for 1 hour.

2 Meanwhile, melt the butter in a large pan. Add the leeks and fry gently for 10 minutes or until softened.

3 Remove the chicken from the pan and leave until cool enough to handle. Strain the stock and put to one side. Strip the chicken from the bones and shred roughly. Add to the stock with the prunes and softened leeks.

4 To make the dumplings, sift the flour and salt into a bowl. Stir in the suet, herbs and about 5 tbsp water to make a fairly firm dough. Lightly shape the dough into 2.5cm (1in) balls. Bring the soup just to the boil and season well. Reduce the heat, add the dumplings and cover the pan with a lid. Simmer for 15–20 minutes until the dumplings are light and fluffy. Serve the soup scattered with chopped parsley.

Serves 4

Chicken Broth

Preparation Time
30 minutes
Cooking Time
15 minutes

- 1 tbsp olive oil
- about 300g (11oz) boneless, skinless chicken thighs, cubed
- 3 garlic cloves, crushed
- 2 medium red chillies, seeded and finely diced (see Cook's Tip)
- 1 litre (1¾ pints) chicken stock
- 250g (9oz) each green beans, broccoli, sugarsnap peas and courgettes, chopped
- 50g (2oz) pasta shapes or spaghetti, broken into short lengths
- salt

NUTRITIONAL INFORMATION
Per Serving 229 calories, 7g fat (of which 1g saturates), 16g carbohydrate, 1.2g salt

1 Heat the oil in a large pan. Add the chicken, garlic and chillies and cook for 5–10 minutes or until the chicken is opaque all over.

2 Add the stock and bring to the boil. Add the vegetables, reduce the heat and simmer for 5 minutes or until the chicken is cooked through.

3 Meanwhile, cook the pasta in a separate pan of lightly salted boiling water for about 5–10 minutes, depending on the type of pasta or until it is just cooked.

4 Drain the pasta and add to the broth. Ladle into warmed bowls and serve immediately.

Healthy Tip

This highly nutritious soup provides an excellent balance of protein (from the chicken), carbohydrate (from the pasta) and healthy unsaturated fats (from the olive oil). The vegetables add valuable amounts of fibre, B vitamins, folate and iron, while the garlic provides numerous health benefits including protection against heart disease.

Cook's Tip

- Chillies vary enormously in strength, from quite mild to blisteringly hot, depending on the type of chilli and its ripeness. Taste a small piece first to check it's not too hot for you.
- Be extremely careful when handling chillies not to touch or rub your eyes with your fingers, as they will sting. Wash knives immediately after handling chillies for the same reason. As a precaution, use rubber gloves when preparing them if you like.

White Bean Salad

Preparation Time
15 minutes

- ½ tbsp red wine vinegar
- 2 tbsp extra virgin olive oil
- ½ red cabbage
- 2 courgettes
- 410g can cannellini beans, drained and rinsed
- 410g can butter beans, drained and rinsed
- ½ red onion, finely chopped
- 100g (3½oz) stale unsliced bread, torn into small chunks
- 125g ball low-fat mozzarella, torn into small pieces
- a handful of fresh basil leaves, chopped
- salt and ground black pepper

NUTRITIONAL INFORMATION
Per serving 346 calories, 13g fat (of which 5g saturates), 40g carbohydrate, 2.2g salt

1 Whisk together the vinegar, oil, plenty of seasoning and a splash of water in a small bowl to make a dressing.

2 Cut out and discard the tough core from the cabbage, then finely shred the leaves and put into a large serving bowl. Peel the courgettes into ribbons, using a y-shaped peeler, and add to the cabbage bowl. Add the remaining ingredients and dressing, and toss well to combine. Serve.

Serves 4

Serves 4

Roasted Root Vegetable Salad

Preparation Time
20 minutes, plus cooling
Cooking Time
40 minutes, plus cooling

- 1 butternut squash, halved, seeded and cubed
- 1½ large carrots, cut into chunks
- 3 fresh thyme sprigs
- 1½ tbsp olive oil
- 2 red onions, cut into wedges
- 1 tbsp balsamic vinegar
- 400g can chickpeas, drained and rinsed
- 25g (1oz) pinenuts, toasted
- 100g (3½oz) wild rocket
- salt and ground black pepper

NUTRITIONAL INFORMATION
Per Serving 290 calories, 14g fat (of which 2g saturates), 33g carbohydrate, 0.7g salt

1 Preheat the oven to 190°C (170°C fan oven) mark 5. Put the squash and carrots into a large deep roasting tin. Scatter the thyme sprigs over them, drizzle with 1 tbsp oil and season with salt and pepper. Roast in the oven for 20 minutes.

2 Remove the tin from the oven, give it a good shake to make sure the vegetables aren't sticking, then add the onions. Drizzle the remaining oil over and toss to coat. Roast for a further 20 minutes or until all the vegetables are tender.

3 Remove the roasted vegetables from the oven and discard any twiggy sprigs of thyme. Drizzle the vinegar over, stir in and leave to cool.

4 To serve, put the chickpeas into a large serving bowl. Add the cooled vegetables, the pinenuts and rocket (reserving a few leaves to garnish). Toss everything together and garnish with the reserved rocket.

Get Ahead

To prepare ahead Complete the recipe to the end of step 3, then cool, cover and chill for up to two days.
To use Complete the recipe.

Healthy Tip

This salad gives you decent amounts of protein, carbohydrate and many vitamins and minerals. Chickpeas are an excellent source of soluble fibre, protein and iron. They contain fructo-oligosaccharides, a type of fibre that promotes healthy gut bacteria, which are important for healthy digestion and healthy immunity.

Melon, Mango & Cucumber Salad with Wasabi Dressing

Preparation Time
15 minutes, plus chilling

- ½ cucumber, halved lengthways and seeded
- 1 Charentais melon, halved and seeded
- 1 mango, peeled and stoned
- freshly chopped flat-leafed parsley and lime wedges to serve

FOR THE WASABI DRESSING

- 3 tsp soy sauce
- 1 tbsp dry sherry
- 1 tbsp rice wine vinegar or white wine vinegar
- ¼ tsp wasabi paste (see Cook's Tip) or finely chopped green chilli (see Cook's Tip, page 55)

NUTRITIONAL INFORMATION

Per Serving 62 calories, trace fat (of which 0g saturates), 14g carbohydrate, 1.5g salt,

Serves 6

Cook's Tip

Wasabi paste is a Japanese condiment, green in colour and extremely hot – a little goes a long way. It is available from larger supermarkets, but if you can't get it use creamed horseradish instead.

Get Ahead

To prepare ahead Complete the recipe, store in an airtight container and chill for up to one day.
To use Serve with lime wedges.

1 Cut the cucumber into slim diagonal slices. Cut the rind off the melon and cut the flesh into similar-size pieces to the cucumber. Cut the mango flesh into similar-size lengths. Mix the cucumber, melon and mango in a large bowl.

2 To make the wasabi dressing, put the soy sauce, sherry, vinegar and wasabi paste or chilli into a small bowl and whisk together, then toss with the salad. Sprinkle with parsley and serve with lime wedges.

Cannellini Bean & Sunblush Tomato Salad

Preparation Time
5 minutes, plus marinating

- ½ red onion, very finely sliced
- 2 tbsp red wine vinegar
- a small handful each of freshly chopped mint and flat-leafed parsley
- 2 × 400g cans cannellini beans, drained and rinsed
- 4 tbsp extra virgin olive oil
- 4 celery sticks, sliced
- 75g (3oz) sunblush tomatoes, snipped in half
- salt and ground black pepper

NUTRITIONAL INFORMATION
Per Serving 163 calories, 8g fat (of which 1g saturates), 17g carbohydrate, 1.3g salt

Healthy Tip
Cannellini beans are a good source of iron needed to prevent anaemia; folate and magnesium needed for energy and cardiovascular health. They also contain fibre, which is needed to regulate bowel function. Their combination of fibre, carbohydrates and protein makes these beans good for prolonged energy and stable blood sugar levels.

1 Put the onion into a small bowl, add the vinegar and toss until the onion is coated. Leave to marinate for 30 minutes – this stage is important as it takes the astringency out of the onion.

2 Tip the onion and vinegar into a large serving bowl, add the remaining ingredients, season to taste with salt and pepper and toss everything together.

Warm Tofu, Fennel & Bean Salad

Preparation Time
10 minutes
Cooking Time
15 minutes

- 1 tbsp olive oil, plus 1 tsp
- 1 red onion, finely sliced
- 1 fennel bulb, finely sliced
- 1 tbsp cider vinegar
- 400g can butter beans, drained and rinsed
- 2 tbsp freshly chopped flat-leafed parsley
- 200g (7oz) smoked tofu
- salt and ground black pepper

NUTRITIONAL INFORMATION
Per Serving 150 calories, 6g fat (of which 1g saturates), 15g carbohydrate, 0.8g salt

Serves 4

Healthy Tip
Tofu is rich in high-quality protein. It is also a good source of calcium, B vitamins and iron. Tofu is also very low in fat and sodium, making it a perfect food for people on sodium-restricted diets. Fennel is a good digestive aid, helping reduce gas and bloating. The butter beans provide good amounts of protein, iron as well as fibre.

1 Heat 1 tbsp oil in a large frying pan. Add the onion and fennel and cook over a medium heat for about 5–10 minutes until soft.

2 Add the cider vinegar and heat through for 2 minutes. Stir in the butter beans and parsley, season to taste with salt and pepper, then tip into a bowl.

3 Slice the smoked tofu horizontally into four and then into eight triangles. Add to the pan with the remaining 1 tsp oil. Cook for 2 minutes on each side or until golden brown.

4 Divide the bean mixture among four plates, then add two slices of tofu to each plate.

Vietnamese Rice Salad

Preparation Time
10 minutes
Cooking Time
20 minutes

- 225g (8oz) mixed basmati and wild rice
- 1 large carrot, coarsely grated
- 1 large courgette, coarsely grated
- 1 red onion, finely sliced
- 4 tbsp roasted salted peanuts, lightly chopped
- 20g (¾oz) each fresh coriander, mint and basil, roughly chopped
- 100g (3½oz) wild rocket

FOR THE VIETNAMESE DRESSING

- 2 tbsp light muscovado sugar
- juice of 2 limes
- 4 tbsp fish sauce
- 6 tbsp rice wine vinegar or white wine vinegar
- 2 tbsp sunflower oil

NUTRITIONAL INFORMATION

Per Serving 294 calories, 14g fat (of which 2g saturates), 38g carbohydrate, 0.6g salt

Get Ahead

To prepare ahead Complete the recipe to the end of step 2 and store in an airtight container in the fridge for up to two days.
To use Complete the recipe.

1 Put the rice into a pan with 500ml (18fl oz) water. Cover and bring to the boil, then reduce the heat and cook for 20 minutes until the rice is just cooked. Tip on to a plastic tray, spread out and leave to cool.

2 Meanwhile, make the dressing. Put the sugar into a small pan and heat gently until it just begins to dissolve. Add the lime juice, fish sauce and vinegar. Stir over a low heat to dissolve the sugar. Take off the heat and add the oil. Stir into the rice with the grated carrot, courgette and sliced onion.

3 Spoon the salad into a large bowl and top with peanuts, herbs and rocket. Cover and keep chilled until ready to serve.

Orange & Chicken Salad

Preparation Time
15 minutes
Cooking Time
10 minutes

Serves 4

- 50g (2oz) cashew nuts
- zest and juice of 2 oranges
- 2 tbsp marmalade
- 1 tbsp honey
- 1 tbsp oyster sauce
- 400g (14oz) roast chicken, shredded
- a handful of chopped raw vegetables, such as cucumber, carrot, red and yellow pepper and Chinese leaves

NUTRITIONAL INFORMATION
Per Serving 252 calories, 8g fat (of which 2g saturates), 20g carbohydrate, 0.5g salt

Cook's Tip

Toasting the cashew nuts in a dry frying pan before adding them to the salad brings out their flavour, giving them an intense, nutty taste and a wonderful golden colour.

1 Put the cashew nuts into a dry frying pan over a medium-high heat and cook for 2–3 minutes, tossing regularly, until golden brown. Tip into a large serving bowl.

2 To make the dressing, put the orange zest and juice into the frying pan with the marmalade, honey and oyster sauce. Bring to the boil, stirring, then reduce the heat and simmer for about 2–3 minutes until thickened.

3 Add the roast chicken to the serving bowl with the chopped raw vegetables. Pour the dressing over the salad, toss everything together and serve immediately.

Chicken Salad

Preparation Time
10 minutes

- 100g (3½oz) shredded roast chicken, skin discarded
- 1 carrot, chopped
- 1 celery stick, chopped
- ¼ cucumber, chopped
- a handful of ripe cherry tomatoes, chopped
- 1 tbsp hummus
- ¼ lemon to serve

NUTRITIONAL INFORMATION
Per Serving 323 calories, 18g fat (of which 5g saturates), 17g carbohydrate, 0.9g salt

Try Something Different

- For an even more nutritious salad, add a few pumpkin seeds or sunflower seeds, or a handful of sprouted seeds such as alfalfa, or chopped watercress.
- For extra bite, add a little finely chopped red chilli; for extra sweetness, add some strips of red pepper.
- For extra flavour, add some freshly chopped coriander or torn fresh basil leaves.

Healthy Tip

Chicken is lower in fat and higher in protein than red meat, and it is a good source of many nutrients, such as vitamins B6 and B12. It also contains selenium (an antioxidant that helps the body fight against cancer) and the amino acids that produce serotonin (the hormone that helps us feel happy).

1 Put the chicken into a shallow bowl. Add the carrot, celery, cucumber and cherry tomatoes.

2 Top with the hummus and serve with a lemon quarter for squeezing over the salad.

Zesty Orange, Chicken & Tarragon Salad

Preparation Time
15 minutes, plus chilling

- 50g (2oz) pecan nuts or walnuts
- 350g (12oz) smoked chicken or cooked chicken breast, skinned and cut into long strips
- 2 oranges
- 2 small chicory heads

FOR THE DRESSING

- grated zest and juice of 2 oranges
- 2 tbsp white wine vinegar
- 1 tsp caster sugar
- 5 tbsp olive oil
- 3 tbsp freshly chopped tarragon
- 1 large egg yolk
- salt and ground black pepper

NUTRITIONAL INFORMATION

Per Serving 252 calories, 8g fat (of which 2g saturates), 20g carbohydrate, 0.5g salt

1 Put the nuts into a dry pan and toast over a medium-high heat, tossing regularly, for 2–3 minutes until golden brown. Chop roughly.

2 Whisk all the dressing ingredients together in a small bowl. Put the chicken strips into a bowl, spoon over the dressing, cover and chill for at least 1 hour.

3 Use a sharp knife to remove the peel and pith from the oranges, then cut into slices.

4 Put a layer of chicory into a large flat salad bowl, add the orange slices, then spoon the chicken and dressing over. Sprinkle the toasted nuts over the top and serve.

Cook's Tip

Instant flavour ideas for chicken

- Snip bacon into a frying pan, cook until crisp and golden, then stir into warm, boiled new potatoes with shredded roast chicken and mustard mayonnaise. Serve with green salad.
- Roast a chicken with lots of tarragon, peppers, whole garlic cloves and olive oil. Serve with couscous, into which you've stirred the roasting juices.
- Pan-fry chicken breasts that have been marinating in olive oil with rosemary, thyme and crushed garlic. Serve with a fresh tomato sauce made by whizzing together ripe tomatoes, olive oil, basil and salt and pepper to taste.
- Pan-fry chicken breasts in butter and set aside. Add flaked almonds and pitted fresh cherries to the pan, toss over a high heat for 1–2 minutes and serve with the cooked chicken.

Serves 4

Warm Chicken Liver Salad

Preparation Time
20 minutes
Cooking Time
8–10 minutes

- 450g (1lb) chicken livers
- 1–2 tbsp balsamic vinegar
- 1 tsp Dijon mustard
- 3 tbsp olive oil
- 50g (2oz) streaky bacon rashers, rind removed and cut into small, neat pieces (lardons)
- 50g (2oz) sun-dried tomatoes or roasted red peppers, cut into thin strips
- ½ curly endive, about 175g (6oz)
- 100g (3½oz) rocket
- 1 bunch of spring onions, sliced
- salt and ground black pepper

NUTRITIONAL INFORMATION
Per Serving 236 calories, 15g fat (of which 3g saturates), 3g carbohydrate, 0.8g salt

Serves 4

1 Drain the chicken livers on kitchen paper, then trim and cut into pieces.

2 To make the dressing, put the vinegar, mustard, 2 tbsp oil, and salt and pepper to taste into a small bowl. Whisk together and put to one side.

3 Fry the lardons in a non-stick frying pan until beginning to brown, stirring from time to time. Add the tomatoes or red peppers and heat through for 1 minute. Add the remaining oil and the chicken livers and stir-fry over a high heat for 2–3 minutes until the livers are just pink in the centre.

4 Meanwhile, toss the endive, rocket and spring onions with the dressing in a large bowl. Divide among four plates, arrange the warm livers and bacon on top and serve at once.

Healthy Tip

Chicken livers provide the richest source of folic acid, with nearly five times the RDA in 100g. They are rich in iron, which is needed for healthy red blood cells and energy, and provide enough vitamin B12 in one portion to satisfy the body's requirements for a month.

Warm Bacon Salad

Preparation Time
10 minutes
Cooking Time
10–15 minutes

Serves 2

- 4 handfuls of soft salad leaves
- 1 small red onion, thinly sliced
- 75g (3oz) cubed pancetta
- 1 thick slice white bread, diced
- 2 medium eggs
- 25g (1oz) Parmesan shavings
- salt and ground black pepper
- fresh flat-leafed parsley sprigs to garnish

FOR THE DRESSING

- 1 tbsp Dijon mustard
- 2 tbsp red wine vinegar
- 2 tbsp fruity olive oil

NUTRITIONAL INFORMATION

Per Serving 375 calories, 29g fat (of which 9g saturates), 11g carbohydrate, 1.7g salt

1 Put the salad leaves and onion into a large bowl. Fry the pancetta in a non-stick frying pan until it begins to release some fat. Add the diced bread and continue to fry until the pancetta is golden and crisp.

2 Put all the dressing ingredients into a small bowl, season with salt and pepper and whisk together.

3 Half-fill a small pan with cold water and bring to the boil. Turn the heat right down – there should be just a few bubbles on the base of the pan. Break the eggs into a cup, then tip them gently into the pan and cook for 3–4 minutes, using a metal spoon to baste the tops with a little of the hot water. Lift the eggs out of the water with a slotted spoon and drain on kitchen paper.

4 Tip the pancetta, bread and any pan juices over the salad leaves. Add the Parmesan, then pour the dressing over the salad. Toss well, then divide between two plates. Top each with an egg, season to taste, then garnish with flat-leafed parsley sprigs and serve.

Couscous & Haddock Salad

Preparation Time
15 minutes
Cooking Time
15 minutes

- 175g (6oz) couscous
- 125g (4oz) cooked smoked haddock, flaked
- 50g (2oz) cooked peas
- a pinch of curry powder
- 2 spring onions, sliced
- 1 tbsp freshly chopped flat-leafed parsley
- 1 small hard-boiled egg, chopped
- 2 tbsp olive oil
- 2 tsp lemon juice
- salt and ground black pepper

NUTRITIONAL INFORMATION
Per Serving 408 calories, 15g fat (of which 2g saturates), 48g carbohydrate, 1.3g salt

Healthy Tip
Couscous is made by rolling and shaping moistened semolina wheat and then coating the granules with finely ground wheat flour. It is very healthy, with a low GI (thus providing sustained energy) and a good profile of vitamins, including thiamin, riboflavin, niacin, vitamin B6 and folate. It is low in fat and sodium and contains useful amounts of selenium.

1 Cook the couscous according to the packet instructions. Drain if necessary.

2 Mix the couscous with the smoked haddock, peas, curry powder, spring onions, parsley and egg.

3 Toss with the oil, lemon juice and plenty of salt and pepper to taste, then serve.

Tuna Salad

Preparation Time
10 minutes

- 2 × 400g can mixed beans, drained and rinsed
- 250g (9oz) flaked tuna
- 1 cucumber, chopped
- 1 large red onion, finely sliced
- 4 ripe tomatoes, chopped
- 4 celery sticks, chopped
- 80g bag baby spinach leaves
- 2 tbsp olive oil
- 1 tsp red wine vinegar
- salt and ground black pepper

NUTRITIONAL INFORMATION
Per Serving 157 calories, 4g fat (of which trace saturates), 9g carbohydrate, 0.5g salt

Cook's Tip

If you prefer tuna in oil, replace the olive oil with the same amount from the tuna can.

1 Put the beans into a bowl and add the tuna, cucumber, red onion, tomatoes, celery and spinach.

2 Mix together the oil and vinegar, season with salt and pepper, then toss through the bean mix and serve immediately.

Trout with Apple & Watercress Salad

Preparation Time
15 minutes
Cooking Time
15–20 minutes

- 4 × 150g (5oz) trout fillets
- 1 tbsp olive oil, plus extra to oil
- 250g (9oz) cooked baby new potatoes, cut into chunks
- 2 apples, cored and cut into chunks
- 4 cooked beetroot in natural juice, cut into chunks
- 150g (5oz) watercress
- salt and ground black pepper

FOR THE DRESSING

- 1 tbsp extra virgin olive oil
- juice of ½ lemon
- 2 tsp Dijon mustard
- 1 tbsp freshly chopped dill

NUTRITIONAL INFORMATION

Per Serving 320 calories, 12g fat (of which 1g saturates), 21g carbohydrate, 0.4g salt

Serves 4

Healthy Tip

Trout is rich in the long-chain omega-3 fatty acids, which help protect against heart disease and stroke. Omega-3 fats may also alleviate inflammatory conditions such as rheumatoid arthritis and some research suggests they may also lower the risk of dementia and depression. Trout is lower in fat than other oily fish such as salmon and is also a good source of iron, selenium, B vitamins and vitamin A.

1 Preheat the oven to 200°C (180°C fan oven) mark 6. Put each piece of fish on a piece of oiled foil, brush the top of the fish with olive oil and season with salt and pepper. Scrunch the foil around the fish and roast for 15–20 minutes until the fish is cooked.

2 Put the potatoes, apples, beetroot and watercress into a large bowl and mix lightly.

3 Mix all the dressing ingredients together in a small bowl and season with salt and pepper. Add to the salad and toss through, then serve with the fish.

Smoked Mackerel Citrus Salad

Preparation Time
10 minutes
Cooking Time
5 minutes

Serves 6

- 200g (7oz) green beans
- 200g (7oz) smoked mackerel fillets
- 125g (4oz) mixed watercress, spinach and rocket
- 4 spring onions, sliced
- 1 avocado, halved, stoned, peeled and sliced

FOR THE DRESSING

- 1 tbsp olive oil
- 1 tbsp freshly chopped coriander
- grated zest and juice of 1 orange

NUTRITIONAL INFORMATION

Per Serving 299 calories, 26g fat (of which 5g saturates), 4g carbohydrate, 1g salt

Cook's Tip

Leftover mackerel fillets can be turned into a quick pâté. Whiz in a food processor with the zest of a lemon and enough crème fraîche to make a spreadable consistency.

1 Preheat the grill. Blanch the green beans in boiling water for 3 minutes until they are just tender. Drain, rinse under cold running water, drain well, then tip into a bowl.

2 Cook the mackerel under the hot grill for 2 minutes until warmed through. Flake into bite-size pieces, discard the skin and add the fish to the bowl with the salad leaves, spring onions and avocado.

3 Whisk all the dressing ingredients together in a small bowl. Pour over the salad, toss well and serve immediately.

Lunch & Light Bites

Serves 6

Cheesy Polenta with Tomato Sauce

Preparation Time
15 minutes, plus cooling
Cooking Time
45 minutes

- oil to oil
- 225g (8oz) polenta
- 4 tbsp freshly chopped herbs, such as oregano, chives and flat-leafed parsley
- 100g (3½oz) freshly grated Parmesan, plus fresh Parmesan shavings to serve
- salt and ground black pepper

FOR THE TOMATO & BASIL SAUCE

- 1 tbsp vegetable oil
- 3 garlic cloves, crushed
- 500g carton creamed tomatoes or passata
- 1 bay leaf
- 1 fresh thyme sprig
- caster sugar
- 3 tbsp freshly chopped basil, plus extra to garnish

NUTRITIONAL INFORMATION
Per serving 249 calories, 9g fat (of which 4g saturates), 31g carbohydrate, 0.9g salt

1 Lightly oil a 25.5 × 18cm (10 × 7in) dish. Bring 1.1 litres (2 pints) water and ¼ tsp salt to the boil in a large pan. Sprinkle in the polenta, whisking constantly. Reduce the heat and simmer, stirring frequently, for 10–15 minutes until the mixture leaves the sides of the pan.

2 Stir in the herbs and Parmesan and season to taste with salt and pepper. Turn into the prepared dish and leave to cool.

3 Next, make the tomato and basil sauce. Heat the oil in a pan and fry the garlic for 30 seconds (do not brown). Add the creamed tomatoes or passata, the bay leaf, thyme and a large pinch of sugar. Season with salt and pepper and bring to the boil, then reduce the heat and simmer, uncovered, for 5–10 minutes. Remove the bay leaf and thyme sprig and add the chopped basil.

4 To serve, preheat a griddle or grill. Cut the polenta into pieces and lightly brush with oil. Fry on the hot griddle for 3–4 minutes on each side or under the hot grill for about 7–8 minutes on each side. Serve with the tomato and basil sauce, fresh Parmesan shavings and chopped basil.

Get Ahead

To prepare ahead Complete the recipe to the end of step 3. Cover and chill separately for up to two days.
To use Complete the recipe.

Mixed Mushroom Frittata

Preparation Time
15 minutes
Cooking Time
15–20 minutes

- 1 tbsp olive oil
- 300g (11oz) mixed mushrooms, sliced
- 2 tbsp freshly chopped thyme
- zest and juice of ½ lemon
- 50g (2oz) watercress, chopped
- 6 medium eggs, beaten
- salt and ground black pepper
- stoneground wholegrain bread (optional) and a crisp green salad to serve

NUTRITIONAL INFORMATION
Per serving 148 calories, 12g fat (of which 3g saturates), 0g carbohydrate, 0.3g salt

Serves 4

Healthy Tip
This dish is rich in protein and a good source of vitamin D. The mushrooms supply useful amounts of fibre, vitamin B6 and potassium while the watercress adds iron and folate.

1 Heat the oil in a large deep frying pan over a medium heat. Add the mushrooms and thyme and stir-fry for 4–5 minutes until starting to soften and brown. Stir in the lemon zest and juice, then bubble for 1 minute. Reduce the heat.

2 Preheat the grill. Add the watercress to the beaten eggs, season with salt and pepper and pour into the pan. Cook on the hob for 7–8 minutes until the sides and base are firm but the centre is still a little soft.

3 Transfer to the grill and cook for 4–5 minutes until just set. Cut into wedges and serve with chunks of bread, if you like, and a salad.

Roast Mushrooms with Pesto

Preparation Time
5 minutes
Cooking Time
15 minutes

- 8 portabella mushrooms
- 8 tbsp fresh Pesto (see Cook's Tip)
- toasted ciabatta, salad and basil leaves to serve

NUTRITIONAL INFORMATION
Per serving 258 calories, 23g fat (of which 6g saturates), 1g carbohydrate, 0.5g salt

Cook's Tip

Pesto Put a 20g pack of roughly chopped basil into a food processor. Add 25g (1oz) finely grated Parmesan, 50g (2oz) pinenuts and 4 tbsp extra virgin olive oil and whiz to a rough paste. Alternatively, grind in a pestle and mortar. Season the pesto with salt and plenty of ground black pepper.

1 Preheat the oven to 200°C (180°C fan oven) mark 6. Put the mushrooms into an ovenproof dish, then spoon 1 tbsp fresh Pesto on top of each one.

2 Pour 150ml (¼ pint) boiling water into the dish, then cook for 15 minutes or until the mushrooms are soft and the topping is hot. Serve with toasted ciabatta and salad, and scatter a few small basil leaves over the mushrooms.

Chickpea Patties

Preparation Time
20 minutes, plus chilling
Cooking Time
15 minutes

- 2 × 400g cans chickpeas, drained and rinsed
- 4 garlic cloves, crushed
- 1 tsp ground cumin
- 1 small red onion, chopped
- 20g pack fresh coriander
- 2 tbsp plain flour, plus extra to dust
- olive oil for frying
- Mixed Salad (see Cook's Tip, page 122) and lemon wedges to serve

NUTRITIONAL INFORMATION
Per serving 344 calories, 17g fat (of which 2g saturates), 37g carbohydrate, 1g salt

1 Pat the chickpeas dry with kitchen paper, then put them into a food processor with the garlic, cumin, onion and coriander. Whiz until smooth, then stir in the flour.

2 With floured hands, shape the chickpea mixture into 12 small, round patties and chill in the fridge for 20 minutes.

3 Heat a little oil in a non-stick frying pan over a medium heat and fry the patties in batches for about 2 minutes on each side or until heated through and golden. Serve the patties warm with a Mixed Salad and lemon wedges.

Freezing Tip

To freeze Make the patties, then cool, put in a freezerproof container and freeze. They will keep for up to one month.
To use Thaw overnight at a cool room temperature, then reheat in the oven at 180°C (160°C fan oven) mark 4 for 20 minutes.

Healthy Tip

Chickpeas are highly nutritious, packed with protein, fibre, B vitamins and iron. They also supply complex carbohydrates and have a low GI, which means they provide long-lasting energy (see page 12). Frying the patties in olive oil is a healthy alternative to frying in a blended vegetable oil, as it contains high levels of heart-healthy monounsaturated fats.

Serves 4

Makes 12

Bubble & Squeak Cakes

Preparation Time
15 minutes
Cooking Time
45 minutes, plus cooling

- 550g (1¼lb) old potatoes
- 125g (4oz) butter
- 175g (6oz) leeks, trimmed and finely shredded
- 175g (6oz) green cabbage, finely shredded
- plain flour to dust
- 1 tbsp oil
- salt and ground black pepper

NUTRITIONAL INFORMATION
Per cake 130 calories, 10g fat (of which 6g saturates), 10g carbohydrate, 0.2g salt

1 Cook the potatoes in a large pan of lightly salted boiling water until tender, then drain and mash.

2 Heat 50g (2oz) butter in a large non-stick frying pan. Add the leeks and cabbage and fry for 5 minutes, stirring, or until soft and beginning to colour. Combine the leeks and cabbage with the potatoes then season well with salt and pepper. Leave to cool. When cool enough to handle, mould into 12 cakes and dust with flour.

3 Heat the oil and remaining butter in a non-stick frying pan and cook the cakes for 4 minutes on each side or until they are golden, crisp and hot right through. Serve.

Rosti Potatoes with Fried Eggs

Preparation Time
20 minutes
Cooking Time
20–25 minutes plus cooling

- 900g (2lb) red potatoes, scrubbed and left whole
- 40g (1½oz) butter
- 4 large eggs
- salt and ground black pepper
- fresh flat-leafed parsley sprigs to garnish

NUTRITIONAL INFORMATION
Per serving 324 calories, 16g fat (of which 7g saturates), 36g carbohydrate, 0.4g salt

Healthy Tip
Potatoes supply vitamin C, vitamin B6 and fibre as well as carbohydrates for energy. Frying them in hot oil minimises the loss of vitamins.

Serves 4

1 Put the potatoes into a pan of cold water. Cover, bring to the boil and parboil for 5–8 minutes. Drain and leave to cool for 15 minutes.

2 Preheat the oven to 150°C (130°C fan oven) mark 2. Put a baking tray inside to warm. Peel the potatoes and coarsely grate them lengthways into long strands. Divide into eight portions and shape into mounds.

3 Melt half the butter in a large non-stick frying pan. When it is beginning to brown, add four of the potato mounds, spacing them well apart, and flatten them a little. Fry slowly for 6–7 minutes until golden brown, then turn them and brown the other side for 6–7 minutes. Transfer to a warmed baking tray and keep warm in the oven while you fry the rest.

4 Just before serving, carefully break the eggs into the hot pan and fry for about 2 minutes until the white is set and the yolk is still soft. Season with salt and pepper and serve at once, with the rösti and garnished with parsley sprigs.

Egg & Pepper Pizza

Preparation Time
15 minutes
Cooking Time
12 minutes

- 150g (5oz) red and yellow marinated peppers in oil, drained and oil reserved
- 8 tbsp (160g) passata
- 4 small (4 × 100g) pizza bases
- 4 medium eggs
- 125g (4oz) watercress, washed and stalks removed

NUTRITIONAL INFORMATION

Per serving 448 calories
16g fat (of which 3g saturates)
63g carbohydrate, 1.2g salt

Cook's Tip
Watercress is the salad superfood par excellence. It is a good source of iron, and vitamins C and E.

1 Preheat the oven to 220°C (200°C fan oven) mark 7. Put two large baking sheets, big enough to hold two pizzas each, into the oven to heat up.

2 Chop the peppers into thin strips. Spoon 2 tbsp passata over each pizza base and scatter strips of pepper around the edges. Make a dip in the passata in the middle of each pizza and break an egg into it. Carefully slide the pizzas on to the preheated baking sheets. Place in the oven and cook for 12 minutes or until the egg is cooked.

3 Top the pizzas with the watercress, drizzle with a little of the reserved oil from the peppers and serve.

Tomato Crostini with Feta & Basil

Preparation Time
20 minutes
Cooking Time
3 minutes

Serves 4

- 1 small garlic clove, crushed
- 3 tbsp freshly chopped basil, plus extra basil leaves to garnish
- 25g (1oz) pinenuts
- 2 tbsp extra virgin olive oil
- grated zest and juice of 1 lime
- 50g (2oz) vegetarian feta cheese
- 4 large tomatoes, preferably vine-ripened, thickly sliced
- 150g tub fresh tomato salsa
- 50g (2oz) pitted black olives, roughly chopped
- 4 thick slices country-style bread
- salt and ground black pepper

NUTRITIONAL INFORMATION
Per serving 242 calories, 17g fat (of which 3g saturates) 18g carbohydrate, 1.5g salt

1 Put the garlic, chopped basil, pinenuts, oil, lime zest and juice into a food processor and whiz to a smooth paste. Add the feta and whiz until smooth. Thin with 1 tbsp water if necessary. Season with salt and pepper.

2 Put the tomatoes, salsa and olives into a bowl and gently toss together.

3 Toast the bread. Divide the tomato mixture among the slices of toast and spoon the basil and feta mixture on top. Garnish with basil leaves and serve immediately.

Chicken Wrap

Preparation Time
10 minutes

- 2 cooked chicken breasts, about 125g (4oz) each, cut into bite-size pieces
- 1 carrot, grated
- 1 avocado, halved, stoned, peeled and chopped
- a small handful of rocket
- juice of ½ lemon
- 3 tbsp mayonnaise
- 4 flour tortillas
- salt and ground black pepper

NUTRITIONAL INFORMATION
Per serving 269 calories
16g fat (of which 3g saturates)
17g carbohydrate, 1.5g salt

Serves 4

Healthy Tip
Tortillas make a sustaining light meal as they have a lower GI (see page 12) than many other types of bread. These wraps are filled with chicken, which provides protein and B vitamins; as well as avocados, rich in heart-protective vitamin E and healthy unsaturated fats.

1 Mix salt and pepper to taste in a large bowl. Add the chicken, carrot, avocado and rocket and mix well.

2 In a separate bowl, mix the lemon juice with the mayonnaise, then spread over the tortillas. Divide the chicken mixture among the tortillas, then roll up and serve in napkins, if you like

Red Pepper Pesto Croûtes

Makes 24

Preparation Time
20 minutes
Cooking Time
15–20 minutes

- 1 thin French stick, sliced into 24 rounds
- olive oil to brush
- ready-made Pesto (see Cook's Tip)
- 4 pepper pieces (from a jar of marinated peppers), each sliced into 6 strips
- pinenuts to garnish

NUTRITIONAL INFORMATION
Per serving 90 calories, 5g fat (of which 1g saturates), 10g carbohydrate, 0.3g salt

Cook's Tip

Pesto Roughly chop 75g (3oz) basil, 50g (2oz) Parmesan, 25g (1oz) pinenuts and ½ crushed garlic clove and put into a food processor. With the motor running, add 50–75ml (2–3fl oz) extra virgin olive oil to make a paste. Season with salt and pepper.

1 Preheat the oven to 200°C (180°C fan oven) mark 6. Brush both sides of the bread with oil and put on a baking sheet. Cook in the oven for 15–20 minutes.

2 Spread 1 tsp Pesto on each croûte, top with a pepper strip and pinenuts and serve.

Bruschetta with Tapenade

Preparation Time
10 minutes
Cooking Time
5 minutes

- 1 ciabatta loaf
- olive oil to brush
- 6 tbsp Tapenade (see Cook's Tip)
- selection of vegetable antipasti, such as marinated red peppers and artichokes, drained
- a few basil sprigs to garnish

NUTRITIONAL INFORMATION
Per slice 119 calories, 4g fat (of which trace saturates), 19g carbohydrate, 0.7g salt

Makes 12

Cook's Tip

- Tapenade is a black olive paste from Provence in the south of France. You can buy ready-made tapenade, or make your own by whizzing 75g (3oz) pitted black olives in a food processor with 4 anchovies, 2 tbsp olive oil and 1 tbsp freshly chopped flat-leafed parsley.
- Instead of spreading it on bread, serve tapenade as a dip for crisp raw carrots, red pepper strips or chicory leaves.

1 Cut the ciabatta on the diagonal to make 12 slices. Brush both sides of the slices with a little oil. Heat a griddle pan until hot, add the ciabatta slices and toast for a couple of minutes on each side.

2 Spread a thin layer of Tapenade on each slice of bread, then top with a little of the antipasti. Garnish with basil and serve. Alternatively, arrange the antipasti in separate bowls and let your guests assemble their own bruschettas.

Chicken & Salsa Verde Crostini

Preparation Time
20 minutes, plus chilling
Cooking Time
2 minutes

Makes 15

- 50g (2oz) walnuts
- 1 loaf walnut bread, cut into 15 × 1cm (½in) slices
- 2 tbsp olive oil
- 1 tbsp sea salt flakes
- 175g (6oz) cooked chicken breast, thinly sliced
- 125g (4oz) sun-dried tomatoes in oil, drained and thinly sliced
- freshly chopped flat-leafed parsley to garnish

FOR THE SALSA VERDE

- 3 tbsp each freshly chopped coriander, mint and basil
- 1 garlic clove, roughly chopped
- 2 tbsp Dijon mustard
- 3 anchovy fillets
- 1 tbsp capers
- 50ml (2fl oz) olive oil
- juice of ½ lemon

NUTRITIONAL INFORMATION

Per serving 208 calories, 9g fat (of which 1g saturates), 24g carbohydrate, 1.7g salt

1 Put the walnuts into a dry pan and toast over a medium-high heat, tossing regularly, for 2–3 minutes until golden brown. Finely chop and set aside.

2 Put all the salsa verde ingredients into a food processor or blender and whiz until it is smooth. (Alternatively, use a pestle and mortar.) Cover and chill in the fridge.

3 Preheat the grill to high. Put the bread on a baking sheet, brush with oil and sprinkle with sea salt flakes. Grill for 1 minute on each side or until lightly toasted.

4 To serve, put two or three chicken slices on each crostini base, top with a spoonful of salsa verde and slices of sun-dried tomato, then garnish with a sprinkling of walnuts and flat-leafed parsley.

Lime & Chilli Chicken Goujons

Preparation Time
15 minutes
Cooking Time
20 minutes

- 300g (11oz) boneless, skinless chicken thighs
- 50g (2oz) fresh breadcrumbs
- 50g (2oz) plain flour
- 2 tsp dried chilli flakes
- grated zest of 1 lime
- 1 medium egg, beaten
- 2 tbsp sunflower oil
- salt and ground black pepper
- lime wedges to serve

FOR THE DIP

- 6 tbsp (240g) natural yogurt
- 6 tbsp (60g) mayonnaise
- ¼ cucumber, halved lengthways, seeded and finely diced
- 25g (1oz) freshly chopped coriander
- juice of 1 lime

NUTRITIONAL INFORMATION

Per serving 337 calories, 21g fat (of which 4g saturates), 24g carbohydrate, 0.7g salt

Cook's Tip

For a lower-fat version, bake the goujons in the oven. Preheat the oven to 200°C (180°C fan oven) mark 6. Put the goujons on a lightly oiled baking sheet, brush each with a little oil and bake for 12–15 minutes until golden and cooked through.

1 Put all the dip ingredients into a bowl. Season to taste with salt and pepper and mix well, then chill in the fridge.

2 Cut the chicken into strips. Put the breadcrumbs into a bowl with the flour, chilli flakes and lime zest and mix well. Pour the egg on to a plate. Dip the chicken in egg, then coat in the breadcrumbs.

3 Heat the oil in a frying pan over a medium heat. Fry the chicken in batches for 7–10 minutes until golden and cooked through. Keep each batch warm while cooking the remainder. Transfer to a serving plate, sprinkle with a little salt, then serve with the dip and lime wedges.

Squid with Haricot Beans & Rocket

Preparation Time
20 minutes, plus marinating
Cooking Time
about 2 minutes

Serves 6

- 450g (1lb) prepared squid, cut into thick rings
- 3 tbsp extra virgin olive oil
- 1 rosemary sprig, cut into four pieces
- 1 chilli, seeded and finely chopped (see Cook's Tip, page 55)
- zest and juice of 1 lemon
- 2 × 400g cans no-added-sugar-or-salt haricot beans, drained and rinsed
- 2 tbsp olive oil
- 6 slices sourdough bread (about 40g each slice)
- 55g pack rocket
- salt and ground black pepper
- lemon wedges to serve

NUTRITIONAL INFORMATION

Per serving 308 calories, 12g fat (of which 2g saturates), 33g carbohydrate, 0.8g salt

Healthy Tip

Squid is a good source of protein, and contains approx 8g of fat per 100g. It is rich in vitamin B6, selenium and phosphorus. The haricot beans in this recipe add protein, complex carbohydrate and iron.

1 Put the squid into a non-metallic bowl. Add 1 tbsp extra virgin olive oil, the rosemary, chilli and half the lemon zest. Season to taste with salt and pepper, then leave to marinate for 30 minutes.

2 Put the beans into a large bowl with the remaining lemon zest and extra virgin olive oil and the lemon juice. Season with salt and pepper, then use a potato masher to pound into a rough purée.

3 Heat the olive oil in a wok or a non-stick frying pan. Add the squid and cook for 1–2 minutes until opaque. Toast the bread.

4 Spread the bean purée over the toast. Top with the squid and rocket and serve with lemon wedges.

Sardines on Toast

Preparation Time
5 minutes
Cooking Time
8–10 minutes

Serves 4

- 4 thick slices wholemeal bread
- 2 large tomatoes, sliced
- 2 × 120g cans sardines in olive oil, drained
- juice of ½ lemon
- ground black pepper
- a small handful of parsley, chopped to garnish

NUTRITIONAL INFORMATION
Per serving 240 calories, 9g fat (of which 2g saturates), 25g carbohydrate, 1.6g salt

Cook's Tip
Oily fish such as sardines are one of the best sources of essential heart-protecting omega-3 oils. Eat them at least once a week. Fresh Cornish sardines, when they are available, are a treat and are cheap. Look out for them at your fishmonger's or on the fresh fish counter at the supermarket.

Try Something Different
Instead of sardines, use a 200g can salmon in oil.

1 Preheat the grill. Toast the bread on both sides.

2 Divide the tomato slices and the sardines among the toast slices, squeeze the lemon juice over them, then put back under the grill for 2–3 minutes to heat through. Season with pepper, then scatter the parsley over the sardines to garnish and serve immediately.

Quick Crab Cakes

Preparation Time
15 minutes
Cooking Time
6 minutes

- 200g (7oz) fresh crabmeat
- 2 spring onions, finely chopped
- 2 red chillies, seeded and finely chopped (see Cook's Tip, page 55)
- finely grated zest of 1 lime
- 4 tbsp freshly chopped coriander
- about 40g (1½oz) wholemeal breadcrumbs
- 1 tbsp groundnut oil
- 1 tbsp plain flour
- salt and ground black pepper
- 1 red chilli, seeded and thinly sliced, to garnish (see Cook's Tip, page 55)
- 1 lime, cut into wedges, and salad leaves to serve

NUTRITIONAL INFORMATION

Per serving 124 calories, 4g fat (of which 1g saturates), 12g carbohydrate, 0.9g salt

1 Put the crabmeat into a bowl, then add the spring onions, chillies, lime zest, coriander and salt and pepepr to taste and stir to mix. Add enough breadcrumbs to hold the mixture together, then form the mixture into four small patties.

2 Heat ½ tbsp oil in a pan. Dredge the patties with flour and fry on one side for 3 minutes. Add the rest of the oil, then turn the patties over and fry for a further 2–3 minutes. Garnish the crab cakes with the sliced red chilli and serve with lime wedges to squeeze over them, and salad leaves.

Healthy Tip

Crabmeat is low in fat and relatively low in calories. It contains high levels of protein, vitamin B6 and the antioxidant selenium. The overall salt content of this recipe is low thanks to the addition of strongly flavoured ingredients such as chilli, lime and spring onions.

Cook's Tip

Use leftover bread to make breadcrumbs and then freeze them – they're a great timesaver. You can use them from frozen.

Serves 4

Trout & Dill Fishcakes

Preparation Time
15 minutes
Cooking Time
25 minutes

- 4 medium potatoes, roughly chopped
- 2 trout fillets
- 3 spring onions, finely chopped
- 2 fresh dill sprigs, finely chopped
- zest of 1 lemon
- 1 tbsp olive oil
- a little plain gluten-free flour
- salt
- watercress to serve

NUTRITIONAL INFORMATION

Per serving 196 calories, 5g fat (of which 1g saturates), 27g carbohydrate, 0.1g salt

Try Something Different

Replace the trout with 225g (8oz) cooked salmon, haddock or smoked haddock: skin, flake and add at step 2.

Healthy Tip

Trout is lower in fat than other types of oily fish. It contains omega-3 fatty acids, which help protect against heart disease, stroke, rheumatoid arthritis and depression. In this recipe the fishcakes are grilled rather than fried, which helps reduce the overall fat content of the dish.

1 Cook the potatoes in a pan of lightly salted boiling water for about 6–8 minutes until tender. Drain, put back into the pan and mash.

2 Preheat the grill to high. Grill the trout fillets for 8–10 minutes until cooked through and firm to the touch. Skin the fish, flake into pieces, removing any bones, then put into the pan with the mashed potato.

3 Add the spring onions, dill and lemon zest to the pan with the oil, season with salt and mix well.

4 Shape the mixture into eight small patties. Dust with flour and put on a non-stick baking sheet. Cook the fishcakes under the hot grill for 3 minutes on each side. Serve the fishcakes hot, with watercress.

Cheese Coleslaw with Roast Chicken

Preparation Time
15 minutes

Serves 4

- 1 baby white cabbage, thinly shredded
- 4 spring onions, finely chopped
- 1 large carrot, finely shredded
- 75g (3oz) mature Cheddar, grated
- 6 tbsp mayonnaise
- ground black pepper
- cress to garnish
- sliced roast chicken to serve

NUTRITIONAL INFORMATION
Per serving 270 calories, 23g fat (of which 7g saturates), 8g carbohydrate, 0.6g salt

1 Put the white cabbage, spring onions, carrot, cheese and mayonnaise into a large bowl and season with pepper.

2 Divide the coleslaw among four small bowls or plates and snip some cress over them. Serve with slices of roast chicken.

Healthy Tip

Cabbage is rich in fibre, vitamin C and cancer-protective nutrients called glucosinolates. It may aid the liver's detoxifying function. Carrots are rich in betacarotene, an antioxidant that helps fight cancer and heart disease. The cheese adds protein and calcium.

Try Something Different

- Use either Gruyère or Emmenthal instead of the Cheddar.
- Add freshly chopped chives or flat-leafed parsley.
- Sprinkle with 1 tbsp mixed seeds just before serving.

Serves 2

Chicken Tarragon Burgers

Preparation Time
30 minutes, plus chilling
Cooking Time
12 minutes

- 225g (8oz) minced chicken
- 2 shallots, finely chopped
- 1 tbsp freshly chopped tarragon
- 25g (1oz) fresh breadcrumbs
- 1 large egg yolk
- vegetable oil to oil
- salt and ground black pepper
- toasted burger buns, mayonnaise or Greek yogurt, salad leaves and tomato salad to serve

NUTRITIONAL INFORMATION
Per serving 205 calories, 4g fat (of which 1g saturates), 12g carbohydrate, 0.4g salt

1 Put the chicken into a bowl with the shallots, tarragon, breadcrumbs and egg yolk. Mix well, then beat in about 75ml (2½fl oz) cold water and season with salt and pepper.

2 Lightly oil a foil-lined baking sheet. Divide the chicken mixture into two or four portions (depending on how large you want the burgers) and put on the foil. Using the back of a wet spoon, flatten each portion to a thickness of 2.5cm (1in). Cover and chill for 30 minutes.

3 Preheat the barbecue or grill. If cooking on the barbecue, lift the burgers straight on to the grill rack; if cooking under the grill, slide the baking sheet under the grill. Cook the burgers for 5–6 minutes on each side until they are cooked through, then serve in a toasted burger bun with a dollop of mayonnaise or Greek yogurt, a few salad leaves and tomato salad.

Try Something Different
Pork and Apricot Burgers Replace the chicken with minced pork, use freshly chopped sage instead of the tarragon, and add 100g (3½oz) chopped ready-to-eat dried apricots to the mixture before shaping into burgers.

Speedy Burgers

Preparation Time
10 minutes
Cooking Time
8–12 minutes

- 450g (1lb) lean minced beef
- 1 onion, very finely chopped
- 1 tbsp dried Herbes de Provence
- 2 tsp sun-dried tomato paste
- 1 medium egg, beaten
- ground black pepper
- Chilli Coleslaw to serve (see Cook's Tip)

NUTRITIONAL INFORMATION
Per serving 80 calories, 20g fat (of which 8g saturates), 2g carbohydrate, 0.3g salt

Serves 4

Cook's Tip
Chilli Coleslaw Put 3 peeled and finely shredded carrots into a large bowl. Add ½ finely shredded white cabbage, 1 seeded and finely sliced red pepper and ½ chopped cucumber. Mix ½ tsp harissa paste with 100g (3½oz) natural yogurt and 1 tbsp white wine vinegar. Add to the vegetables and toss well.

1. Put the minced beef, onion, herbs, tomato paste and beaten egg into a large bowl and mix well. Season with pepper, then shape the mixture into four round burgers about 2cm (¾in) thick.

2. Preheat the grill or griddle pan. Cook the burgers for 4–6 minutes on each side and serve immediately with the Chilli Coleslaw.

Piperade

Preparation Time
20 minutes
Cooking Time
20 minutes

- 2 tbsp olive oil
- 1 medium onion, finely chopped
- 1 garlic clove, finely chopped
- 1 red pepper, seeded and chopped
- 375g (13oz) tomatoes, peeled, seeded and chopped
- a pinch of cayenne pepper
- 8 large eggs
- salt and ground black pepper
- freshly chopped flat-leafed parsley to garnish
- fresh bread to serve (optional)

NUTRITIONAL INFORMATION

Per serving 232 calories, 17g fat (of which 4g saturates), 7g carbohydrate, 0.4g salt

Serves 4

1 Heat the oil in a heavy-based frying pan. Add the onion and garlic and cook gently for 5 minutes. Add the red pepper and cook for 10 minutes or until softened.

2 Add the tomatoes, increase the heat and cook until they are reduced to a thick pulp. Season well with cayenne pepper, salt and pepper.

3 Lightly whisk the eggs and add to the frying pan. Using a wooden spoon, stir gently until they've just begun to set but are still creamy. Garnish with parsley and serve with bread, if you like.

Weekday Suppers

Serves 4

Spicy Beans with Jazzed-up Potatoes

Preparation Time
12 minutes
Cooking Time
about 1½ hours

- 4 baking potatoes
- 1 tbsp olive oil, plus extra to rub
- 1 tsp smoked paprika, plus a pinch
- 2 shallots, finely chopped
- 1 tbsp freshly chopped rosemary
- 400g can cannellini beans, drained and rinsed
- 400g can chopped tomatoes
- 1 tbsp light muscovado sugar
- 1 tsp vegetarian Worcestershire sauce
- 75ml (2½fl oz) red wine
- 75ml (2½fl oz) hot vegetable stock
- a small handful of freshly chopped flat-leafed parsley
- grated mature vegetarian Cheddar to sprinkle
- sea salt and ground black pepper

NUTRITIONAL INFORMATION
Per Serving 298 calories, 4g fat (of which 1g saturates), 56g carbohydrate, 0.8g salt

1 Preheat the oven to 200°C (180°C fan oven) mark 6. Rub the potatoes with a little oil and put them on a baking tray. Scatter with sea salt and a pinch of smoked paprika. Bake for 1–1½ hours.

2 Meanwhile, heat the 1 tbsp oil in a large pan, then fry the shallots over a low heat for 1–2 minutes until they start to soften.

3 Add the rosemary and 1 tsp paprika and fry for 1–2 minutes, then add the beans, tomatoes, sugar, Worcestershire sauce, wine and hot stock. Season, then bring to the boil, reduce the heat and simmer, uncovered, for 10–15 minutes. Serve with the baked potatoes, scattered with parsley and grated Cheddar.

Healthy Tip

Baked potatoes are a useful source of vitamin C, which is preserved well in this cooking method. Much of the vitamin content is found just beneath the skin so you should eat the skin for maximum nutritional benefits. The cannellini beans add protein, fibre, iron and zinc while the canned tomatoes are rich in the anti-cancer phytochemical, lycopene.

Try Something Different

For a quick meal that takes less than 25 minutes, the spicy beans are just as good served with toast.

Italian Meatballs

Preparation Time
15 minutes
Cooking Time
50 minutes

- 50g (2oz) fresh breadcrumbs
- 450g (1lb) minced lean pork
- 1 tsp fennel seeds, crushed
- ¼ tsp chilli flakes, or to taste
- 3 garlic cloves, crushed
- 4 tbsp freshly chopped flat-leafed parsley
- 3 tbsp red wine
- oil-water spray (see Cook's Tip)
- roughly chopped fresh oregano to garnish
- spaghetti to serve

FOR THE TOMATO SAUCE

- oil-water spray (see Cook's Tip)
- 2 large shallots, finely chopped
- 3 pitted black olives, shredded
- 2 garlic cloves, crushed
- 2 pinches of chilli flakes
- 250ml (9fl oz) vegetable or chicken stock
- 500g carton passata
- 2 tbsp each freshly chopped flat-leafed parsley, basil and oregano
- salt and ground black pepper

NUTRITIONAL INFORMATION

Per Serving 275 calories, 12g fat (of which 4g saturates), 16g carbohydrate, 1.8g salt

1 To make the tomato sauce, spray a pan with the oil-water spray and add the shallots. Cook gently for 5 minutes. Add the olives, garlic, chilli flakes and stock and bring to the boil, then reduce the heat, cover and simmer for 3–4 minutes.

2 Uncover and simmer for 10 minutes or until the shallots and garlic are soft and the liquid syrupy. Stir in the passata and season with salt and pepper. Bring to the boil, then reduce the heat and simmer for 10–15 minutes. Stir in the herbs.

3 Meanwhile, put the breadcrumbs, pork, fennel seeds, chilli flakes, garlic, parsley and wine into a large bowl, season and mix together, using your hands, until thoroughly combined. (If you wish to check the seasoning, fry a little mixture, taste and adjust if necessary.)

4 Preheat the grill. Line a grill pan with foil, shiny side up, and spray with the oil-water spray. With wet hands, roll the mixture into balls. Cook the meatballs under the hot grill for 3–4 minutes on each side. Serve with the tomato sauce and spaghetti, garnished with oregano.

Cook's Tip

Oil-water spray is far lower in calories than oil alone and, as it sprays on thinly and evenly, you'll use less. Fill one-eighth of a travel-sized spray bottle with oil such as sunflower, light olive or vegetable (rapeseed) oil, then top up with water.
To use, shake well before spraying. Store in the fridge.

Serves 4

Steak & Chips

Preparation Time
10 minutes
Cooking Time
35–45 minutes

Serves 4

- 2 large potatoes, cut into chips
- 2 tbsp olive oil
- 4 sirloin steaks, 125g (4oz) each, fat trimmed
- 25g (1oz) Roquefort cheese, cut into four small pieces
- salt and ground black pepper
- watercress to garnish

NUTRITIONAL INFORMATION
Per Serving 318 calories, 13g fat (of which 5g saturates), 18g carbohydrate, 0.4g salt

Healthy Tip
The overall fat and saturated fat content of dish is dramatically lower than steak and chips cooked the traditional way. Here the chips are sealed with just a little oil and baked in the oven instead of deep-frying them, which saves around 10g fat per portion. Pan-frying the steak in minimal oil further cuts the fat and calorie content.

1 Preheat the oven to 220°C (200°C fan oven) mark 7. Put the potato chips into a pan of lightly salted water. Bring to the boil, then reduce the heat and simmer for about 4–5 minutes. Drain well.

2 Put the chips into a roasting tin, toss with 1 tbsp oil and bake, turning once, for about 30–40 minutes until cooked through and golden.

3 When the chips are nearly done, heat a non-stick frying pan until really hot. Brush the remaining oil over the steaks and season with salt and pepper. Add to the pan and fry for 3 minutes on each side for medium-rare, or 2 minutes more if you prefer the meat well done. Put on to warmed plates, top each steak with a small piece of Roquefort while still hot and serve with the chips. Garnish with watercress.

Spicy Pork & Bean Stew

Preparation Time
15 minutes
Cooking Time
50–55 minutes

- 3 tbsp olive oil
- 400g (14oz) pork escalopes, cut into cubes
- 1 red onion, sliced
- 2 leeks, trimmed and cut into chunks
- 2 celery sticks, cut into chunks
- 1 tbsp harissa paste
- 1 tbsp tomato purée
- 400g (14oz) cherry tomatoes
- 300ml (½ pint) hot vegetable or chicken stock
- 400g can cannellini beans, drained and rinsed
- 1 marinated red pepper, sliced
- salt and ground black pepper
- freshly chopped flat-leafed parsley to garnish
- Greek yogurt, lemon wedges and bread to serve

NUTRITIONAL INFORMATION
Per Serving 348 calories, 14g fat (of which 3g saturates), 27g carbohydrate, 1.5g salt

1 Preheat the oven to 180°C (160°C fan oven) mark 4. Heat 2 tbsp oil in a flameproof casserole and fry the pork in batches until golden. Remove from the pan and put to one side.

2 Heat the remaining oil in the pan and fry the onion for 5–10 minutes until softened. Add the leeks and celery and cook for about 5 minutes. Return the pork to the pan, and add the harissa and tomato purée. Cook for 1–2 minutes, stirring all the time. Add the tomatoes and hot stock and season well with salt and pepper. Bring to the boil, then transfer to the oven and cook for 25 minutes.

3 Add the drained beans and red pepper to the mixture and put back into the oven for 5 minutes to warm through. Garnish with parsley and serve with a dollop of Greek yogurt, lemon wedges for squeezing over the stew, and chunks of crusty baguette or wholegrain bread.

Serves 4

Pork Fillet with Apricots

Preparation Time
10 minutes, plus marinating
Cooking Time
about 20 minutes, plus resting

- 700g (1½lb) pork fillet (tenderloin), trimmed
- 4 tbsp light soy sauce
- 150ml (5fl oz) red wine
- 4 tbsp dry sherry
- 1 tbsp clear honey
- 1 fresh thyme sprig or a pinch of dried thyme
- 75g (3oz) dried apricots
- 100ml (3½fl oz) dry white wine
- 2 tbsp olive oil
- 175g (6oz) onions, sliced
- 2 tsp cornflour
- ground black pepper
- green vegetables to serve

NUTRITIONAL INFORMATION
Per Serving 387 calories, 13g fat (of which 3g saturates), 16g carbohydrate, 0.3g salt

1 Put the pork into a non-metallic dish. Combine the soy sauce, red wine, sherry, honey and thyme, season with pepper and spoon over the pork. Cover with clingfilm and leave to marinate in the fridge for at least 2 hours or overnight.

2 Meanwhile, put the apricots and white wine into a pan. Bring to the boil, then reduce the heat, cover and simmer for about 20 minutes or until the apricots are soft. Strain, reserving the liquid, and chop the apricots roughly.

3 Preheat the oven to 200°C (180°C fan oven) mark 6. Lift the pork from the marinade; reserve the marinade. Heat 1 tbsp oil in a casserole. Add the meat and brown over a high heat, then roast in the oven for about 20 minutes or until cooked.

4 Meanwhile, heat 1 tbsp oil in a pan. Add the onions and cook, stirring, for 10–12 minutes until softened. Add the apricots. Keep warm.

5 When the meat is cooked, remove from the casserole and keep warm. Add the marinade and the reserved liquid from the apricots to the juices in the casserole. Blend the cornflour with 1 tbsp cold water and stir into the sauce. Bring to the boil and cook over a medium heat, stirring constantly, for 2 minutes until the sauce thickens.

6 Cut the pork into slices about 1cm (½ in) thick. To serve, spoon a little apricot and onion mixture on to four warmed plates. Put the sliced pork on top and pour a little sauce over it. Serve with green vegetables.

Garlic Pork

Preparation Time
5 minutes
Cooking Time
20–25 minutes

- 1 tbsp olive oil
- 2 garlic cloves, crushed
- 5cm (2in) piece fresh root ginger, peeled and grated
- 4 pork chops
- salt
- stir-fried shredded cabbage to serve

NUTRITIONAL INFORMATION

Per Serving 181 calories, 8g fat (of which 2g saturates), 1g carbohydrate, 0.2g salt

Healthy Tip

Garlic contains allicin, an antioxidant nutrient that helps combat heart disease, high blood pressure, high blood cholesterol levels and certain cancers, particularly cancer of the colon. It also has anti-viral and antibacterial properties.

1 Preheat the grill to high. Put the oil into a small bowl, add the garlic and ginger and a pinch of salt and stir well to mix.

2 Cook the pork chops under the hot grill for 7–10 minutes on each side, then remove from the grill. Brush the oil mixture all over the chops, then put back under the grill and cook for a further 2 minutes on each side. Serve with stir-fried shredded cabbage.

Sticky Chicken Thighs

Preparation Time
5 minutes
Cooking Time
20 minutes

- 1 garlic clove, crushed
- 1 tbsp clear honey
- 1 tbsp Thai sweet chilli sauce
- 4 chicken thighs
- rice (optional) and green salad to serve

NUTRITIONAL INFORMATION
Per Serving 218 calories, 12g fat (of which 3g saturates), 5g carbohydrate, 0.4g salt

Serves 4

Try Something Different
Try this with sausages instead of the chicken.
Italian Marinade Mix 1 crushed garlic clove with 4 tbsp olive oil, the juice of 1 lemon and 1 tsp dried oregano. If you like, then leave to marinate for 1–2 hours before cooking.
Oriental Marinade Mix 2 tbsp soy sauce with 1 tsp demerara sugar, 2 tbsp dry sherry or apple juice, 1 tsp chopped fresh root ginger and 1 crushed garlic clove.
Honey and Mustard Marinade Mix together 2 tbsp grain mustard, 3 tbsp clear honey and the grated zest and juice of 1 lemon.

1 Preheat the oven to 200°C (180°C fan oven) mark 6. Put the garlic into a large bowl with the honey and chilli sauce and stir to mix. Add the chicken thighs and toss to coat.

2 Put the chicken into a roasting tin and roast in the oven for 15–20 minutes until golden and cooked through and the juices run clear when the thighs are pierced with a skewer. Serve with rice, if you like, and a crisp green salad.

One-pan Chicken with Tomatoes

Preparation Time
5 minutes
Cooking Time
20–25 minutes

- 4 chicken thighs
- 1 red onion, sliced
- 400g can chopped tomatoes with herbs
- 400g can mixed beans, drained and rinsed
- 2 tsp balsamic vinegar
- freshly chopped flat-leafed parsley to garnish

NUTRITIONAL INFORMATION
Per Serving 238 calories, 4g fat (of which 1g saturates), 20g carbohydrate, 1g salt

Serves 4

Healthy Tip

Tomatoes are packed with vitamin C and lycopene, a powerful antioxidant linked with a lower risk of cancer of the prostate. It is absorbed more readily from cooked tomatoes, including the canned variety, which makes this dish a healthy option. The mixed beans add useful amounts of fibre, protein and iron.

Try Something Different

Use flageolet beans or other canned beans instead of the mixed beans, and garnish with freshly chopped basil or oregano.

1 Heat a non-stick pan and fry the chicken thighs, skin side down, until golden. Turn over and fry for 5 minutes.

2 Add the onion and fry for a further 5 minutes. Add the tomatoes, mixed beans and vinegar, cover the pan and simmer for 10–12 minutes until piping hot. Garnish with parsley and serve immediately.

Spiced Chicken with Garlic Butter Beans

Preparation Time
10 minutes
Cooking Time
15 minutes

- 4 boneless, skinless chicken breasts, about 100g (3½oz) each
- 1 tbsp olive oil
- 1 tsp ground coriander
- 1 tsp ground cumin
- 100g (3½oz) couscous
- 3 tbsp extra virgin olive oil
- 1 garlic clove, sliced
- 2 × 400g cans no-added-sugar-or-salt butter beans, drained and rinsed
- juice of 1 lemon
- 1 small red onion, thinly sliced
- 50g (2oz) marinated roasted peppers, drained
- 2 medium tomatoes, seeded and chopped
- 1 tbsp freshly chopped coriander
- 1 tbsp freshly chopped flat-leafed parsley
- salt and ground black pepper
- green salad and lemon wedges to serve

NUTRITIONAL INFORMATION
Per Serving 443 calories, 16g fat (of which 3g saturates), 42g carbohydrate, 0.2g salt

1 Put the chicken on a board, cover with clingfilm and flatten lightly with a rolling pin. Put the olive oil into a large bowl with the ground coriander and cumin. Mix together, then add the chicken and turn until the chicken is coated in the mixture.

2 Heat a large frying pan and cook the chicken for 5–7 minutes on each side until golden and the juices run clear when pierced with a sharp knife.

3 While the chicken is cooking, put the couscous into a bowl and add 100ml (3½fl oz) boiling water. Cover with clingfilm and put to one side.

4 Put the extra virgin olive oil into a small pan with the garlic and butter beans and warm through for 3–4 minutes over a low heat. Stir in the lemon juice and season with salt and pepper.

5 Fluff up the couscous with a fork and tip in the warm butter beans. Add the onion, peppers, tomatoes and herbs and stir together. Slice each chicken breast into four pieces and arrange alongside the bean salad. Serve with a green salad and lemon wedges to squeeze over it.

Chicken with Spicy Couscous

Preparation Time
15 minutes, plus soaking

Serves 4

- 125g (4oz) couscous
- 1 ripe mango, peeled, stoned and cut into 2.5cm (1in) chunks
- 1 tbsp lemon or lime juice
- 125g tub fresh tomato salsa
- 3 tbsp mango chutney
- 3 tbsp orange juice
- 2 tbsp freshly chopped coriander, plus extra to garnish
- 200g (7oz) chargrilled chicken fillets
- 4 tbsp fromage frais (optional)
- salt and ground black pepper
- lime wedges to garnish

NUTRITIONAL INFORMATION
Per Serving 223 calories, 6g fat (of which 2g saturates), 30g carbohydrate, 0.2g salt

Healthy Tip
Couscous is made from semolina flour and has a low GI (see page 12), helping to make you feel fuller longer. It provides B vitamins and valuable amounts of selenium. Mango is rich in betacarotene, an antioxidant which helps combat harmful free radicals and promotes healthy skin.

1 Put the couscous into a large bowl and pour 300ml (½ pint) boiling water over. Season well with salt and pepper, then leave to soak for 15 minutes.

2 Put the mango chunks on a large plate and sprinkle with the lemon or lime juice.

3 Mix the tomato salsa with the mango chutney, orange juice and coriander in a small bowl.

4 Drain the couscous if necessary, fluff the grains with a fork, then stir in the salsa mixture and check the seasoning. Turn out on to a large serving dish and arrange the chicken and mango on top.

5 Just before serving, spoon the fromage frais over the chicken, if you like, then garnish with chopped coriander and lime wedges.

Mild Spiced Chicken & Quinoa

Preparation Time
15 minutes
Cooking Time
20 minutes

- 2 tbsp mango chutney
- juice of ½ lemon
- 1 tbsp olive oil
- 2 tsp mild curry powder
- 1 tsp paprika
- 350g (12oz) skinless chicken breast, cut into thick strips
- 200g (7oz) quinoa (see Cook's Tip)
- 1 cucumber, roughly chopped
- ½ bunch of spring onions, sliced
- 75g (3oz) ready-to-eat dried apricots, sliced
- 2 tbsp freshly chopped mint, basil or tarragon
- salt and ground black pepper
- fresh mint sprigs to garnish

NUTRITIONAL INFORMATION
Per Serving 268 calories, 3g fat (of which trace saturates), 37g carbohydrate, 0.4g salt

Cook's Tip

Quinoa is a tiny, bead-shaped grain with a slightly nutty flavour. It's easy to prepare and nearly quadruples in size and looks translucent when cooked. It can be substituted for rice or couscous.

1 Put the chutney, lemon juice, ½ tbsp oil, the curry powder, paprika and salt and pepper into a bowl and mix together. Add the chicken strips and toss to coat.

2 Cook the quinoa in boiling water for 10–12 minutes until tender or according to the pack instructions. Drain thoroughly. Put into a bowl, then stir in the cucumber, spring onions, apricots, herbs and remaining oil.

3 Put the chicken and marinade into a pan and fry over a high heat for 2–3 minutes, then add 150ml (¼ pint) water. Bring to the boil, then reduce the heat and simmer for 5 minutes or until the chicken is cooked through. Serve with the quinoa garnished with mint.

Quick Chicken Stir-fry

Preparation Time
10 minutes
Cooking Time
12 minutes

- 1 tsp groundnut oil
- 300g (11oz) boneless, skinless chicken breasts, sliced
- 4 spring onions, chopped
- 200g (7oz) medium rice noodles
- 100g (3½oz) mangetouts
- 200g (7oz) purple sprouting broccoli, chopped
- 2–3 tbsp sweet chilli sauce
- coriander leaves to garnish
- lime wedges (optional) to serve

NUTRITIONAL INFORMATION
Per Serving 316 calories, 3g fat (of which 1g saturates), 46g carbohydrate, 0.5g salt

1 Heat the oil in a wok or large frying pan. Add the chicken and spring onions and stir-fry over a high heat for 5–6 minutes until the chicken is golden brown.

2 Meanwhile, soak the rice noodles in boiling water for 4 minutes or according to the pack instructions.

3 Add the mangetouts, broccoli and chilli sauce to the chicken. Continue to stir-fry for 4 minutes.

4 Drain the noodles, then add to the pan and toss everything together. Scatter the coriander over the top and serve with lime wedges to squeeze over the stir-fry, if you like.

Try Something Different

Other vegetables are just as good in this dish: try pak choi, button mushrooms, carrots cut into matchsticks, or baby sweetcorn.

Healthy Tip

Stir-frying is a healthy cooking method as it uses only minimal amounts of oil, thus helping keep the calorie and overall fat content of the dish low. It also seals in the vitamins so losses are kept to a minimum. Purple sprouting broccoli contains the phytochemical sulphoraphane (thought to help prevent cancer) and may provide resistance against heart disease and Type 2 diabetes. It is packed with vitamin C and is a good source of carotenoids, iron, folate, calcium, fibre and vitamin A.

Serves 4

Chicken Stir-fry with Noodles

Preparation Time
20 minutes
Cooking Time
20 minutes

- 250g pack thick egg noodles
- 2 tbsp vegetable oil
- 2 garlic cloves, crushed
- 4 boneless, skinless chicken breasts, each sliced into 10 pieces
- 3 medium carrots, about 450g (1lb), cut into thin strips, about 5cm (2in) long
- 1 bunch of spring onions, sliced
- 200g (7oz) mangetouts
- 155g jar sweet chilli and lemongrass sauce

NUTRITIONAL INFORMATION
Per Serving 355 calories, 10g fat (of which 2g saturates), 29g carbohydrate, 0.5g salt

Serves 4

Try Something Different
Use turkey or pork escalopes instead of the chicken, if you like: you will need 450g (1lb), cut into thin strips.

1 Cook the noodles in boiling water according to the pack instructions.

2 Meanwhile, heat the oil in a wok or frying pan. Add the garlic and stir-fry for 1–2 minutes. Add the chicken pieces and stir-fry for 5 minutes, then add the carrot strips and stir-fry for a further 5 minutes.

3 Add the spring onions, mangetouts and sauce to the wok and stir-fry for 5 minutes.

4 Drain the cooked noodles well and add to the wok. Toss everything together and serve.

Chicken Falafels

Preparation Time
20 minutes, plus soaking
Cooking Time
20 minutes

Serves 4

- 450g (1lb) minced chicken
- 3 shallots, finely chopped
- 125g (4oz) canned chickpeas (½ can), drained and rinsed
- 2.5cm (1in) piece fresh root ginger, peeled and grated
- ½ tsp salt
- 20g (¾oz) freshly chopped coriander
- 1 medium egg
- 3 tbsp olive oil
- 400g can chopped tomatoes
- 1 tsp caster sugar

FOR THE COUSCOUS SALAD

- 200g (7oz) couscous
- 350ml (12fl oz) hot chicken stock
- grated zest and juice of ½ lemon
- 25g (1oz) pinenuts
- seeds from ½ pomegranate
- 3 tbsp extra virgin olive oil
- 2–3 tbsp freshly chopped parsley

NUTRITIONAL INFORMATION

Per Serving 287 calories, 14g fat (of which 3g saturates), 10g carbohydrate, 1.1g salt

1 First, make the couscous salad. Put the couscous into a bowl and add the hot stock and lemon zest. Leave to soak for 20 minutes. Meanwhile, toast the pinenuts in a dry pan, tossing regularly, until golden. Use a fork to fluff up the couscous, then stir in the pinenuts, pomegranate seeds, lemon juice, extra virgin olive oil and parsley.

2 Put the minced chicken into a food processor. Add 1 chopped shallot, the chickpeas, grated ginger and salt and whiz to combine.

3 Add the coriander and egg and whiz again briefly. With damp hands, shape into 12 balls, each measuring 6.5cm (2½in).

4 Heat 2 tbsp olive oil in a frying pan. Fry the patties for 2–3 minutes on each side until golden brown.

5 Meanwhile, fry the remaining shallots in a pan with the remaining olive oil. Stir in the tomatoes and sugar and simmer for 10 minutes or until slightly thickened. Serve the patties with the couscous salad, and with the sauce on the side.

Spiced Tikka Kebabs

Preparation Time
10 minutes
Cooking Time
20 minutes

Serves 4

- 2 tbsp tikka paste
- 150g (5oz) natural yogurt
- juice of ½ lime
- 4 spring onions, chopped
- 350g (12oz) skinless chicken, cut into bite-size pieces
- lime wedges and Mixed Salad (see Cook's Tip) to serve

NUTRITIONAL INFORMATION

Per Serving 150 calories, 5g fat (of which 1g saturates), 4g carbohydrate, 0.3g salt

Healthy Tip

This dish is cooked in a yogurt marinade, which means that no additional oil is required for cooking and is therefore a great low fat cooking method. Chicken is a rich source of protein and B vitamins; the yogurt adds valuable calcium.

Cook's Tip

Mixed Salad Put 75g (3oz) green salad leaves into a large bowl. Add ¼ chopped avocado, a handful of halved cherry tomatoes, ½ chopped cucumber and the juice of 1 lime. Season to taste with salt and pepper and mix together well.

1 Preheat the grill. Put the tikka paste, yogurt, lime juice and spring onions into a large bowl. Add the chicken and toss well until coated. Thread the chicken on to metal skewers.

2 Grill the chicken for 8–10 minutes on each side, turning and basting with the paste, until cooked through. Serve with lime wedges to squeeze over the kebabs, and Mixed Salad.

Moroccan Spiced Chicken Kebabs

Preparation Time
10 minutes, plus marinating
Cooking Time
10–12 minutes

- 2 tbsp olive oil
- 15g (½oz) fresh flat-leafed parsley
- 1 garlic clove
- ½ tsp paprika
- 1 tsp ground cumin
- zest and juice of 1 lemon
- 4 skinless chicken breasts, cut into bite-size chunks
- salt
- shredded lettuce, sliced cucumber and tomatoes, and lime wedges to serve

NUTRITIONAL INFORMATION
Per Serving 190 calories, 7g fat (of which 1g saturates), 1g carbohydrate, 0.2g salt

Serves 4

Try Something Different
Instead of chicken, use 700g (1½lb) lean lamb fillet or leg of lamb, cut into chunks.

1 Put the oil into a blender and add the parsley, garlic, paprika, cumin, lemon zest and juice and a pinch of salt. Whiz to make a paste.

2 Put the chicken into a medium-sized shallow dish and rub in the spice paste. Leave to marinate for at least 20 minutes. Soak some wooden skewers in water. Preheat the grill to high.

3 Thread the marinated chicken on to the soaked skewers and grill for 10–12 minutes, turning every now and then, until the meat is cooked through. Serve with shredded lettuce, sliced cucumber and tomatoes, and lime wedges.

Serves 6

Oven-baked Chicken with Garlic Potatoes

Preparation Time
10 minutes
Cooking Time
1½ hours

- 2 medium baking potatoes, thinly sliced
- a little freshly grated nutmeg
- 600ml (1 pint) white sauce (use a ready-made sauce or make your own, see Cook's Tip)
- ½ × 390g can fried onions
- 250g (9oz) frozen peas
- 450g (1lb) cooked chicken, shredded
- 20g pack garlic butter, sliced
- a little butter to grease
- salt and ground black pepper
- Granary bread to serve (optional)

NUTRITIONAL INFORMATION
Per Serving 376 calories, 16g fat (of which 5g saturates), 32g carbohydrate, 1.2g salt

1 Preheat the oven to 180°C (160°C fan oven) mark 4. Layer half the potatoes over the base of a 2.4 litre (4¼ pint) shallow ovenproof dish and season with the nutmeg, salt and pepper. Pour the white sauce over and shake the dish, so that the sauce settles through the gaps in the potatoes.

2 Spread half the onions on top, then scatter on half the peas. Arrange the shredded chicken on top, then add the remaining peas and onions. Finish with the remaining potatoes, arranged in an even layer, and dot with garlic butter. Season with salt and pepper.

3 Cover tightly with buttered foil and cook in the oven for 1 hour. Increase the heat to 200°C (180°C fan oven) mark 6, remove the foil and cook for 20–30 minutes until the potatoes are golden and tender. Serve with Granary bread, if you like, to mop up the juices.

Cook's Tip

White Sauce To make 600ml (1 pint) white sauce, melt 25g (1oz) butter in a pan, then stir in 25g (1oz) plain flour. Cook, stirring constantly, for 1 minute. Remove from the heat and gradually pour in 600ml (1 pint) milk, beating after each addition. Return to the heat and cook, stirring, until the sauce has thickened and is velvety and smooth. Season with salt, pepper and freshly grated nutmeg.

Oven-baked Mediterranean Chicken

Preparation Time
5 minutes
Cooking Time
20 minutes

- 1 red pepper, seeded and chopped
- 2 tbsp capers
- 2 tbsp freshly chopped rosemary
- 2 tbsp olive oil
- 4 skinless chicken breasts, about 125g (4oz) each
- salt and ground black pepper
- rice or new potatoes to serve

NUTRITIONAL INFORMATION
Per Serving 223 calories, 7g fat (of which 1g saturates), 3g carbohydrate, 0.2g salt

Serves 4

Healthy Tip

Red peppers are a rich source of vitamin C, betacarotene and beta-cryptoxanthin, all powerful antioxidants that help protect the body from heart disease and certain cancers. Oven-roasting the peppers in olive oil is healthy way of preserving the vitamin content.

Try Something Different

Use chopped black olives instead of the capers.

1 Preheat the oven to 200°C (180°C fan oven) mark 6. Put the red pepper into a bowl with the capers, rosemary and oil. Season with salt and pepper and mix well.

2 Put the chicken breasts into an ovenproof dish and spoon the pepper mixture over the top. Roast for 15–20 minutes or until the chicken is cooked through and the topping is hot. Serve with rice or new potatoes.

Grilled Spicy Chicken

Serves 4

Preparation Time
10 minutes, plus marinating
Cooking Time
about 20 minutes

- 4 boneless, skinless chicken breasts
- 1 tbsp coriander seeds, crushed
- 1 tsp ground cumin
- 2 tsp mild curry paste
- 1 garlic clove, crushed
- 450g (1lb) natural yogurt
- 3 tbsp freshly chopped coriander
- salt and ground black pepper
- fresh coriander sprigs to garnish
- rice and Mixed Salad (see Cook's Tip, page 122) to serve

NUTRITIONAL INFORMATION
Per Serving 157 calories, 2g fat (of which 1g saturates), 3g carbohydrate, 0.2g salt

Healthy Tip
This dish is low in fat as it is marinated in a low fat yogurt mixture instead of an oil-based version. Yogurt is rich in calcium, important for maintaining bone strength and, according to recent studies has been linked with reduced blood pressure and heart disease risk.

1 Prick the chicken breasts all over with a fork, cover with clingfilm and lightly beat with a rolling pin to flatten them slightly.

2 Mix the coriander seeds with the cumin, curry paste, garlic and yogurt in a large shallow dish. Season with salt and pepper and stir in the chopped coriander.

3 Add the chicken and turn to coat with the spiced yogurt. Cover and leave to marinate in the fridge for at least 30 minutes or overnight.

4 Preheat the barbecue or griddle. Lift the chicken out of the marinade and cook over a medium-high heat, turning occasionally, for about 20 minutes or until cooked through. Serve immediately, with rice and a Mixed Salad, garnished with coriander sprigs.

Garlic & Thyme Fish Steaks

Preparation Time
10 minutes, plus marinating
Cooking Time
5–10 minutes

- 2 garlic cloves, crushed
- 2 tbsp chopped thyme leaves
- 4 tbsp olive oil
- 2 lemons
- 4 × 200g (7oz) firm fish steaks, such as tuna, swordfish or shark
- salt and ground black pepper
- Barbecued Red Peppers (see Cook's Tip) and salad leaves to serve

NUTRITIONAL INFORMATION
Per Serving 299 calories, 12g fat (of which 3g saturates), trace carbohydrate, 0.2g salt

1 Put the garlic, thyme, oil and juice of one lemon into a large shallow container and mix well.

2 Add the fish steaks and season with salt and pepper, then cover and chill in the refrigerator for 20 minutes. Cut the other lemon into four slices and put to one side.

3 Preheat the barbecue or a griddle pan.

4 Cook the fish on the barbecue or griddle for 4–5 minutes on one side and brush with a little of the marinade. Turn over, put a slice of reserved lemon on top of each steak and continue to cook for 3–4 minutes until cooked through. Serve with Barbecued Red Peppers and salad leaves.

Cook's Tip

Barbecued Red Peppers Halve 3 red peppers, seed, then cut into thick strips. Brush with 1 tbsp olive oil and season with salt and pepper. Cook on the barbecue or on a preheated griddle pan for 15–20 minutes until the peppers are tender.

Serves 4

Cod with Cherry Tomatoes

Preparation Time
15 minutes
Cooking Time
20–25 minutes

- 4 × 100g (3½oz) cod steaks
- 1 tbsp plain flour
- 2 tbsp olive oil
- 1 small onion, sliced
- 1 large red chilli, seeded and chopped (see Cook's Tip, page 55)
- 1 garlic clove, crushed
- 250g (9oz) cherry tomatoes, halved
- 4 spring onions, chopped
- 2 tbsp freshly chopped coriander
- salt and ground black pepper

NUTRITIONAL INFORMATION
Per Serving 168 calories, 7g fat (of which 1g saturates), 8g carbohydrate, 0.2g salt

Try Something Different
Use another white fish such as sea bass or pollack fillets instead of the cod, if you like.

1 Season the cod with salt and pepper, then dust lightly with the flour. Heat 1 tbsp oil in a large frying pan. Add the onion and fry for 5–10 minutes until golden.

2 Pour the remaining oil into the pan. Add the cod and fry for 3 minutes on each side. Add the chilli, garlic, cherry tomatoes, spring onions and coriander and season with salt and pepper. Cover and continue to cook for 5–10 minutes until everything is heated through. Serve immediately.

Oven-poached Cod with Spring Onions & Herbs

Preparation Time
10 minutes
Cooking Time
10 minutes

- 10 spring onions, sliced
- 2 garlic cloves, crushed
- 6 tbsp shredded fresh mint
- 6 tbsp freshly chopped flat-leafed parsley
- juice of ½ lemon
- 150ml (¼ pint) fish, chicken or vegetable stock
- 4 cod fillets, about 200g (7oz) each
- salt and ground black pepper
- lemon wedges to garnish
- mashed potatoes to serve

NUTRITIONAL INFORMATION

Per Serving 170 calories, 2g fat (of which trace saturates), 1g carbohydrate, 0.5g salt

Healthy Tip

The flat-leafed parsley used in this dish is rich in vitamin C (it contains three times as much vitamin C as oranges weight for weight), betacarotene, folate and iron. It contains flavanoids and other phytochemicals, recognised as having cancer-fighting properties. Mint is also a source of anti-cancer substances and well-recognised for soothing the digestive tract.

Try Something Different

There are lots of alternatives to cod: try sea bass, gurnard or pollack.

1 Preheat the oven to 230°C (210°C fan oven) mark 8. Combine the spring onions (putting some of the green part to one side), garlic, mint, parsley, lemon juice and stock in an ovenproof dish that can hold the cod in a single layer.

2 Put the cod on the herb and garlic mixture and turn to moisten. Season with salt and pepper, then roast for 8–10 minutes.

3 Sprinkle with the reserved spring onion, garnish with lemon wedges and serve with mashed potatoes.

Serves 4

Cod Steaks with Fennel

Preparation Time
10 minutes, plus marinating
Cooking Time
30 minutes

- 1 tbsp hoisin sauce
- 4 tbsp light soy sauce
- 4 tbsp dry vermouth
- 4 tbsp orange juice
- ½ tsp Chinese five-spice powder
- ½ tsp ground cumin
- 1 garlic clove, crushed
- 4 × 150g (5oz) thick cod fillets or steaks (see Cook's Tip)
- 1 tbsp vegetable oil
- 2 fennel bulbs, about 700g (1½lb), thinly sliced and tops put to one side
- 2 tsp sesame seeds

NUTRITIONAL INFORMATION
Per Serving 209 calories, 6g fat (of which 1g saturates), 6g carbohydrate, 1.4g salt

1 For the marinade, combine the hoisin sauce, soy sauce, vermouth, orange juice, five-spice powder, cumin and garlic. Put the cod into a shallow dish and pour the marinade over it. Cover and leave to marinate in a cool place for at least 1 hour.

2 Preheat the grill or a lightly oiled griddle. Remove the fish and put the marinade to one side. Cook the fish under the hot grill or on the hot griddle for 4 minutes, then turn over and cook for a further 3–4 minutes until cooked.

3 Heat the oil in a sauté pan. Add the fennel and cook briskly for 5–7 minutes until brown and beginning to soften. Add the marinade, bring to the boil and bubble until reduced and sticky.

4 Put the fish on a bed of fennel, spoon any pan juices around it and sprinkle with the sesame seeds. Garnish with the reserved fennel tops.

Healthy Tip

Fennel is packed with antioxidants that helps protect the body from free radical damage. It is believed to help combat certain cancers. It is also a good source of fibre, vitamin C, folate, magnesium, calcium, iron, and phosphorus, and helpful in easing digestive problems such as gas and bloating.

Cook's Tip

Ask your fishmonger to remove the scales from the cod's skin. When grilled, the skin will be crisp and delicious to eat.

Sardines with Mediterranean Vegetables

Preparation Time
15 minutes
Cooking Time
20 minutes

- 3 tbsp olive oil
- 2 red onions, about 300g (11oz), halved and cut into petals
- 2 garlic cloves, crushed
- 2 red peppers, about 375g (12oz), seeded and cut into chunks
- 225g (8oz) courgettes, cut into small chunks
- 900g (2lb) sardines (about 16), cleaned
- olive oil and lemon juice to drizzle
- salt and ground black pepper
- small fresh basil sprigs to garnish

NUTRITIONAL INFORMATION
Per Serving 409 calories, 23g fat (of which 5g saturates), 13g carbohydrate, 0.5g salt

1 Heat the oil in a large griddle pan, or preheat the grill. Add the onions and fry for 2–3 minutes until almost soft. Add the garlic and peppers and stir-fry for 5 minutes, then add the courgettes and stir-fry for 4–5 minutes until almost soft. Remove from the griddle and keep warm.

2 Season the sardines and cook on the griddle or under the hot grill for 3–4 minutes on each side until cooked in the centre.

3 Drizzle the sardines with a little olive oil and lemon juice. Garnish with basil sprigs and serve with the vegetables.

Healthy Tip

Sardines are an excellent source of omega-3s, which help prevent clots forming in the arteries (thrombosis), stroke and high blood pressure. They are also beneficial for promoting healthy joints and alleviating rheumatoid arthritis. They also provide plenty of protein and iron.

Get Ahead

To prepare ahead Complete the recipe to the end of step 1, cover and chill for up to 3 hours.
To use Stir-fry the vegetables for 2–3 minutes until hot. Complete the recipe.

Serves 4

Chinese-style Sesame-crusted Trout

Preparation Time
10 minutes
Cooking Time
10–13 minutes

- 1 tbsp sesame oil
- 1 tbsp soy sauce
- juice of 1 lime
- 4 × 150g (5oz) trout fillets
- 2 tbsp sesame seeds
- lime wedges, herb salad and fennel to serve

NUTRITIONAL INFORMATION
Per Serving 259 calories, 15g fat (of which 3g saturates) 1g carbohydrate, 0.8g salt

Serves 4

Cook's Tip

Sesame seeds are deliciously nutty and highly nutritious. They are a valuable source of protein, good omega fats and vitamin E. Lightly toasted sesame seeds, crushed with a little salt and stirred into 1–2 tbsp olive oil, make an excellent dressing for lightly cooked green beans, broccoli florets and carrots.

1 Preheat the grill. Put the oil into a bowl, add the soy sauce and lime juice and whisk together.

2 Put the trout fillets on a baking sheet, pour the sesame mixture over them and cook under the hot grill for 8–10 minutes. Sprinkle with the sesame seeds and grill for a further 2–3 minutes until the seeds are golden. Serve with lime wedges, a herb salad and finely sliced fennel.

Crispy Crumbed Fish

Preparation Time
5 minutes
Cooking Time
10–15 minutes

Serves 4

- 50g (2oz) fresh breadcrumbs
- a small handful of freshly chopped flat-leafed parsley
- 2 tbsp capers, chopped
- grated zest of 1 lemon
- 4 haddock or pollack fillets, about 150g (5oz) each
- ½ tbsp Dijon mustard
- juice of ½ lemon
- salt and ground black pepper
- new potatoes and Mixed Salad (see Cook's Tip, page 122) to serve

NUTRITIONAL INFORMATION
Per Serving 171 calories, 1g fat (of which trace saturates), 10g carbohydrate, 0.8g salt

1 Preheat the oven to 180°C (160°C fan oven) mark 4. Put the breadcrumbs into a bowl with the parsley, capers and lemon zest. Mix well, then set aside.

2 Put the fish fillets on a baking tray. Mix the mustard and half the lemon juice in a bowl with a little salt and pepper, then spread over the top of each piece of fish. Spoon the breadcrumb mixture on top – don't worry if some falls off.

3 Cook in the oven for 10–15 minutes until the fish is cooked and the breadcrumbs are golden. Pour the remaining lemon juice over the top and serve with new potatoes and a Mixed Salad.

Serves 6

Red Mullet with Cherry Tomatoes & Basil Oil

Preparation Time
10 minutes
Cooking Time
about 40 minutes

- 450g (1lb) cherry tomatoes, mixture of red and yellow
- 2 tbsp green peppercorns in brine, drained
- 8 garlic cloves, bruised not peeled
- zest and juice of 1 small lemon
- 75ml (2½fl oz) basil oil
- 12 × 50g (2oz) red mullet fillets, descaled
- a small handful of fresh basil leaves, shredded
- salt and ground black pepper
- steamed new potatoes to serve

NUTRITIONAL INFORMATION

Per Serving (without potatoes) 282 calories, 17g fat (of which 2g saturates), 4g carbohydrates, 0.4g salt

1 Preheat the oven to 180°C (160°C fan oven) mark 4. Halve the larger tomatoes, then put them all into a shallow roasting tin. Add the peppercorns, garlic and lemon zest, drizzle with half the oil and bake for 20 minutes.

2 Add the fish to the tin and drizzle with the remaining oil. Cook for a further 15–20 minutes until golden and cooked through.

3 Pour the lemon juice over the fish and sprinkle with basil leaves and salt and pepper. Serve with steamed new potatoes.

Healthy Tip

Red mullet is classified as a white fish but it has a richer and more satisfying flavour than most other white fish thanks to its slightly higher fat content – around 4g per fillet. It is baked with basil oil – a good source of monounsaturates – and tomatoes, which are a rich source of vitamin C and betacarotene.

Pasta, Rice, Noodles & Grains

Tomato & Artichoke Pasta

Preparation Time
10 minutes
Cooking Time
10–12 minutes

Serves 4

- 300g (11oz) penne
- 6 pieces sunblush tomatoes in oil
- 1 red onion, sliced
- about 10 pieces roasted artichoke hearts in oil, drained and roughly chopped
- 50g (2oz) pitted black olives, roughly chopped
- 50g (2oz) pecorino cheese, grated
- 100g (3½oz) rocket
- salt

NUTRITIONAL INFORMATION

Per Serving 380 calories, 11g fat (of which 4g saturates), 59g carbohydrate, 1.3g salt

Healthy Tip

Artichokes are a good source of vitamin C, folate, magnesium and dietary fibre. They contain the powerful phytonutrients cynarin and silymarin, which have beneficial effects on the liver. The olives contain useful amounts of vitamin E while the rocket adds iron and folate.

1 Cook the pasta in a large pan of lightly salted boiling water according to the pack instructions until al dente. Drain well.

2 Meanwhile, drain the sunblush tomatoes, reserving the oil, and roughly chop. Heat 1 tbsp oil from the tomatoes in a large frying pan. Add the onion and fry for 5–6 minutes until softened and turning golden. Add the tomatoes, artichokes and olives to the pan and heat for 3–4 minutes until hot.

3 Add half the pecorino cheese and stir through. Remove from the heat and stir in the rocket and pasta. Divide the pasta among four bowls and sprinkle the remaining pecorino over the top to serve.

Ham & Mushroom Pasta

Preparation Time
5 minutes
Cooking Time
15 minutes

- 350g (12oz) penne
- 1 tbsp olive oil
- 2 shallots, sliced
- 200g (7oz) small button mushrooms
- 3 tbsp crème fraîche
- 125g (4oz) smoked ham, roughly chopped
- 2 tbsp freshly chopped flat-leafed parsley
- salt and ground black pepper

NUTRITIONAL INFORMATION

Per Serving 415 calories, 10g fat (of which 4g saturates), 67g carbohydrate, 1g salt

Healthy Tip

Mushrooms contain significant amounts of selenium, which may help prevent certain cancers, in particular prostate cancer. They also supply B vitamins and potassium and are very low in fat.

1 Cook the pasta in a large pan of lightly salted boiling water according to the pack instructions until al dente.

2 Meanwhile, heat the oil in a pan. Add the shallots and fry gently for 3 minutes or until starting to soften. Add the mushrooms and fry for 5–6 minutes.

3 Drain the pasta, put back in the pan and add the shallots and mushrooms. Stir in the crème fraîche, ham and parsley. Toss everything together, season to taste with salt and pepper and heat through to serve.

Penne with Smoked Salmon

Preparation Time
5 minutes
Cooking Time
10–15 minutes

Serves 4

- 350g (12oz) penne or other short tubular pasta
- 200ml (7fl oz) half-fat crème fraîche
- 150g (5oz) smoked salmon, roughly chopped
- 20g (¾oz) fresh dill, finely chopped
- salt and ground black pepper
- lemon wedges to serve (optional)

NUTRITIONAL INFORMATION

Per Serving 432 calories, 11g fat (of which 6g saturates), 67g carbohydrate, 1.7g salt

1 Cook the pasta in a large pan of lightly salted boiling water according to the pack instructions until al dente. Drain well.

2 Meanwhile, put the crème fraîche into a large bowl. Add the smoked salmon and dill, season well with salt and pepper and mix together. Gently stir into the drained penne and serve immediately with lemon wedges, if you like, to squeeze over the salmon and pasta.

Stuffed Pasta Shells

Preparation Time
15 minutes
Cooking Time
about 1 hour

- 2 tbsp olive oil
- 1 large onion, finely chopped
- a few fresh rosemary or oregano sprigs, chopped
- 125g (4oz) small flat mushrooms, sliced
- 6 plump coarse sausages, skinned
- 175ml (6fl oz) red wine
- 300ml (½ pint) passata
- 4 tbsp sun-dried tomato paste
- sugar to taste, if necessary
- 250g (9oz) large pasta shells, such as conchiglioni rigati
- 150ml (¼ pint) half-fat single cream (optional)
- salt
- freshly grated Parmesan to garnish
- green salad to serve

NUTRITIONAL INFORMATION

Per Serving 378 calories, 17g fat (of which 5g saturates), 41g carbohydrate, 1.1g salt

1 Preheat the oven to 180°C (160°C fan oven) mark 4. Heat the oil in a deep frying pan. Stir in the onion and rosemary or oregano and cook over a gentle heat for 10 minutes or until the onion is soft and golden. Add the mushrooms and cook over a medium heat until the vegetables are soft and beginning to brown at the edges. Tip the onion mixture into a bowl.

2 Crumble the sausagemeat into the hot pan and stir over a high heat with a wooden spoon, breaking the meat up as you do so, until browned all over. Reduce the heat slightly and pour in the wine. Leave to bubble and reduce by about half. Return the onion mixture to the pan and add the passata and sun-dried tomato paste. Bubble gently for a further 10 minutes. Add a pinch of sugar if the sauce tastes a little sharp.

3 Meanwhile, cook the pasta shells in a large pan of lightly salted boiling water for 10 minutes or until al dente. Drain well and run under the cold tap to cool.

4 Fill the shells with the sauce and put into a shallow ovenproof dish. Drizzle with any extra sauce and the cream, if using, and bake for 30 minutes or until piping hot. Sprinkle with Parmesan and serve with a big bowl of green salad.

Pasta with Goat's Cheese & Sunblush Tomatoes

Preparation Time
5 minutes
Cooking Time
10 minutes

Serves 4

- 300g (11oz) pasta shells, such as conchiglie
- 2 tbsp olive oil
- 1 red pepper, seeded and chopped
- 1 yellow pepper, seeded and chopped
- ½ tbsp sun-dried tomato paste
- 75g (3oz) sunblush tomatoes
- 75g (3oz) soft goat's cheese
- 2 tbsp freshly chopped parsley
- salt and ground black pepper

NUTRITIONAL INFORMATION

Per Serving 409 calories, 12g fat (of which 4g saturates), 64g carbohydrate, 0.4g salt

1 Cook the pasta in a large pan of lightly salted boiling water according to the pack instructions until al dente.

2 Meanwhile, heat the oil in a pan and fry the red and yellow peppers for 5–7 minutes until softened and just beginning to brown. Add the tomato paste and cook for a further minute. Add a ladleful of pasta cooking water to the pan and simmer for 1–2 minutes to make a sauce.

3 Drain the pasta and put back in the pan. Pour the sauce on top, then add the tomatoes, goat's cheese and parsley. Toss together until the cheese begins to melt, then season with pepper and serve.

Borlotti, Anchovy & Spinach Pasta

Preparation Time
10 minutes
Cooking Time
1 hour

Serves 4

- 300g (11oz) pasta shells, such as conchiglie
- 30g can anchovies, drained and chopped, oil from the can put to one side
- 400g can borlotti beans, drained and rinsed
- a handful of spinach leaves

FOR THE TOMATO SAUCE

- 2 tbsp oil from the drained anchovies
- 2 carrots, diced
- 1 large onion, diced
- 2 celery sticks, diced
- 1 bay leaf
- 250ml (9fl oz) dry white wine
- 300ml (½ pint) hot vegetable stock
- 2 × 400g cans chopped tomatoes
- 1 tsp caster sugar or to taste (optional)
- salt and ground black pepper

NUTRITIONAL INFORMATION

Per Serving 518 calories, 9g fat (of which 1g saturates), 86g carbohydrate, 1.8g salt

1 To make the tomato sauce, preheat the oven to 180°C (160°C fan oven) mark 4. Heat the oil in a flameproof casserole on the hob. Add the carrots, onion, celery and bay leaf and season to taste. Cook gently for 15–20 minutes, stirring occasionally, until soft and golden.

2 Add the wine, hot stock and tomatoes. Bring to the boil, then cover and cook in the oven for 20 minutes. Uncover and cook for a further 20 minutes until the sauce is thick. Taste the sauce – if it's a little acidic, add the sugar.

3 Cook the pasta in a large pan of lightly salted boiling water according to the pack instructions until al dente.

4 Meanwhile, add the anchovies to the simmering tomato sauce with 1 tbsp of the oil from the can, the beans and spinach. Heat for 5 minutes. Drain the pasta and toss through the sauce. Serve.

Serves 4

Seafood Spaghetti with Pepper & Almond Sauce

Preparation Time
20 minutes
Cooking Time
25 minutes

- 1 small red pepper
- 1 red chilli (see Cook's Tip, page 55)
- 50g (2oz) blanched almonds
- 2–3 garlic cloves, chopped
- 2 tbsp red wine vinegar
- 350ml (12fl oz) tomato juice
- a small handful of flat-leafed parsley
- 300g (11oz) spaghetti
- 450g (1lb) mixed cooked seafood, such as prawns, mussels and squid
- salt and ground black pepper

NUTRITIONAL INFORMATION
Per Serving 426 calories, 9g fat (of which 1g saturates), 62g carbohydrate, 0.9g salt

1 Preheat the grill. Grill the red pepper and chilli, turning occasionally, until the skins char and blacken. Cover and leave to cool slightly, then peel off the skins. Halve, seed, then put the flesh into a food processor.

2 Toast the almonds under the grill until golden. Add the toasted almonds and garlic to the processor with the vinegar, tomato juice and half the parsley, then season with salt and pepper. Whiz until almost smooth, then transfer the sauce to a large pan.

3 Meanwhile, cook the spaghetti in a pan of lightly salted boiling water according to the pack instructions until al dente.

4 Heat the sauce gently until it simmers, then add the mixed cooked seafood. Simmer for 3–4 minutes until the sauce and seafood have heated through, stirring frequently.

5 Roughly chop the remaining parsley. Drain the pasta and put back in the pan, then add the sauce together with the chopped parsley and toss well. Serve immediately.

Healthy Tip

Red peppers are rich in vitamin C, betacarotene and other phytochemicals that help combat cancer and heart disease. Almonds supply useful amounts of calcium and protein and although high in fat, it is the healthy unsaturated kind. Seafood such as prawns and mussels are good sources of protein and zinc, and low in fat.

Pappardelle with Spinach

Preparation Time
5 minutes
Cooking Time
12 minutes

- 350g (12oz) pappardelle
- 350g (12oz) baby leaf spinach, roughly chopped
- 2 tbsp olive oil
- 75g (3oz) ricotta
- freshly grated nutmeg
- salt and ground black pepper

NUTRITIONAL INFORMATION
Per Serving 404 calories, 11g fat (of which 3g saturates), 67g carbohydrate, 0.3g salt

Serves 4

Healthy Tip

Spinach is rich in iron, calcium, betacarotene (which the body converts to vitamin A), vitamin C and folate. Ricotta is a type of whey cheese, containing just 9g of fat per 100g – considerably less than cream cheese at 45g per 100g. It is a good source of protein, calcium, magnesium and also selenium.

1 Cook the pappardelle in a large pan of boiling water according to the pack instructions until al dente.

2 Drain the pasta well, put back in the pan and add the spinach, oil and ricotta, tossing for 10–15 seconds until the spinach has wilted. Season with a little nutmeg, salt and pepper and serve immediately.

Pea, Mint & Ricotta Pasta

Preparation Time
5 minutes
Cooking Time
10 minutes

- 300g (11oz) farfalle
- 200g (7oz) frozen peas
- 175g (6oz) ricotta cheese
- 3 tbsp freshly chopped mint
- 2 tbsp extra virgin olive oil
- salt and ground black pepper

NUTRITIONAL INFORMATION
Per Serving 431 calories, 14g fat (of which 5g saturates), 63g carbohydrate, trace salt

Serves 4

1 Cook the pasta according to the pack instructions until al dente. Add the frozen peas for the last 4 minutes of cooking.

2 Drain the pasta and peas, reserving a ladleful of pasta cooking water, then put back in the pan. Stir in the ricotta and mint with the pasta water. Season well with salt and pepper, drizzle with the oil and serve at once.

Spaghetti with Mussels

Preparation Time
20 minutes
Cooking Time
35 minutes

- 1kg (2lb) fresh mussels in their shells, cleaned (see Cook's Tip)
- 1kg (2lb) ripe, flavourful tomatoes, quartered
- 1 onion, chopped
- 4 garlic cloves
- 6 basil leaves, plus extra to garnish
- 150ml (¼ pint) white wine
- 400g (14oz) dried spaghetti
- 2 tbsp olive oil
- 2 red chillies, halved, seeded and chopped (see Cook's Tip, page 55)
- salt and ground black pepper

NUTRITIONAL INFORMATION

Per Serving 530 calories, 10g fat (of which 2g saturates), 83g carbohydrate, 0.5g salt

1 Put the mussels into a large pan with a cupful of water. Cover and cook for 3–4 minutes, shaking the pan occasionally, until the mussels open. Using a slotted spoon, transfer the mussels to a bowl; discard any unopened ones. Strain the cooking juices through a muslin-lined sieve and put to one side.

2 Put the tomatoes and onion into a shallow pan. Crush 2 garlic cloves and add them to the pan with the basil. Bring to the boil, then reduce the heat and simmer for 20 minutes or until the tomatoes disintegrate. Press the tomato mixture through a nylon sieve into a clean pan. Pour in the cooking juices and the wine. Bring to the boil and leave to bubble until reduced by half.

3 Cook the spaghetti according to the pack instructions. Meanwhile, heat the oil in another pan. Chop the remaining garlic and add to the pan with the chillies. Cook until golden, then stir in the tomato sauce and mussels. Cover and simmer for 2–3 minutes. Season with salt and pepper.

4 Drain the spaghetti, keeping 2 tbsp of the pasta cooking water. Toss the spaghetti and reserved water with the sauce. Serve, garnished with basil.

Cook's Tip

To clean mussels, scrape off the fibres (beards) attached to the shells. If the mussels are very clean, give them a quick rinse under the cold tap. If they are very sandy, scrub them with a stiff brush, then rinse thoroughly. If the shells have sizeable barnacles on them, it's best (though not essential) to remove them. Rap them sharply with a metal spoon or the back of a washing-up brush, then scrape off. Discard any open mussels that don't shut when sharply tapped; this means they are dead and may cause food poisoning.

Serves 4

Clams with Chilli

Preparation Time
15 minutes
Cooking Time
about 10 minutes

- 300g (11oz) linguine
- 2 tbsp olive oil
- 1 garlic clove, crushed
- 1 red chilli, seeded and finely chopped (see Cook's Tip, page 55)
- 4 tomatoes, seeded and chopped
- 900g (2lb) clams in their shells, washed and scrubbed
- 150ml (¼ pint) light dry white wine
- 2 tbsp freshly chopped parsley
- salt and ground black pepper

NUTRITIONAL INFORMATION
Per Serving 512 calories, 9g fat (of which 1g saturates), 64g carbohydrate, 0.3g salt

Healthy Tip
Clams are very low in fat and saturated fat. They provide good amounts of protein, vitamin A, iron, manganese, B vitamins and zinc. Chilli adds vitamin C to the dish. There is also some evidence that, eaten regularly, chilli may help to ward off certain types of cancer.

1 Cook the linguine in a pan of lightly salted boiling water according to the pack instructions until al dente.

2 Meanwhile, heat the oil in a large pan. Add the garlic, chilli and tomatoes and fry for 4 minutes, stirring gently. Add the clams and wine. Cover and cook over a high heat for 3–4 minutes until the clam shells spring open – discard any that remain closed.

3 Drain the pasta and put back in the pan, then add the clams with the sauce and the parsley. Toss together gently, season and serve immediately.

Butternut Squash & Spinach Lasagne

Preparation Time
30 minutes
Cooking Time
about 1 hour

- 1 butternut squash, peeled, halved, seeded and cut into 3cm (1¼in) cubes
- 2 tbsp olive oil
- 1 onion, sliced
- 25g (1oz) butter
- 25g (1oz) plain flour
- 600ml (1 pint) milk
- 250g (9oz) ricotta cheese
- 1 tsp freshly grated nutmeg
- 225g bag baby leaf spinach
- 6 'no need to pre-cook' lasagne sheets
- 50g (2oz) pecorino cheese or Parmesan, freshly grated
- salt and ground black pepper

NUTRITIONAL INFORMATION
Per Serving 273 calories, 17g fat (of which 7g saturates), 18g carbohydrate, 0.6g salt

Healthy Tip
Butternut squash is super-rich in betacarotene, which helps to protect against heart disease and cancer. Spinach adds folate, vitamin C, calcium and iron to the dish.

1 Preheat the oven to 200°C (180°C fan oven) mark 6. Put the squash into a roasting tin with the oil, onion and 1 tbsp water. Mix well and season with salt and pepper. Roast for 25 minutes, tossing halfway through.

2 To make the sauce, melt the butter in a pan, then stir in the flour and cook over a medium heat for 1–2 minutes. Gradually add the milk, stirring constantly. Reduce the heat to a simmer and cook, stirring, for 5 minutes or until the sauce has thickened. Crumble the ricotta into the sauce and add the nutmeg. Mix together thoroughly and season with salt and pepper.

3 Heat 1 tbsp water in a pan. Add the spinach, cover and cook until just wilted. Season generously.

4 Spoon the squash mixture into a 1.7 litre (3 pint) ovenproof dish. Layer the spinach on top, then cover with one-third of the sauce, then the lasagne. Spoon the remaining sauce on top, season and sprinkle with the grated cheese. Cook for 30–35 minutes until the cheese topping is golden and the pasta is cooked.

Serves 6

Classic Lasagne

Preparation Time
about 1 hour, plus infusing
Cooking Time
45 minutes

- butter to grease
- 350g (12oz) fresh lasagne, or 225g (8oz) 'no need to pre-cook' lasagne (12–15 sheets, see Cook's Tip)
- 3 tbsp freshly grated Parmesan
- mixed salad leaves to serve

FOR THE BOLOGNESE SAUCE

- 2 tbsp olive oil
- 1 onion, finely chopped
- 2 garlic cloves, crushed
- 450g (1lb) extra-lean minced beef
- 2 tbsp sun-dried tomato paste
- 300ml (½ pint) red wine
- 400g can chopped tomatoes
- 125g (4oz) chestnut mushrooms, sliced
- 2 tbsp Worcestershire sauce
- salt and ground black pepper

FOR THE BÉCHAMEL SAUCE

- 300ml (½ pint) semi-skimmed milk
- 1 onion slice
- 6 peppercorns
- 1 mace blade
- 1 bay leaf
- 15g (½oz) butter
- 15g (½oz) plain flour
- freshly grated nutmeg
- salt and ground black pepper

NUTRITIONAL INFORMATION
Per Serving 326 calories, 13g fat (of which 6g saturates), 37g carbohydrate, 0.5g salt

1 To make the Bolognese sauce, heat the oil in a large pan. Add the onion and fry over a medium heat for 10 minutes or until softened and golden. Add the garlic and cook for 1 minute. Add the beef and brown evenly, using a wooden spoon to break up the pieces. Stir in the tomato paste and wine, cover and bring to the boil. Add the tomatoes, mushrooms and Worcestershire sauce and season well with salt and pepper. Bring back to the boil, reduce the heat and simmer for 20 minutes.

2 To make the béchamel sauce, pour the milk into a pan and add the onion, peppercorns, mace and bay leaf. Bring almost to the boil, then remove from the heat, cover and leave to infuse for about 20 minutes. Strain. Melt the butter in a pan, stir in the flour and cook, stirring, for 1 minute or until cooked but not coloured. Remove from the heat and gradually pour in the milk, whisking constantly. Season lightly with nutmeg, salt and pepper. Put back on the heat and cook, stirring constantly, until the sauce is thickened and smooth, then simmer gently for 2 minutes.

3 Preheat the oven to 180°C (160°C fan oven) mark 4. Spoon one-third of the Bolognese sauce over the base of a greased 2.3 litre (4 pint) ovenproof dish. Cover with a layer of lasagne sheets, then a layer of béchamel. Repeat these layers twice more, finishing with a layer of béchamel to cover the lasagne.

4 Sprinkle the Parmesan over the top and stand the dish on a baking sheet. Cook in the oven for 45 minutes or until well browned and bubbling. Serve with mixed salad leaves.

Cook's Tip

If using 'no need to pre-cook' lasagne, add a little extra stock or water to the sauce.

Pasta & Pastrami Salad

Preparation Time
10 minutes
Cooking Time
20 minutes

- 300g (11oz) cooked pasta, cooled
- 125g (4oz) pastrami, diced
- 4 tomatoes, chopped
- 1 cucumber, chopped
- 3 tbsp freshly chopped parsley
- 1 medium red onion, finely chopped

FOR THE DRESSING

- wholegrain mustard to taste
- 6 tbsp Vinaigrette Dressing (see Cook's Tip)

NUTRITIONAL INFORMATION

Per Serving 72 calories, 1g fat (of which 0.5g saturates), 12g carbohydrate, 0.4g salt

Serves 4

Cook's Tip

Vinaigrette Dressing Put 100ml (3½fl oz) extra virgin olive oil, 100ml (3½fl oz) grapeseed oil, 75ml (2fl oz) white wine vinegar, pinch each sugar and English mustard powder and 1 crushed garlic clove (optional) in a large screw-topped jar. Shake well, season to taste with salt and ground black pepper and store in a cool place. Makes about 300ml (½ pint).

1 Combine all the ingredients for the salad in a large salad bowl.

2 To make the dressing, mix the mustard into the vinaigrette, then pour on to the salad and toss.

Greek Pasta Salad

Preparation Time
10 minutes
Cooking Time
10–15 minutes

- 3 tbsp olive oil
- 2 tbsp lemon juice
- 150g (5oz) cooked pasta shapes, cooled
- 75g (3oz) vegetarian feta cheese, crumbled
- 3 tomatoes, roughly chopped
- 2 tbsp small pitted black olives
- ½ cucumber, roughly chopped
- 1 small red onion, finely sliced
- salt and ground black pepper
- freshly chopped mint and lemon zest to garnish
- crusty bread to serve

NUTRITIONAL INFORMATION

Per Serving 382 calories, 27g fat (of which 8g saturates), 25g carbohydrate, 2.5g salt

Serves 2

Healthy Tip

This salad provides many vitamins and minerals. Tomatoes are rich in vitamins A and C, as well as the cancer-protective phytochemical lycopene. Olives supply high levels of vitamin E and heart-healthy monounsaturated fats while the cucumber supplies potassium, important for regulating blood pressure and fluid balance.

1 Mix the oil and lemon juice together in a large salad bowl, then add the pasta, feta cheese, tomatoes, olives, cucumber and onion.

2 Season with salt and pepper and stir to mix, then garnish with chopped mint and lemon zest and serve with chunks of crusty bread.

Prawn & Peanut Noodles

Preparation Time
10 minutes, plus soaking

- 300g (11oz) straight-to-wok noodles
- 360g pack stir-fry vegetables
- 4 tbsp coconut cream
- 4 tbsp smooth peanut butter
- 1 tbsp Thai red or green curry paste
- juice of ½ lime
- 225g (8oz) cooked and peeled king prawns
- a small handful of freshly chopped coriander
- 25g (1oz) peanuts, chopped

NUTRITIONAL INFORMATION
Per Serving 579 calories, 24g fat (of which 7g saturates) 67g carbohydrate, 0.7g salt

Serves 4

Cook's Tip

Ready-prepared stir-fry vegetables make this extra-quick, but if you can't find them, try a mixture of three or four of the following: strips of red, orange or yellow peppers, baby sweetcorn, mangetouts or sugarsnaps, carrots cut into matchsticks and bean sprouts.

1 Put the noodles and stir-fry vegetables into a large bowl or wok and cover with boiling water. Cover with clingfilm and leave for 5 minutes.

2 Meanwhile, mix the coconut cream with the peanut butter, curry paste and lime juice in a bowl.

3 Drain the noodles and vegetables in a colander. Put back into the bowl and toss with the prawns, coriander and half the dressing. Sprinkle with the peanuts and serve with the remaining dressing.

Salmon & Bulgur Wheat Pilau

Preparation Time
5 minutes
Cooking Time
20 minutes

Serves 4

- 1 tbsp olive oil
- 1 onion, chopped
- 175g (6oz) bulgur wheat
- 450ml (¾ pint) vegetable stock
- 400g can pink salmon, drained and flaked
- 125g (4oz) spinach, roughly chopped
- 225g (8oz) frozen peas
- zest and juice of 1 lemon
- salt and ground black pepper

NUTRITIONAL INFORMATION

Per Serving 323 calories, 11g fat (of which 2g saturates), 30g carbohydrate, 1.5g salt

Healthy Tip

Salmon is a rich source of omega-3 fats, which helps promote cardiovascular health and protects against heart disease. It also helps maintain brain function and eyesight. Bulgur wheat is made from wholegrain wheat so is a good source of fibre, iron and B vitamins.

Try Something Different

Instead of salmon, use 200g (7oz) cooked peeled prawns and 200g (7oz) cherry tomatoes.

1 Heat the oil in a large pan. Add the onion and cook until softened. Stir in the bulgur wheat to coat in the oil, then stir in the stock and bring to the boil. Cover, reduce the heat and simmer for 10–15 minutes until the stock has been fully absorbed.

2 Stir in the chopped salmon, spinach, peas and lemon juice and cook until the spinach has wilted and the salmon and peas are heated through. Season to taste with salt and pepper and sprinkle with lemon zest before serving.

Prawn & Vegetable Pilau

Preparation Time
10 minutes
Cooking Time
15–20 minutes

- 250g (9oz) long-grain rice
- 1 broccoli head, broken into florets
- 150g (5oz) baby sweetcorn, halved
- 200g (7oz) sugarsnap peas
- 1 red pepper, seeded and sliced into thin strips
- 400g (14oz) cooked and peeled king prawns

FOR THE DRESSING

- 1 tbsp sesame oil
- 5cm (2in) piece fresh root ginger, peeled and grated
- juice of 1 lime
- 1–2 tbsp light soy sauce

NUTRITIONAL INFORMATION

Per Serving 360 calories, 5g fat (of which 1g saturates), 61g carbohydrate, 1.8g salt

Cook's Tip

The word 'pilau', or 'pilaf', comes from the Persian 'pilaw'. The dish consists of rice flavoured with spices, to which vegetables, poultry, meat, fish or shellfish are added.

1 Put the rice into a large wide pan – it needs to be really big, as you'll be cooking the rice and steaming the vegetables on top, then tossing it all together. Add 600ml (1 pint) boiling water. Cover with the lid and bring to the boil, then reduce the heat to low and cook the rice according to the pack instructions.

2 About 10 minutes before the end of the rice cooking time, add the broccoli, corn, sugarsnaps and red pepper. Stir well, then cover the pan and cook until the vegetables and rice are just tender.

3 Meanwhile, put the prawns into a bowl. Add the sesame oil, ginger, lime and soy sauce. Mix the prawns and dressing into the cooked vegetables and rice and toss well. Serve immediately.

Coconut Fish Pilau

Preparation Time
15 minutes
Cooking Time
30 minutes

- 2 tsp olive oil
- 1 shallot, chopped
- 1 tbsp Thai green curry paste
- 225g (8oz) brown basmati rice
- 600ml (1 pint) hot fish or vegetable stock
- 150ml (¼ pint) reduced-fat coconut milk
- 350g (12oz) skinless white fish fillet, cut into bite-size pieces
- 350g (12oz) sugarsnap peas
- 125g (4oz) cooked and peeled prawns
- 25g (1oz) flaked almonds, toasted
- a squeeze of lemon juice
- salt and ground black pepper
- 2 tbsp freshly chopped coriander to garnish

NUTRITIONAL INFORMATION
Per Serving 398 calories, 7g fat (of which 1g saturates), 53g carbohydrate, 0.4g salt

Try Something Different
There are plenty of alternatives to cod: try coley (saithe), sea bass or pollack.

1 Heat the oil in a frying pan. Add the shallot and 1 tbsp water and fry for 4–5 minutes until golden. Stir in the curry paste and cook for a further 1–2 minutes.

2 Add the rice, hot stock and coconut milk and bring to the boil. Cover the pan, reduce the heat and simmer for 15–20 minutes until all the liquid has been absorbed.

3 Add the fish and cook for 3–5 minutes. Add the sugarsnap peas, prawns, almonds and lemon juice and stir over the heat for about 3–4 minutes or until heated through. Check the seasoning and serve immediately, garnished with chopped coriander.

Aubergine & Chickpea Pilau

Preparation Time
10 minutes
Cooking Time
20 minutes, plus standing

- 4–6 tbsp olive oil
- 275g (10oz) aubergine, roughly chopped
- 225g (8oz) onions, finely chopped
- 25g (1oz) butter
- ½ tsp cumin seeds
- 175g (6oz) long-grain rice
- 600ml (1 pint) vegetable stock
- 400g can chickpeas, drained and rinsed
- 225g (8oz) baby spinach leaves
- salt and ground black pepper

NUTRITIONAL INFORMATION

Per Serving 462 calories, 20g fat (of which 5g saturates), 58g carbohydrate, 0.9g salt

1 Heat half the oil in a large pan or flameproof casserole over a medium heat. Fry the aubergine for 4–5 minutes, in batches, until deep golden brown. Remove from the pan with a slotted spoon and put to one side. Add the remaining oil to the pan, then add the onions and cook for 5 minutes until golden.

2 Add the butter, then stir in the cumin seeds and rice. Fry for 1–2 minutes. Pour in the stock, season with salt and pepper and bring to the boil. Reduce the heat, then simmer, uncovered, for 10–12 minutes until most of the liquid has evaporated and the rice is tender.

3 Remove the pan from the heat. Stir in the chickpeas, spinach and reserved aubergine. Cover with a tight-fitting lid and leave to stand for 5 minutes until the spinach has wilted and the chickpeas are heated through. Adjust the seasoning to taste. Fork through the rice grains to separate and make the rice fluffy before serving.

Healthy Tip

Chickpeas are excellent sources of fibre, protein and iron. They contain a type of fibre called fructo-oligosaccharides, which help promote the friendly gut bacteria, and boost immunity. Spinach supplies plenty of vitamins A and C.

Get Ahead

To prepare ahead Fry the aubergine and onion as in step 1. Cover and keep in a cool place for 1½ hours.
To use Complete the recipe.

Serves 4

Serves 4

Prawn & Lemon Risotto

Preparation Time
15 minutes
Cooking Time
40 minutes

- 225g (8oz) sugarsnap peas, sliced diagonally
- 175g (6oz) baby courgettes, sliced diagonally
- 2 tbsp olive oil
- 1 onion, finely chopped
- ¼ tsp saffron (optional)
- 225g (8oz) arborio rice
- 1 garlic clove, crushed
- 225g (8oz) brown-cap mushrooms, quartered
- zest and juice of 1 lemon
- 750ml (1¼ pints) hot fish, chicken or vegetable stock
- 300g (11oz) cooked and peeled prawns
- 3 tbsp freshly chopped chives
- salt and ground black pepper
- spring onion curls (see Cook's Tips) and grated lemon zest to garnish

NUTRITIONAL INFORMATION

Per Serving 405 calories, 8g fat (of which 1g saturates), 59g carbohydrate, 0.9g salt

1 Put the sugarsnap peas and courgettes into a pan of lightly salted boiling water and bring to the boil. Cook for 1–2 minutes. Drain and plunge into ice-cold water.

2 Heat the oil in a medium non-stick pan. Add the onion and saffron, if using, and cook over a medium heat for 10 minutes or until soft. Add the rice, garlic and mushrooms and cook, stirring, for 1–2 minutes. Season with salt and pepper.

3 Add the grated lemon zest and about one-third of the hot stock. Simmer gently, stirring frequently, until most of the liquid has been absorbed. Add another one-third of the stock, then repeat the process.

4 Add the remaining stock. Cook, stirring, for 10 minutes or until the rice is tender and most of the stock has been absorbed. Add the prawns, drained vegetables, 1–2 tbsp lemon juice and the chives, then heat for 3–4 minutes. Garnish with spring onion curls and lemon zest.

Cook's Tips

- Adding the hot stock gradually gives the risotto its deliciously creamy texture.
- To make spring onion curls, thinly slice the onions lengthways, soak in ice-cold water for 30 minutes, then drain well.

Prawn, Courgette & Leek Risotto

Preparation Time
10 minutes
Cooking Time
30 minutes, plus standing

- 1 tbsp olive oil
- 25g (1oz) butter
- 1 leek, finely chopped
- 2 courgettes, thinly sliced
- 2 garlic cloves, crushed
- 350g (12oz) arborio rice
- 1.6 litres (2¾ pints) vegetable stock
- 200g (7oz) cooked and peeled prawns
- small bunch of parsley or mint, or a mixture of both, chopped
- salt and ground black pepper

NUTRITIONAL INFORMATION
Per Serving 320 calories, 7g fat (of which 3g saturates), 49g carbohydrate, 1.3g salt

Serves 6

Healthy Tip

Arborio rice is the classic risotto rice. It is a medium- to long-grain white rice that can absorb a lot of cooking liquid yet still retain a good 'bite' when fully cooked. Like other types of white rice it is low in fat and high in complex carbohydrates, and contains small amounts of B vitamins. The prawns add protein to the dish while the courgettes provide valuable vitamins A and C.

1 Heat the oil and half the butter in a large shallow pan. Add the leek, courgettes and garlic and soften over a low heat. Add the rice and cook, stirring well, for 1 minute.

2 Meanwhile, heat the stock in a separate pan to a steady low simmer. Add a ladleful of the hot stock to the rice and simmer, stirring, until absorbed. Continue adding the hot stock, a ladleful at a time.

3 When nearly all the stock has been added and the rice is al dente, add the prawns. Season to taste with salt and pepper and stir in the remaining stock and the rest of the butter. Stir through and remove from the heat. Cover and leave to stand for a couple of minutes, then stir the chopped herbs through it. Serve immediately.

Squash & Bacon Risotto

Preparation Time
10 minutes
Cooking Time
40 minutes

- 125g (4oz) smoked bacon, chopped
- 1 small butternut squash, peeled and cut into small chunks
- 1 onion, finely chopped
- 300g (11oz) arborio rice
- 1 litre (1¾ pints) hot vegetable stock

NUTRITIONAL INFORMATION

Per Serving 390 calories, 9g fat (of which 3g saturates), 65g carbohydrate, 2g salt

Try Something Different

- Instead of the squash, use 750g (1lb 11oz) peeled and seeded pumpkin.
- Instead of the onion, use a fennel bulb.

Healthy Tip

Butternut squash is a very good source of betacarotene and vitamin C as well as magnesium, manganese, calcium and potassium. Smoked bacon supplies protein to the dish but is high in salt so keep portion sizes small.

1 Put the bacon and the butternut squash into a large deep frying pan and fry over a medium heat for 8–10 minutes.

2 When the bacon is golden and the squash has softened, add the onion to the pan and continue to fry for 5 minutes until softened.

3 Stir in the rice, cook for 1–2 minutes, then add the hot stock. Bring to the boil, reduce the heat and simmer for 15–20 minutes, stirring occasionally to ensure the rice doesn't stick, until almost all the stock has been absorbed and the rice and squash are tender. Serve immediately.

Simple Fried Rice

Preparation Time
5 minutes
Cooking Time
15–20 minutes

- 150g (5oz) long-grain rice
- 2 tbsp sesame oil
- 3 medium eggs, lightly beaten
- 250g (9oz) frozen petits pois
- 250g (9oz) cooked and peeled prawns

NUTRITIONAL INFORMATION

Per Serving 339 calories, 11g fat (of which 2g saturates), 37g carbohydrate, 0.4g salt

Serves 4

1 Cook the rice in boiling water for about 10 minutes or according to the pack instructions. Drain well.

2 Heat 1 tsp oil in a large non-stick frying pan. Pour in half the beaten eggs and tilt the pan around over the heat for about 1 minute until the egg is set. Tip the omelette on to a warmed plate. Repeat with another 1 tsp oil and the remaining beaten egg to make another omelette. Tip on to another warmed plate.

3 Add the remaining oil to the pan and stir in the rice and peas. Stir-fry for 2–3 minutes until the peas are cooked. Stir in the prawns.

4 Roll up the omelettes, roughly chop one-third of one, then slice the remainder into strips. Add the chopped omelette to the rice, peas and prawns and cook for 1–2 minutes until heated through. Divide the fried rice among four bowls, top with the sliced omelette and serve immediately.

Rice & Red Pepper Stir-fry

Preparation Time
5 minutes
Cooking Time
15 minutes

- 75g (3oz) long-grain rice
- 200ml (7fl oz) hot vegetable stock
- 2 tsp vegetable oil
- ½ onion, sliced
- 2 rashers streaky bacon
- 1 small red pepper, halved, seeded and cut into chunks
- a handful of frozen peas
- a dash of Worcestershire sauce

NUTRITIONAL INFORMATION
Per Serving 584 calories, 20g fat (of which 5g saturates), 82g carbohydrate, 1.7g salt

Serves 1

Healthy Tip
Red peppers are rich in vitamin C – one pepper supplies 100% of your daily needs – as well as betacarotene, a powerful cancer-fighting nutrient. Peas add valuable amounts of fibre to the dish as well as vitamin C and protein. Streaky bacon is high in fat so use smaller amounts if you want to reduce the overall fat content of the dish.

1 Put the rice into a pan and pour in the hot stock. Cover and bring to the boil, then reduce the heat and simmer for 10 minutes or until the rice is tender and the liquid has been absorbed.

2 Heat the oil in a frying pan over a medium heat. Add the onion and fry for 5 minutes, then add the bacon and red pepper. Fry for 5 minutes or until the bacon is crisp. Stir in the cooked rice and the peas. Cook, stirring occasionally, for 2–3 minutes until the rice is hot and the peas are tender. Add a dash of Worcestershire sauce and serve.

Weekend & Special Meals

Serves 8

Leek, Artichoke & Mushroom Croute

Preparation Time
30 minutes, plus chilling
Cooking Time
30–35 minutes, plus cooling

- 3 tbsp olive oil
- 2 garlic cloves, crushed
- 125g (4oz) shiitake mushrooms, sliced
- 1 tbsp balsamic vinegar
- 50g (2oz) peeled cooked (or vacuum-packed) chestnuts, roughly chopped
- 1½ tsp fresh thyme leaves
- 400g can artichoke hearts, drained and quartered
- 350g (12oz) leeks, sliced
- 375g pack ready-rolled puff pastry
- butter to grease
- 1 medium egg, lightly beaten
- salt and ground black pepper
- cranberry sauce and a little extra virgin olive oil to serve

NUTRITIONAL INFORMATION
Per Serving 236 calories, 17g fat (of which 1g saturates), 20g carbohydrate, 0.4g salt

1 Heat 2 tbsp olive oil in a large pan and fry the garlic for 1 minute. Add the mushrooms and cook over a low heat for 3 minutes to soften. Add the vinegar, chestnuts, ½ tsp thyme leaves and the artichokes, then cook for 1 minute. In a separate pan, soften the leeks in the remaining 1 tbsp oil for 4 minutes. Tip into a bowl and leave to cool for 5 minutes.

2 Unroll the pastry and sprinkle with the remaining thyme; roll it lightly into the pastry. Flip the pastry over so that the herbs are on the underside, then lightly roll out to a 38 × 25.5cm (15 × 10in) rectangle. Using a sharp knife, cut the pastry in half to create two long thin rectangles. Spoon half the mushroom mixture down the centre of each. Top with the leeks and season. Brush the pastry edges with water, then fold each side of the pastry up over the filling and seal. Cut both rolls in half and put on to a greased baking sheet. Cover and chill overnight.

3 Preheat the oven to 200°C (180°C fan oven) mark 6. Brush the pastry with beaten egg to glaze. Cook for 20 minutes until the pastry is golden. Slice each croûte into six and serve three slices per person, with cranberry sauce and a light drizzle of extra virgin olive oil.

Freezing Tip

To freeze Complete the recipe to the end of step 2, then wrap and freeze for up to one month.
To use Cook from frozen in a preheated oven at 200°C (180°C fan oven) mark 6 for 25 minutes until the pastry is golden brown. Complete the recipe.

Lamb, Orange & Apricot Kebabs

Preparation Time
45 minutes, plus chilling
Cooking Time
25–30 minutes

- 700g (1½lb) boned leg of lamb
- 75g (3oz) ready-to-eat dried apricots
- 150g (5oz) ready-to-eat dried figs
- 1 garlic clove, crushed
- 50g (2oz) spring onions, finely chopped
- juice of 2 lemons
- 6 tbsp Greek yogurt
- 5 tbsp smooth peanut butter
- 2 tsp each ground coriander and cumin seeds
- 1 tsp ground fenugreek
- ½ tsp chilli powder
- 3 tbsp olive oil
- 225g (8oz) onions
- 2 large oranges
- salt and ground black pepper
- salad leaves to serve

NUTRITIONAL INFORMATION
Per Serving 260 calories, 14g fat (of which 5g saturates), 15g carbohydrate, 0.2g salt

1 Trim the lamb and cut into large cubes, allowing about three pieces per skewer. Put the apricots and figs into a bowl and add enough water to cover completely, then cover and chill.

2 In a large bowl, mix the garlic and spring onions with 8 tbsp lemon juice and all the remaining ingredients except the whole onions and oranges. Add the lamb to the marinade, season and stir to coat well. Cover and chill for at least 6 hours or overnight.

3 Preheat the barbecue and, if using wooden skewers, soak eight in water for 20 minutes. Quarter the onions, then separate the quarters into petals. Thickly slice the oranges. Thread the meat, onions, oranges, apricots and figs on to the skewers.

4 Barbecue for 25–30 minutes until the lamb is pink to the centre. Serve hot, with salad leaves.

Fennel Pork with Cabbage & Apple

Preparation Time
10 minutes
Cooking Time
6–10 minutes

Serves 4

- 2 tbsp olive oil
- ½ tbsp fennel seeds, crushed
- 1 tbsp freshly chopped sage
- 4 lean pork medallions, 125g (4oz) each
- ½ small red cabbage, shredded
- 450g (1lb) purple sprouting broccoli, tough ends removed
- 1 apple, cored and sliced into rings
- salt and ground black pepper

NUTRITIONAL INFORMATION
Per Serving 276 calories, 12g fat (of which 3g saturates), 9g carbohydrate, 0.3g salt

Healthy Tip
Red cabbage is rich in natural pigments called anthocyanins, which act not only as powerful antioxidants but also have anti-inflammatory effects and help protect against cardiovascular disease, and may also help lower blood sugar levels. It is also rich in immunity-boosting vitamin C, vitamin K and fibre.

1 Put 1 tbsp oil into a large shallow bowl. Add the fennel seeds and sage, season with salt and pepper and mix well. Add the pork and rub the mixture into the meat.

2 Heat the remaining oil in a wok or large frying pan and stir-fry the cabbage and broccoli for 6–8 minutes until starting to char.

3 Meanwhile, heat a non-stick griddle until hot and fry the pork for 2–3 minutes on each side until cooked through. Remove and put to one side. Add the apple rings to the griddle and cook for 1–2 minutes on each side until starting to char and caramelise. Serve with the pork and vegetables.

Lemon-roasted Pork with Garlic & Basil

Preparation Time
20 minutes, plus marinating
Cooking Time
40 minutes

- 2 pork tenderloins, about 350g (12oz) each, trimmed
- finely grated zest and juice of 2 lemons, sieved
- 6 tbsp freshly chopped basil or parsley
- 12 garlic cloves, blanched and halved if large
- 2–3 bay leaves
- 2 tbsp olive oil
- salt and ground black pepper
- fresh herbs and lemon slices to garnish
- sautéed shallots to serve

NUTRITIONAL INFORMATION
Per Serving 185 calories, 9g fat (of which 2g saturates), 1.5g carbohydrate, 0.2g salt

1 Split the pork lengthways without cutting right through and open each piece out flat. Sprinkle with the lemon zest and basil or parsley. Lay the garlic cloves evenly along the middle of each fillet and season with salt and pepper.

2 Close the pork and tie loosely at 2.5cm (1in) intervals with string. Put in a shallow non-metallic dish with the bay leaves and sieved lemon juice. Cover, and marinatein the fridge overnight.

3 Preheat the oven to 200°C (180°C fan oven) mark 6. Remove the pork and put the marinade to one side. Heat the oil in a sauté pan. Add the meat and fry until browned. Transfer to a shallow roasting tin with the marinade. Season the pork and cook in the oven for about 35 minutes, basting frequently.

4 Serve the pork sliced, garnished with herbs and lemon slices, and with sautéed shallots.

Healthy Tip
Garlic is rich in antioxidants and other chemicals that support many aspects of health, from heart and circulatory health to immunity and anti-ageing. Garlic has been found to lower LDL ('bad') cholesterol, blood pressure, and atherosclerosis.

Serves 6

Pork with Basil, Tomato & Stilton

Preparation Time
10 minutes
Cooking Time
10–14 minutes

- 4 pork loin steaks
- 1 ripe beef tomato, sliced
- a few basil leaves
- 50g (2oz) Stilton, sliced
- new potatoes and runner beans to serve

NUTRITIONAL INFORMATION
Per Serving 212 calories, 9g fat (of which 5g saturates), 2g carbohydrate, 0.5g salt

Try Something Different
Instead of pork, use 4 boneless, skinless chicken breasts: season lightly, place between two pieces of clingfilm and beat with a rolling pin until about 1cm (½in) thick. Brush lightly with olive oil before grilling.

1 Preheat the grill. Grill the pork for 4–5 minutes on each side.

2 Divide the sliced tomato among the steaks, add a few basil leaves and the sliced Stilton and grill for a further 1–2 minutes or until the cheese has melted and the pork is cooked through. Serve with new potatoes and runner beans.

Calf's Liver with Fried Sage & Balsamic Vinegar

Preparation Time
5 minutes
Cooking Time
5 minutes

- 15g (½oz) butter plus a little olive oil to fry
- 12 sage leaves
- 4 thin slices of calf's liver
- 1–2 tbsp balsamic vinegar
- rice, with freshly chopped parsley stirred through, or grilled polenta to serve

NUTRITIONAL INFORMATION
Per Serving 88 calories, 6g fat (of which 3g saturates), trace carbohydrate, 0.1g salt

Healthy Tip
Liver is an excellent source of the minerals iron and selenium as well as vitamin A, vitamin B2, vitamin B12 and folate. In addition, it is also a good source of protein, zinc, niacin and vitamin B6.

1 Preheat the oven to a low setting. Melt the butter with a little oil in a heavy-based frying pan and when hot add the sage leaves. Cook briefly for 1 minute or so until crisp. Remove, put in a single layer in a shallow dish and keep hot in the oven.

2 Add a little extra oil to the pan, put in two slices of calf's liver and cook quickly for 30 seconds on each side over a high heat. Remove and place on a plate while you quickly cook the remaining two slices.

3 Return all four slices to the pan, splash the balsamic vinegar over the top and cook for another minute or so. Serve immediately with rice or grilled polenta.

Mustard Roast Beef

Preparation Time
10 minutes, plus marinating
Cooking Time
50–60 minutes, plus resting

- 1.1kg (2½lb) boned, rolled sirloin of beef
- 1 tbsp olive oil
- 5 bay leaves
- 200ml (7fl oz) red wine
- 2 onions, sliced
- 2 tbsp English mustard
- 300ml (½ pint) hot vegetable stock
- salt and ground black pepper
- new potatoes and broccoli to serve

NUTRITIONAL INFORMATION
Per Serving 469 calories, 19g fat (of which 6g saturates), 3g carbohydrate, 0.5g salt

1 Put the beef into a bowl and add the oil, bay leaves, wine and onions. Cover and marinate in the fridge for 4 hours or overnight.

2 Preheat the oven to 200°C (180°C fan oven) mark 6. Put the beef into a roasting tin with all the marinade ingredients. Spread the mustard over the meat, then season well with salt and pepper. Pour in the stock, then roast in the oven for 50–60 minutes. Cover and leave to rest for 10 minutes, then carve and serve with new potatoes and broccoli.

Sesame Beef

Preparation Time
20 minutes
Cooking Time
10 minutes

- 2 tbsp soy sauce
- 2 tbsp Worcestershire sauce
- 2 tsp tomato purée
- juice of ½ lemon
- 1 tbsp sesame seeds
- 1 garlic clove, crushed
- 400g (14oz) rump steak, sliced
- 1 tbsp vegetable oil
- 3 small pak choi, chopped
- 1 bunch of spring onions, sliced
- egg noodles or tagliatelle to serve

NUTRITIONAL INFORMATION
Per Serving 207 calories, 10g fat (of which 3g saturates), 4g carbohydrate, 2g salt

Healthy Tip

In addition to being a very good source of protein, beef is a good source of vitamin B12, and vitamin B6. It is one of the richest dietary sources of iron, needed to carry oxygen around the body.

Try Something Different

Use 400g (14oz) pork escalope cut into strips instead of beef. Cook for 5 minutes before removing from the pan at step 2.

1 Put the soy and Worcestershire sauces, tomato purée, lemon juice, sesame seeds and garlic into a bowl and mix well. Add the steak and toss to coat.

2 Heat the oil in a large wok or non-stick frying pan until hot. Add the steak and sear well. Remove from the wok and put to one side.

3 Add any sauce from the bowl to the wok and heat for 1 minute. Add the pak choi, spring onions and steak and stir-fry for 5 minutes. Add freshly cooked and drained noodles or pasta, then toss and serve immediately.

Chicken & Artichoke Pie

Preparation Time
20 minutes
Cooking Time
45 minutes

- 3 boneless, skinless chicken breasts, about 350g (12oz)
- 150ml (¼ pint) dry white wine
- 225g (8oz) reduced-fat cream cheese with garlic and herbs
- 400g can artichoke hearts, drained and quartered
- 4 sheets filo pastry, thawed if frozen
- olive oil to brush
- 1 tsp sesame seeds
- salt and ground black pepper

NUTRITIONAL INFORMATION
Per Serving 241 calories, 9g fat (of which 5g saturates), 7g carbohydrate, 0.2g salt

Try Something Different
Replace the artichoke hearts with 225g (8oz) brown-cap mushrooms, cooked in a little water with some salt and pepper and lemon juice.

Healthy Tip
This recipe uses filo pastry, which is almost fat free, and therefore a healthy alternative to traditional shortcrust pastry, which contains around 30g of fat and 500 calories per 100g. Artichokes have cholesterol-lowering properties and help protect the liver from damage by toxins.

1 Preheat the oven to 200°C (180°C fan oven) mark 6. Put the chicken and wine into a pan and bring to the boil, then cover, reduce the heat and simmer for 10 minutes. Remove the chicken with a slotted spoon and put to one side. Add the cheese to the wine and mix until smooth. Bring to the boil, then reduce the heat and simmer until thickened.

2 Cut the chicken into bite-size pieces, then add to the sauce with the artichokes. Season and mix well.

3 Put the mixture into an ovenproof dish. Brush the pastry lightly with oil, scrunch slightly and put on top of the chicken. Sprinkle with sesame seeds, then cook in the oven for 30–35 minutes until crisp. Serve hot.

Stuffed Chicken Breasts

Preparation Time
5 minutes
Cooking Time
20 minutes

- vegetable oil to oil
- 150g (5oz) ball mozzarella
- 4 skinless chicken breasts, about 125g (4oz) each
- 4 sage leaves
- 8 slices Parma ham
- ground black pepper
- baby new potatoes and wilted spinach to serve

NUTRITIONAL INFORMATION
Per Serving 297 calories, 13g fat (of which 7g saturates), trace carbohydrate, 1.4g salt

Serves 4

Cook's Tip

Sage has a strong, pungent taste, so you need only a little to flavour the chicken. Don't be tempted to add more than just one leaf to each chicken breast or it will overpower the finished dish.

1 Preheat the oven to 200°C (180°C fan oven) mark 6. Lightly oil a baking sheet. Slice the mozzarella into eight, then put two slices on each chicken piece. Top each with a sage leaf.

2 Wrap each piece of chicken in two slices of Parma ham, covering the mozzarella. Season with pepper.

3 Put on the prepared baking sheet and cook in the oven for 20 minutes or until the chicken is cooked through. Serve with baby new potatoes and wilted spinach.

Chicken with Wine & Capers

Preparation Time
5 minutes
Cooking Time
25 minutes

Serves 4

- 1 tbsp olive oil
- 15g (½ oz) butter
- 4 small skinless chicken breasts
- ground black pepper
- lemon wedges to garnish
- boiled rice to serve

FOR THE WINE AND CAPER SAUCE

- 125ml (4fl oz) white wine
- 3 tbsp capers, rinsed and drained
- juice of 1 lemon
- 15g (½oz) butter
- 1 tbsp freshly chopped flat-leafed parsley

NUTRITIONAL INFORMATION

Per Serving 234 calories, 10g fat (of which 5g saturates), trace carbohydrate, 0.3g salt

1 Heat the oil and butter in a frying pan over a medium heat. Add the chicken breasts and fry for 10–12 minutes on each side until cooked through. Transfer to a warmed plate, cover and keep warm.

2 To make the sauce, add the wine and capers to the same pan. Bring to the boil, then reduce the heat and simmer for 2–3 minutes until the wine is reduced by half. Add the lemon juice and butter and stir in the parsley.

3 Divide the chicken among four warmed plates, pour the sauce over the chicken, season with pepper, garnish each serving with a lemon wedge and serve immediately with boiled rice.

Thai Red Chicken Curry

Preparation Time
5 minutes
Cooking Time
20 minutes

Serves 4

- 1 tbsp vegetable oil
- 3 tbsp Thai red curry paste
- 4 boneless, skinless chicken breasts, about 600g (1lb 5oz) total weight, sliced
- 400ml can coconut milk
- 300ml (½ pint) hot chicken or vegetable stock
- juice of 1 lime, plus lime halves to serve
- 200g pack mixed baby sweetcorn and mangetouts
- 2 tbsp freshly chopped coriander, plus sprigs to garnish
- rice or rice noodles to serve

NUTRITIONAL INFORMATION
Per Serving 248 calories, 8g fat (of which 1g saturates), 16g carbohydrate, 1g salt

Healthy Tip
Coconut milk is made from the pressed flesh of coconut. It contains around 18g of fat per 100ml, which is lower than coconut cream used in many Asian recipes (about 20–25g/100g). You can cut the fat content of the dish further by using half-fat coconut milk (6–9g fat/100ml).

1 Heat the oil in a wok or large pan over a low heat. Add the curry paste and cook for 2 minutes or until fragrant.

2 Add the chicken and fry gently for about 10 minutes or until browned.

3 Add the coconut milk, hot stock, lime juice and sweetcorn to the pan and bring to the boil. Add the mangetouts, reduce the heat and simmer for 4–5 minutes until the chicken is cooked.

4 Stir in the chopped coriander, garnish with coriander sprigs and serve immediately with rice or noodles and lime halves to squeeze over.

Serves 4

Chicken Cacciatore

Preparation Time
5 minutes
Cooking Time
40 minutes

- 2 tbsp olive oil
- 8 boneless, skinless chicken thighs
- 2 garlic cloves, crushed
- 1 tsp dried thyme
- 1 tsp dried tarragon
- 150ml (¼ pint) white wine
- 400g can chopped tomatoes
- 12 pitted black olives
- 12 capers, rinsed and drained
- ground black pepper
- brown rice and broad beans or peas to serve

NUTRITIONAL INFORMATION
Per Serving 327 calories, 17g fat (of which 4g saturates), 3g carbohydrate, 1.3g salt

1 Heat the oil in a flameproof casserole over a high heat. Add the chicken and brown all over. Reduce the heat and add the garlic, thyme, tarragon and wine to the casserole. Stir for 1 minute, then add the tomatoes and season with pepper.

2 Bring to the boil, then reduce the heat, cover the casserole and simmer for 20 minutes or until the chicken is tender.

3 Lift the chicken out of the casserole and put to one side. Bubble the sauce for 5 minutes or until thickened, add the olives and capers, stir well and cook for a further 2–3 minutes.

4 Put the chicken into the sauce. Serve immediately with brown rice and broad beans or peas.

Chicken with Mango & Fennel Salsa

Preparation Time
12 minutes
Cooking Time
20 minutes

- 4 skinless chicken breasts
- juice of ½ lime
- oil-water spray (see Cook's Tip, page 106)
- salt and ground black pepper
- rocket to serve

FOR THE SALSA

- 1 mango, peeled, stoned and diced
- 1 small fennel bulb, trimmed and diced
- 1 fresh chilli, seeded and finely diced (see Cook's Tips, page 94)
- 1 tbsp balsamic vinegar
- juice of ½ lime
- 2 tbsp freshly chopped flat-leafed parsley
- 2 tbsp freshly chopped mint

NUTRITIONAL INFORMATION

Per Serving 161 calories, 2g fat (of which trace saturates), 6g carbohydrate, 0.2g salt

Serves 4

Try Something Different

Replace the chicken with 4 duck breasts with skin; score the skin in a crisscross pattern and grill for 5–8 minutes on each side.

1 Preheat the grill to medium. Put the chicken on a grill pan and season well with salt and pepper. Pour the lime juice over it and spray with the oil-water spray. Grill for 8–10 minutes on each side until cooked and the juices run clear when pierced with a skewer. Remove from the grill and put the chicken to one side

2 Combine all the salsa ingredients in a bowl and season generously with salt and pepper. Spoon on top of the chicken and serve with rocket.

Thai Green Curry

Preparation Time
10 minutes
Cooking Time
15 minutes

- 2 tsp vegetable oil
- 1 green chilli, seeded and finely chopped (see Cook's Tip, page 55)
- 4cm (1½in) piece fresh root ginger, peeled and finely grated
- 1 lemongrass stalk, trimmed and cut into three pieces
- 225g (8oz) brown-cap or oyster mushrooms
- 1 tbsp Thai green curry paste
- 300ml (½ pint) coconut milk
- 150ml (¼ pint) chicken stock
- 1 tbsp Thai fish sauce
- 1 tsp light soy sauce
- 350g (12oz) boneless, skinless chicken breasts, cut into bite-size pieces
- 350g (12oz) cooked peeled large prawns
- fresh coriander sprigs to garnish
- Thai fragrant rice to serve

NUTRITIONAL INFORMATION
Per Serving 132 calories, 2g fat (of which 0g saturates), 4g carbohydrate, 1.4g salt

1 Heat the oil in a wok or large frying pan. Add the chilli, ginger, lemongrass and mushrooms and stir-fry for about 3 minutes or until the mushrooms begin to turn golden. Add the curry paste and fry for a further 1 minute.

2 Pour in the coconut milk, stock, fish sauce and soy sauce and bring to the boil. Stir in the chicken, then reduce the heat and simmer for about 8 minutes or until the chicken is cooked.

3 Add the prawns and cook for a further 1 minute. Garnish with coriander sprigs and serve immediately, with Thai fragrant rice.

Garlic & Thyme Chicken

Preparation Time
10 minutes
Cooking Time
10–15 minutes

- 2 garlic cloves, crushed
- 2 tbsp freshly chopped thyme leaves
- 2 tbsp olive oil
- 4 chicken thighs
- salt and ground black pepper

NUTRITIONAL INFORMATION
Per Serving 135 calories, 6g fat (of which 1g saturates), trace carbohydrate, 0.2g salt

1 Preheat the barbecue or grill. Mix the garlic with the thyme and oil in a large bowl. Season with salt and pepper.

2 Using a sharp knife, make two or three slits in each chicken thigh. Put the chicken into the bowl and toss to coat thoroughly. Barbecue or grill for 5–7 minutes on each side until golden and cooked through.

Healthy Tip

Chicken is a rich source of protein and B vitamins. Chicken thighs contain more iron than chicken breast. Garlic has many health benefits: it has been shown to lower the risk of heart disease, high blood pressure, high blood cholesterol levels and certain cancers.

Serves 4

Chicken in Lemon Vinaigrette

Preparation Time
10 minutes
Cooking Time
40 minutes

Serves 6

- 2 lemons
- 175g (6oz) shallots or onions, sliced
- 2 tbsp balsamic vinegar
- 2 tbsp sherry vinegar
- 4 tbsp clear honey
- 150ml (¼ pint) olive oil
- 6 boneless chicken breasts or
- 12 boneless thighs, with skin
- salt and ground black pepper
- mashed potatoes to serve

NUTRITIONAL INFORMATION
Per Serving 353 calories, 21g fat (of which 4g saturates), 10g carbohydrate, 0.3g salt

Get Ahead
To prepare ahead Complete the recipe to the end of step 2, then cool, cover and chill in the fridge for up to one day in a non-metallic dish. Transfer the chicken to a roasting tin before cooking.
To use Complete the recipe.

1 Preheat the oven to 200°C (180°C fan oven) mark 6. Grate the zest and squeeze the juice of one lemon, then put to one side. Thinly slice the remaining lemon, then scatter the lemon slices and shallots or onions in a small roasting tin – it should be just large enough to hold the chicken comfortably in a single layer.

2 Whisk the lemon zest and juice, vinegars, honey and oil together in a bowl. Put the chicken into the roasting tin, season with salt and pepper and pour the lemon vinaigrette over it.

3 Roast in the oven, basting regularly, for about 35 minutes or until the chicken is golden and cooked through. Transfer the chicken to a serving dish and keep warm in a low oven. Put the roasting tin, with the juices, over a medium heat on the hob. Bring to the boil and bubble for 2–3 minutes until syrupy. Spoon over the chicken and serve with mashed potatoes.

Orange & Herb Chicken

Preparation Time
10 minutes
Cooking Time
20–30 minutes

- 125ml (4fl oz) orange juice
- grated zest of 1 unwaxed orange
- 2 tbsp freshly chopped tarragon
- 2 tbsp freshly chopped flat-leafed parsley
- 1 tbsp olive oil
- 1 garlic clove, crushed
- 4 skinless chicken breasts, about 125g (4oz) each
- 4 small orange wedges
- salt and ground black pepper
- brown rice and watercress to serve

NUTRITIONAL INFORMATION
Per Serving 180 calories, 4g fat (of which 1g saturates), 5g carbohydrate, 0.2g salt

Healthy Tip
This recipe is very low in fat – skinless chicken breast contains just 3g of fat per portion – making this an ideal dish for those on a low fat or low calorie diet. The orange juice adds vitamin C.

1 Preheat the oven to 200°C (180°C fan oven) mark 6. Whisk the orange juice, orange zest, herbs, oil and garlic together in a large bowl. Season with salt and pepper.

2 Slash the chicken breasts several times and put into a large ovenproof dish. Pour the marinade over them and top each chicken breast with an orange wedge.

3 Cook in the oven for 20–30 minutes until cooked through. Serve with brown rice and watercress.

Prawns in Yellow Bean Sauce

Preparation Time
10 minutes, plus standing
Cooking Time
5 minutes

- 250g pack medium egg noodles
- 1 tbsp stir-fry oil or sesame oil
- 1 garlic clove, sliced
- 1 tsp freshly grated ginger
- 1 bunch of spring onions, each stem cut into four lengthways
- 250g (9oz) frozen raw peeled tiger prawns, thawed
- 200g (7oz) pak choi, leaves separated and the white base cut into thick slices
- 160g jar Chinese yellow bean stir-fry sauce

NUTRITIONAL INFORMATION
Per Serving 394 calories, 10g fat (of which 2g saturates), 59g carbohydrate, 0.9g salt

Try Something Different
Instead of the prawns, use skinless chicken breast, cut into thin strips.

Serves 4

Healthy Tip
Prawns are good sources of protein and zinc, while being low in fat. The egg noodles have a low GI (see page 12), which means they are digested more slowly, keeping you satisfied longer. The pak choi adds valuable vitamins A and C.

1 Put the noodles into a bowl, pour 2 litres (3½ pints) boiling water over them and leave for 4 minutes. Drain and put to one side.

2 Heat the oil in a wok over a medium heat. Add the garlic and ginger and stir-fry for 30 seconds. Add the spring onions and prawns and cook for 2 minutes.

3 Add the chopped white part of the pak choi and the yellow bean sauce. Fill the empty sauce jar with boiling water and pour this into the wok too.

4 Add the noodles to the wok and continue to cook for 1 minute, tossing every now and then to heat through. Finally, stir in the green pak choi leaves and serve immediately.

Cod with Sweet Chilli Glaze

Preparation Time
10 minutes
Cooking Time
20 minutes

- 1 red chilli, seeded and finely chopped (see Cook's Tip, page 55)
- 2 tsp dark soy sauce
- grated zest and juice of 1 lime
- ¼ tsp ground allspice or 6 allspice berries, crushed
- 50g (2oz) light muscovado sugar
- 4 thick cod fillets, with skin, about 175g (6oz) each
- finely sliced red chilli and finely sliced lime zest to garnish
- lime wedges to serve

FOR THE SAFFRON MASH
- 900g (2lb) potatoes, roughly chopped
- a pinch of saffron
- 50g (2oz) butter
- salt and ground black pepper

NUTRITIONAL INFORMATION
Per Serving 193 calories, 1g fat (of which trace saturates), 13g carbohydrate, 0.7g salt

1 To make the saffron mash, cook the potatoes in lightly salted boiling water until tender. Meanwhile, soak the saffron in 2 tbsp boiling water. Drain the potatoes and mash with the butter, then beat in the saffron liquid. Season to taste with salt and pepper.

2 Meanwhile, preheat the grill or griddle pan until hot. Stir the chopped chilli, soy sauce, lime zest and juice, allspice and sugar together in a bowl.

3 Grill the cod for about 1 minute on the flesh side. Turn skin side up and grill for 1 minute. Spoon the chilli glaze over the fish and grill for a further 2–3 minutes until the skin is crisp and golden.

4 Garnish with finely sliced chilli and lime zest. Serve with the saffron mash and lime wedges.

Try Something Different
Use sea bass, gurnard, coley (saithe) or pollack instead of the cod.

Serves 4

Cod with Oriental Vegetables

Preparation Time
10 minutes, plus marinating
Cooking Time
6 minutes

- 4 thick cod fillets, 175g (6oz) each
- grated zest of 1 lime
- 1 tbsp chilli oil
- 1 tbsp sesame oil
- 1 red chilli, seeded and chopped (see Cook's Tip, page 55)
- 2 garlic cloves, chopped
- 8 spring onions, trimmed and sliced
- 125g (4oz) shiitake mushrooms, sliced
- 225g (8oz) carrots, cut into strips
- 300g (11oz) pak choi, chopped
- 1 tbsp soy sauce
- salt and ground black pepper
- lime wedges to serve

NUTRITIONAL INFORMATION
Per Serving 284 calories, 9g fat (of which 1g saturates), 12g carbohydrate, 1g salt

1 Put the cod into a shallow non-metallic dish. Mix the lime zest with the chilli oil and rub all over the fillets. Cover and leave to marinate in a cool place for 30 minutes.

2 Preheat the grill to medium-hot. Heat the sesame oil in a large frying pan. Add the chilli, garlic, spring onions, mushrooms and carrots and stir-fry for 2–3 minutes until the vegetables begin to soften. Add the pak choi and stir-fry for 1–2 minutes. Add the soy sauce and cook for a further minute. Season with salt and pepper.

3 Meanwhile, grill the cod fillets under the hot grill for 2–3 minutes on each side until the flesh has turned opaque and is firm to the touch.

4 Pile the stir-fried vegetables on top of the cod and serve immediately with lime wedges.

Healthy Tip

Cod contains less than 1g of fat per 100g and practically no saturated fat. It is a good source of protein, vitamin B6, niacin, vitamin B12 and potassium. The carrots provide high levels of betacarotene while the pak choi provides vitamin C.

Try Something Different

Replace the cod with any firm-fleshed fish: try salmon, coley (saithe), pollack or whiting.

Smoked Salmon Salad with Mustard & Dill Dressing

Preparation Time
15 minutes, plus chilling

- 4 tbsp extra virgin olive oil
- juice of 1 lemon
- ½ tsp golden caster sugar
- 2 tsp wholegrain mustard
- 4 tsp freshly chopped dill
- salt and ground black pepper

FOR THE SALAD

- 1 small head of fennel
- 110g bag baby leaf salad
- 75g (3oz) wild rocket
- 400g (14oz) oak-smoked wild salmon

NUTRITIONAL INFORMATION

Per Serving 163 calories, 12g fat (of which 2g saturates), 1g carbohydrate, 1g salt

Cook's Tip
Keep the dressing and the salad separately chilled and covered in the fridge.

1 Pour the oil, lemon juice, sugar and mustard into a clean lidded jar and season with salt and pepper. Seal, then shake to combine and chill for up to one day.

2 Using a sharp knife, trim and thinly slice the fennel. Wash the fennel, baby leaf salad and rocket, then dry in a salad spinner, or drain in a colander and spread out on a clean teatowel to remove excess moisture. (Once dried, the salad can be stored, covered, in the fridge for up to one day.)

3 To serve, place twists of salmon on each plate, then pile the salad leaves and fennel alongside and season with pepper. Add the dill to the dressing and shake well to mix. Drizzle the dressing over and around the salad leaves. Serve immediately.

Chinese-style Haddock with Courgettes & Peas

Preparation Time
5 minutes
Cooking Time
10 minutes

Serves 4

- 2 tsp sunflower oil
- 1 small onion, finely chopped
- 1 green chilli, seeded and finely chopped (see Cook's Tips, page 94)
- 2 courgettes, thinly sliced
- 125g (4oz) frozen peas, thawed
- 350g (12oz) skinless haddock fillet, cut into bite-size pieces
- 2 tsp lemon juice
- 4 tbsp hoisin sauce
- lime wedges to serve

NUTRITIONAL INFORMATION
Per Serving 150 calories, 3g fat (of which 1g saturates), 10g carbohydrate, 0.7g salt

Try Something Different
There are plenty of alternatives to haddock: try sea bass, sea bream or gurnard.

1 Heat the oil in a large non-stick frying pan. Add the onion, chilli, courgettes and peas and stir-fry over a high heat for 5 minutes or until the onion and courgettes begin to soften.

2 Add the fish to the pan with the lemon juice, hoisin sauce and 150ml (¼ pint) water. Bring to the boil, then reduce the heat and simmer, uncovered, for 2–3 minutes until the fish is cooked through. Serve with lime wedges.

Salmon with Roasted Vegetables

Preparation Time
10 minutes
Cooking Time
30 minutes

Serves 4

- 2 large leeks, cut into chunks
- 2 large courgettes, sliced
- 2 fennel bulbs, cut into chunks
- 125ml (4fl oz) hot vegetable stock
- zest of ½ lemon
- 4 salmon fillets, 100g (3½oz) each
- 15g (½oz) pinenuts, toasted
- salt and ground black pepper
- lemon wedges to serve

NUTRITIONAL INFORMATION
Per Serving 258 calories, 15g fat (of which 2g saturates), 7g carbohydrate, 0.1g salt

Healthy Tip

Salmon is rich in omega-3 fats, which help reduce the risk of heart disease and stroke, as well as selenium. Fennel contains antioxidants that help combat certain cancers. It is a good source of fibre, vitamin C, folate, magnesium, calcium, iron, and phosphorus, and also promotes healthy digestion.

1 Preheat the oven to 200°C (180°C fan oven) mark 6. Put the leeks into a roasting tin, then add the courgettes and fennel. Pour the hot stock over the vegetables, season well with salt and pepper and roast for 30 minutes or until tender.

2 Meanwhile, sprinkle the lemon zest over the salmon and season with salt and pepper. Put the fish on a baking sheet lined with greaseproof paper and cook in the oven with the vegetables for the last 20 minutes of the cooking time.

3 Scatter the pinenuts over the roasted vegetables and mix well. Divide the vegetables among four plates and top each with a piece of salmon. Serve with lemon wedges.

Mediterranean Salmon

Preparation Time
15 minutes, plus chilling
Cooking Time
10–12 minutes

- 12 × 125g (4oz) salmon fillets, skinned
- 5 tbsp Pesto (see Cook's Tip, page 80)
- 50g (2oz) sun-dried tomatoes, chopped
- 100g (3½oz) black olives
- 3 lemons
- new potatoes and a green salad to serve

NUTRITIONAL INFORMATION
Per Serving 251 calories, 18g fat (of which 3g saturates), 1g carbohydrate, 0.8g salt

Serves 12

Get Ahead

To prepare ahead Complete the recipe to the end of step 1, then cover and chill for up to two days.
To use Complete the recipe.

1 Mix the salmon, Pesto, tomatoes and olives in a large bowl. Sprinkle with the zest of 1 lemon, then cover and chill for 30 minutes.

2 Preheat the oven to 200°C (180°C fan oven) mark 6. Arrange the salmon in a large ovenproof serving dish and spoon the tomato, olive and pesto marinade over it.

3 Cut each of the remaining lemons into six wedges and put around the salmon. Cook in the oven for 10–12 minutes until the fish flakes when pushed with a knife, then serve with new potatoes and salad.

Spicy Monkfish Stew

Preparation Time
10 minutes
Cooking Time
35 minutes

Serves 6

- 1 tbsp olive oil
- 1 onion, finely sliced
- 1 tbsp tom yum paste (see Cook's Tip)
- 450g (1lb) potatoes, cut into 2cm (¾in) chunks
- 400g can chopped tomatoes in rich tomato juice
- 600ml (1 pint) hot fish stock
- 450g (1lb) monkfish, cut into 2cm (¾in) chunks
- 200g (7oz) ready-to-eat baby spinach
- salt and ground black pepper

NUTRITIONAL INFORMATION

Per Serving 142 calories, 3g fat (of which 1g saturates), 16g carbohydrate, 0.2g salt

Cook's Tip

Tom yum paste is a hot and spicy Thai mixture used in soups and stews. It is available from large supermarkets and Asian food shops.

1 Heat the oil in a pan over a medium heat. Add the onion and fry for 5 minutes until golden.

2 Add the tom yum paste and potatoes and stir-fry for 1 minute. Add the tomatoes and hot stock, season well with salt and pepper and cover. Bring to the boil, then reduce the heat and simmer, partially covered, for 15 minutes or until the potatoes are just tender.

3 Add the monkfish to the pan and continue to simmer for 5–10 minutes until the fish is cooked. Add the baby spinach leaves and stir through until wilted. Spoon the fish stew into warmed bowls and serve immediately.

Fish Stew

Preparation Time
15 minutes
Cooking Time
about 30 minutes

- 2 tbsp olive oil
- 1 onion, chopped
- 1 leek, trimmed and chopped
- 2 tsp smoked paprika
- 2 tbsp tomato purée
- 450g (1lb) cod or haddock, roughly chopped
- 125g (4oz) basmati rice
- 175ml (6fl oz) white wine
- 450ml (¾ pint) hot fish stock
- 200g (7oz) cooked and peeled king prawns
- a large handful of spinach leaves
- crusty bread to serve

NUTRITIONAL INFORMATION
Per Serving 280 calories, 7g fat (of which 1g saturates), 34g carbohydrate, 0.3g salt

Healthy Tip
This dish is packed with body-building protein. The onions and leeks are rich in powerful sulphur-containing compounds, including the phytochemical quercetin, which helps keep the heart healthy.

Try Something Different
There are lots of alternatives to cod and haddock: try sea bass, gurnard, coley (saithe) or pollack.

1 Heat the oil in a large pan. Add the onion and leek and fry for 8–10 minutes until they start to soften. Add the smoked paprika and tomato purée and cook for 1–2 minutes.

2 Add the fish, rice, wine and hot stock. Bring to the boil, then cover the pan, reduce the heat and simmer for 10 minutes or until the fish is cooked through and the rice is tender. Add the prawns and cook for 1 minute or until heated through. Stir in the spinach until it wilts, then serve with chunks of bread.

Lemon Tuna

Preparation Time
15–20 minutes, plus marinating
Cooking Time
4–6 minutes

- 3 large lemons
- 2 garlic cloves, crushed
- 100ml (3½fl oz) extra virgin olive oil
- 900g (2lb) fresh tuna in one piece
- 3 tbsp freshly chopped flat-leafed parsley
- ground black pepper
- flatbread to serve

NUTRITIONAL INFORMATION
Per Serving 180 calories, 8g fat (of which 2g saturates), trace carbohydrate, 0.1g salt

1 Finely grate the zest from one lemon and squeeze the juice from the grated lemon and one other lemon. Mix the zest and juice with the garlic and olive oil and season well with pepper.

2 Cut the tuna in half lengthways, then cut into strips about 2cm (¾in) thick. Lay the strips in a shallow dish, pour the marinade over them, then turn the fish to coat. Cover and leave to marinate for at least 30 minutes.

3 Preheat the barbecue or grill. Soak eight bamboo skewers in water for 20 minutes.

4 Fold the strips of tuna and thread on to the soaked skewers. Cut the remaining lemon into eight wedges and push one on to each skewer. Drizzle the skewers with any remaining marinade and sprinkle with the chopped parsley.

5 Lay the skewers on the barbecue or grill and cook for 2–3 minutes on each side. Serve immediately with warmed flatbread.

Serves 8

Meat-free Meals

Serves 12

Red Onion Tarte Tatin

Preparation Time
15 minutes
Cooking Time
35–40 minutes, plus cooling

- 50g (2oz) butter
- 2 tbsp olive oil
- 1.1kg (2½lb) red onions, sliced into rounds
- 1 tbsp light muscovado sugar
- 175ml (6fl oz) white wine
- 4 tsp white wine vinegar
- 1 tbsp freshly chopped thyme, plus extra to garnish (optional)
- 450g (1lb) puff pastry
- plain flour to dust
- salt and ground black pepper

NUTRITIONAL INFORMATION
Per Serving 235 calories, 15g fat (of which 3g saturates), 23g carbohydrate, 0.4g salt

1 Lightly grease two 23cm (9in) non-stick sandwich tins with a little of the butter and put to one side.

2 Melt the remaining butter with the oil in a large non-stick frying pan. Add the onions and sugar and fry for 10–15 minutes until golden, keeping the onions in their rounds.

3 Preheat the oven to 220°C (200°C fan) mark 7. Add the wine, vinegar and thyme to the pan. Bring to the boil and let it bubble until the liquid has evaporated. Season with salt and pepper, then divide the mixture between the tins and leave to cool.

4 Halve the pastry. On a lightly floured surface, roll out each piece thinly into a round shape just larger than the sandwich tin. Put one pastry round over the onion mixture in each tin and tuck in the edges. Prick the pastry dough all over with a fork.

5 Cook the tarts for 15–20 minutes until the pastry is risen and golden. Remove from the oven and put a large warmed plate over the pastry. Turn over and shake gently to release the tart, then remove the tin. Scatter with thyme, if you like, and cut into wedges to serve.

Get Ahead

To prepare ahead Complete the recipe to the end of step 4 up to one day in advance. Cover and keep in the fridge for up to 24 hours.
To use Complete the recipe.

Baked Eggs

Preparation Time
10 minutes
Cooking Time
15 minutes

Serves 2

- 2 tbsp olive oil
- 125g (4oz) mushrooms, chopped
- 225g (8oz) fresh spinach
- 2 medium eggs
- 2 tbsp single cream
- salt and ground black pepper

NUTRITIONAL INFORMATION

Per Serving 238 calories, 21g fat (of which 5g saturates), 2g carbohydrate, 0.6g salt

Healthy Tip

Eggs are a good protein source, with one egg providing about one-sixth of our daily requirement. Spinach is rich in iron, which is better absorbed when you consume a vitamin C-rich source (such as orange juice) at the same meal.

1 Preheat the oven to 200°C (180°C fan oven) mark 6. Heat the oil in a large frying pan. Add the mushrooms and stir-fry for 30 seconds. Add the spinach and stir-fry until wilted. Season to taste, then divide the mixture between two shallow ovenproof dishes.

2 Carefully break an egg into the centre of each dish, then spoon 1 tbsp single cream over it.

3 Cook in the oven for about 12 minutes or until just set – the eggs will continue to cook a little once they're out of the oven. Grind a little more pepper over the top, if you like, and serve.

Tomato & Butter Bean Stew

Preparation Time
10 minutes
Cooking Time
50–55 minutes

- 2 tbsp olive oil
- 1 onion, finely sliced
- 2 garlic cloves, finely chopped
- 2 large leeks, trimmed and sliced
- 2 × 400g cans cherry tomatoes
- 2 × 400g cans no-added-sugar-or-salt butter beans, drained and rinsed
- 150ml (¼ pint) hot vegetable stock
- 1–2 tbsp balsamic vinegar
- salt and ground black pepper

NUTRITIONAL INFORMATION
Per Serving 214 calories, 7g fat (of which 1g saturates), 29g carbohydrate, 0.2g salt

Healthy Tip
Butter beans provide good amounts of protein, complex carbohydrate, iron and fibre; they have a low GI (see page 12), so tend to release their energy over a longer period of time keeping you feeling full longer. They are also high in potassium, which helps to regulate fluid balance in the body.

1 Preheat the oven to 180°C (160°C fan oven) mark 4. Heat the oil in a flameproof casserole over a medium heat. Add the onion and garlic and cook for 10 minutes or until golden and soft. Add the leeks, cover and cook for 5 minutes.

2 Add the tomatoes, beans and hot stock and season well with salt and pepper. Bring to the boil, then cover and cook in the oven for 35–40 minutes until the sauce has thickened. Remove from the oven, stir in the vinegar and spoon into warmed bowls.

Leek & Broccoli Bake

Preparation Time
20 minutes
Cooking Time
45–55 minutes

Serves 4

- 2 tbsp olive oil
- 1 large red onion, cut into wedges
- 1 aubergine, chopped
- 2 leeks, trimmed and cut into chunks
- 1 broccoli head, cut into florets and stalks chopped
- 3 large flat mushrooms, chopped
- 2 × 400g cans cherry tomatoes
- 3 fresh rosemary sprigs, chopped
- 50g (2oz) Parmesan, freshly grated (see Cook's Tips, page 216)
- salt and ground black pepper

NUTRITIONAL INFORMATION

Per Serving 245 calories, 13g fat (of which 4g saturates), 18g carbohydrate, 0.4g salt

Try Something Different
Use sliced courgettes instead of the aubergine.

1 Preheat the oven to 200°C (180°C fan oven) mark 6. Heat the oil in a large flameproof dish, add the onion, aubergine and leeks and cook for 10–12 minutes until golden and softened.

2 Add the broccoli, mushrooms, cherry tomatoes, half the rosemary and 300ml (½ pint) boiling water. Season with salt and pepper. Stir well, then cover and cook in the oven for 30 minutes.

3 Meanwhile, put the Parmesan into a bowl. Add the remaining rosemary and season with pepper. When the vegetables are cooked, remove the lid and sprinkle the Parmesan mixture on top. Cook, uncovered, in the oven for a further 5–10 minutes until the topping is golden.

Roasted Stuffed Peppers

Preparation Time
20 minutes
Cooking Time
45 minutes

- 40g (1½oz) butter
- 4 Romano peppers, halved, with stalks on and seeded
- 3 tbsp olive oil
- 350g (12oz) chestnut mushrooms, roughly chopped
- 4 tbsp finely chopped fresh chives
- 100g (3½oz) vegetarian feta cheese
- 50g (2oz) fresh white breadcrumbs
- 25g (1oz) freshly grated Parmesan (see Cook's Tips, page 216)
- salt and ground black pepper

NUTRITIONAL INFORMATION
Per Serving 189 calories, 14g fat (of which 6g saturates), 11g carbohydrate, 0.9g salt

Get Ahead
To prepare ahead Complete the recipe to the end of step 4, up to one day ahead. Cover and chill.
To use Reheat under the grill for 5 minutes.

1 Preheat the oven to 180°C (160°C fan oven) mark 4. Use a little of the butter to grease a shallow ovenproof dish and put the peppers in it side by side, ready to be filled.

2 Heat the remaining butter and 1 tbsp oil in a pan. Add the mushrooms and fry until they're golden and there's no excess liquid left in the pan. Stir in the chives, then spoon the mixture into the pepper halves.

3 Crumble the feta over the mushrooms. Mix the breadcrumbs and Parmesan in a bowl, then sprinkle over the peppers.

4 Season with salt and pepper and drizzle with the remaining oil. Roast in the oven for 45 minutes or until golden and tender. Serve warm.

Cheese & Vegetable Bake

Preparation Time
15 minutes
Cooking Time
15 minutes

- 250g (9oz) macaroni
- 1 cauliflower, cut into florets
- 2 leeks, trimmed and finely chopped
- 100g (3½oz) frozen peas
- 25g (1oz) wholemeal breadcrumbs
- crusty bread to serve

FOR THE CHEESE SAUCE
- 15g (½oz) butter
- 15g (½oz) plain flour
- 200ml (7fl oz) skimmed milk
- 75g (3oz) Parmesan, grated (see Cook's Tips)
- 2 tsp Dijon mustard
- salt and ground black pepper

NUTRITIONAL INFORMATION
Per Serving 471 calories, 13g fat (of which 7g saturates), 67g carbohydrate, 0.8g salt

1 Cook the macaroni in a large pan of boiling water for 6 minutes, adding the cauliflower and leeks for the last 4 minutes and the peas for the last 2 minutes.

2 Meanwhile, make the cheese sauce. Melt the butter in a pan and add the flour. Cook for 1–2 minutes, then take off the heat and gradually stir in the milk. Bring to the boil slowly, stirring until the sauce thickens. Stir in 50g (2oz) Parmesan and the mustard. Season to taste with salt and pepper.

3 Preheat the grill to medium. Drain the pasta and vegetables and put back into the pan. Add the cheese sauce and mix well. Spoon into a large shallow 2 litre (3½ pint) ovenproof dish and scatter the remaining Parmesan and the breadcrumbs over the top. Grill for 5 minutes or until golden and crisp. Serve hot with bread.

Cook's Tips

Microwave Cheese Sauce Put the butter, flour and milk into a large microwave-proof bowl and whisk together. Cook in a 900W microwave oven on full power for 4 minutes, whisking every minute, until the sauce has thickened. Stir in the cheese until it melts. Stir in the mustard and season to taste.

Vegetarian cheeses Some vegetarians prefer to avoid cheeses that have been produced by the traditional method, because this uses animal-derived rennet. Most supermarkets and cheese shops now stock an excellent range of vegetarian cheeses, produced using vegetarian rennet, which comes from plants, such as thistle and mallow, that contain enzymes capable of curdling milk.

Serves 4

Serves 4

Spicy Vegetable Kebabs

Preparation Time
30 minutes, plus chilling
Cooking Time
25 minutes

- 12 baby onions
- 12 new potatoes
- 12 button mushrooms
- 2 courgettes
- 2 garlic cloves, crushed
- 1 tsp each ground coriander and turmeric
- ½ tsp ground cumin
- 1 tbsp sun-dried tomato paste
- 1 tsp chilli sauce
- juice of ½ lemon
- 4 tbsp olive oil
- 275g (10oz) smoked tofu, cut into 2.5cm (1in) cubes
- salt and ground black pepper
- Yogurt Sauce (see Cook's Tip) and lemon wedges to serve

NUTRITIONAL INFORMATION
Per Serving 247 calories, 14g fat (of which 3g saturates), 22g carbohydrate, 0.1g salt

1 Blanch the baby onions in a pan of lightly salted boiling water for 3 minutes, then drain, refresh in cold water and peel away the skins. Put the potatoes into a pan of lightly salted cold water, bring to the boil and parboil for 8 minutes, then drain and refresh under cold water. Blanch the button mushrooms in boiling water for 1 minute, then drain and refresh under cold water. Cut each courgette into six chunky slices and blanch for 1 minute, then drain and refresh under cold water.

2 Mix the garlic, spices, tomato paste, chilli sauce, lemon juice, oil, salt and pepper together in a shallow dish. Add the well-drained vegetables and tofu and toss to coat. Cover and chill in the fridge for several hours or overnight.

3 Preheat the barbecue or grill. Soak six wooden skewers in water for 20 minutes. Thread the vegetables and tofu on to the soaked skewers. Cook the kebabs for 8–10 minutes until the vegetables are charred and tender, turning frequently and basting with the marinade. Serve with the Yogurt Sauce and lemon wedges.

Cook's Tip
Yogurt Sauce Mix 225g (8oz) Greek yogurt with 1 crushed garlic clove and 2 tbsp freshly chopped coriander. Season to taste with salt and pepper. Chill until ready to serve.

Beef Tomatoes with Bulgur

Preparation Time
10 minutes
Cooking Time
30–35 minutes

Serves 4

- 125g (4oz) bulgur wheat
- 20g (¾oz) flat-leafed parsley, finely chopped
- 75g (3oz) vegetarian feta cheese, chopped
- 1 courgette, chopped
- 50g (2oz) flaked almonds, toasted
- 4 large beef tomatoes
- 1 tbsp olive oil

NUTRITIONAL INFORMATION

Per Serving 245 calories, 14g fat (of which 4g saturates), 21g carbohydrate, 0.7g salt

Try Something Different

Try quinoa instead of the bulgur wheat. Put the quinoa in a bowl of cold water and mix well, then soak for 2 minutes. Drain. Put into a pan with twice its volume of water and bring to the boil. Reduce the heat and simmer for 20 minutes. Remove from the heat, cover and leave to stand for 10 minutes.

Healthy Tip

Tomatoes are full of betacarotene and vitamin C, both antioxidants with heart-protective properties. They also contain the antioxidant lycopene, which helps to combat prostate cancer. It is more readily absorbed by the body when the tomatoes are cooked.

1 Preheat the oven to 180°C (160°C fan oven) mark 4. Cook the bulgur according to the pack instructions. Chop the parsley, feta and courgette and stir into the bulgur with the almonds.

2 Chop the top off each tomato and scoop out the seeds. Put on to a baking sheet and spoon in the bulgur mixture. Drizzle with the oil and cook in the oven for 15–20 minutes until the cheese is starting to soften. Serve.

Mediterranean Halloumi & Vegetable Kebabs

Preparation Time
15 minutes
Cooking Time
8–10 minutes

- 1 large courgette, cut into chunks
- 1 red pepper, seeded and cut into chunks
- 12 cherry tomatoes
- 125g (4oz) halloumi cheese, cubed
- 100g (3½oz) natural yogurt
- 1 tsp ground cumin
- 2 tbsp olive oil
- squeeze of lemon
- 1 lemon, cut into eight wedges
- couscous tossed with freshly chopped flat-leafed parsley to serve

NUTRITIONAL INFORMATION
Per Serving 164 calories, 13g fat (of which 5g saturates), 7g carbohydrate, 1.1g salt

Healthy Tip
These kebabs are packed with vitamins and minerals. Both the tomatoes and red peppers supply vitamin C and betacarotene, which assist the immune system. Halloumi cheese is a semi-hard cheese traditionally prepared from a mixture of sheep's and goat's milk. It contains 25g fat per 100g, which is lower than Cheddar cheese (35g per 100g).

1 Preheat the barbecue or grill. Soak eight wooden skewers in water for 20 minutes. Put the courgette into a large bowl with the red pepper, cherry tomatoes and halloumi cheese. Add the yogurt, cumin, oil and a squeeze of lemon and mix.

2 Push a lemon wedge on to each skewer, then divide the vegetables and cheese among the skewers. Grill the kebabs, turning regularly, for 8–10 minutes until the vegetables are tender and the halloumi is nicely charred. Serve with couscous.

Sesame & Cabbage Rolls

Preparation Time
30 minutes, plus soaking
Cooking Time
about 15 minutes, plus cooling

- 50g (2oz) dried shiitake mushrooms
- 3 tbsp sesame oil
- 4 garlic cloves, crushed
- 4 tbsp sesame seeds
- 450g (1lb) cabbage, finely shredded
- 1 bunch of spring onions, chopped
- 225g can bamboo shoots, drained
- 3 tbsp soy sauce
- ½ tsp caster sugar
- 2 × 270g packs filo pastry
- 1 large egg, beaten
- vegetable oil for deep-frying
- Spiced Plum Sauce or Thai Chilli Dipping Sauce to serve (see Cook's Tip)

NUTRITIONAL INFORMATION
Per Roll 224 calories, 13g fat (of which 2g saturates), 23g carbohydrate, 0.7g salt

1 Put the mushrooms into a heatproof bowl and cover with boiling water. Soak for 20 minutes.

2 Heat the sesame oil in a wok or large frying pan. Add the garlic and sesame seeds and fry gently until golden brown. Add the cabbage and spring onions and fry, stirring, for 3 minutes.

3 Drain and slice the mushrooms. Add them to the pan with the bamboo shoots, soy sauce and sugar and stir until well mixed. Remove the pan from the heat and leave to cool.

4 Cut the filo pastry into 24 × 18cm (7in) squares. Keep the filo squares covered with a damp teatowel as you work. Place one square of filo pastry on the worksurface and cover with a second square. Place a heaped tablespoon of the cabbage mixture across the centre of the top square to within 2.5cm (1in) of the ends. Fold the 2.5cm (1in) ends of pastry over the filling. Brush one unfolded edge of the pastry with a little beaten egg, then roll up to make a thick parcel shape. Shape the remaining pastry and filling in the same way to make 12 parcels.

5 Heat a 5cm (2in) depth of vegetable oil in a deep-fryer or large heavy-based saucepan to 180°C (test by frying a small cube of bread: it should brown in 30 seconds). Fry the rolls in batches for about 3 minutes or until crisp and golden. Remove with a slotted spoon and drain on kitchen paper; keep them warm while you fry the remainder. Serve hot with a sauce for dipping.

Cook's Tip

Spiced Plum Sauce Slice 2 spring onions as thinly as possible. Put them in a small pan with 6 tbsp plum sauce, the juice of 1 lime, ½ tsp Chinese five-spice powder and 2 tbsp water. Heat gently for 2 minutes.

Thai Chilli Dipping Sauce Put 200ml (7fl oz) white wine vinegar and 6 tbsp caster sugar in a small pan, bring to the boil, then reduce the heat and simmer for 2 minutes. Add 1 finely chopped red chilli and 50g (2oz) each finely chopped cucumber, onion and pineapple.

Makes 12

Serves 4

Chilli Vegetable & Coconut Stir-fry

Preparation Time
25 minutes
Cooking Time
about 10 minutes

- 2 tbsp sesame oil
- 2 green chillies, seeded and finely chopped (see Cook's Tip, page 55)
- 2.5cm (1in) piece fresh root ginger, peeled and finely grated
- 2 garlic cloves, crushed
- 1 tbsp Thai green curry paste
- 125g (4oz) carrots, cut into fine matchsticks
- 125g (4oz) baby sweetcorn, halved
- 125g (4oz) mangetouts, halved on the diagonal
- 2 large red peppers, seeded and finely sliced
- 2 small pak choi, quartered
- 4 spring onions, finely chopped
- 300ml (½ pint) coconut milk
- 2 tbsp peanut satay sauce
- 1 tbsp light soy sauce
- 1 tsp soft brown sugar
- 4 tbsp freshly chopped coriander, plus extra sprigs to garnish
- ground black pepper
- 25g (1oz) roasted peanuts to garnish
- rice or noodles to serve

NUTRITIONAL INFORMATION
Per Serving 191 calories, 11g fat (of which 2g saturates), 18g carbohydrate, 1.3g salt

1 Heat the oil in a wok or large non-stick frying pan over a medium heat. Add the chillies, ginger and garlic and stir-fry for 1 minute. Add the curry paste and fry for a further 30 seconds.

2 Add the carrots, sweetcorn, mangetouts and red peppers. Stir-fry over a high heat for 3–4 minutes, then add the pak choi and spring onions. Cook, stirring, for a further 1–2 minutes.

3 Pour in the coconut milk, satay sauce, soy sauce and sugar. Season with pepper, bring to the boil and cook for 1–2 minutes, then add the chopped coriander. Garnish with the peanuts and coriander sprigs and serve with rice or noodles.

Cook's Tip

Check the ingredients in the Thai curry paste: some contain shrimp and are therefore not suitable for vegetarians.

Couscous-stuffed Mushrooms

Preparation Time
3 minutes
Cooking Time
12 minutes

Serves 4

- 125g couscous
- 20g pack fresh flat-leafed parsley, roughly chopped
- 280g jar mixed antipasti in oil, drain and oil put to one side
- 8 large, flat large flat mushrooms
- green salad to serve

FOR THE SAUCE

- 25g (1oz) butter
- 25g (1oz) plain flour
- 300ml (½ pint) skimmed milk
- 75g (3oz) mature Cheddar, grated, plus extra to sprinkle

NUTRITIONAL INFORMATION

Per Serving 340 calories, 21.1g fat (of which 8.9g saturates), 25.5g carbohydrate, 0.6g salt

1 Preheat the oven to 220°C (200°C fan oven) mark 7. Put the couscous in a bowl with 200ml (7fl oz) boiling water, the parsley, antipasti and 1 tbsp of the reserved oil. Stir well. Put the mushrooms on a non-stick baking tray and spoon a little of the couscous mixture into the centre of each. Cook in the oven while you make the sauce.

2 Meanwhile, whisk together the butter, flour and milk in a small pan over a high heat until the mixture comes to the boil. Reduce the heat as soon as it starts to thicken, then whisk until smooth. Take the pan off the heat and stir in the cheese. Spoon the sauce over the mushrooms and sprinkle with the extra cheese. Put back into the oven for a further 7–10 minutes until golden. Serve with a green salad.

Black-eye Bean Chilli

Preparation Time
10 minutes
Cooking Time
20 minutes

- 1 tbsp olive oil
- 1 onion, chopped
- 3 celery sticks, finely chopped
- 2 × 400g no-added-sugar-or-salt cans black-eye beans, drained and rinsed
- 2 × 400g cans chopped tomatoes
- 2 or 3 splashes of Tabasco sauce
- 3 tbsp freshly chopped coriander
- 4 warmed tortillas and soured cream to serve

NUTRITIONAL INFORMATION
Per Serving 332 calories, 4g fat (of which 1g saturates), 61g carbohydrate, 0.7g salt

Healthy Tip
Black-eye beans are a good source of protein, soluble fibre, iron, zinc and B vitamins. The fibre increases satiety (so you feel satisfied longer) and helps lower blood cholesterol levels. Tomatoes add valuable vitamin C and betacarotene.

Try Something Different
Replace half the black-eye beans with red kidney beans.

1 Heat the oil in a frying pan. Add the onion and celery and cook for 10 minutes or until softened.

2 Add the beans, tomatoes and Tabasco to the pan. Bring to the boil, then reduce the heat and simmer for 10 minutes.

3 Just before serving, stir in the coriander. Spoon the chilli on to the warmed tortillas, roll up and serve with soured cream.

Chilli Bean Cake

Preparation Time
10 minutes
Cooking Time
20 minutes

Serves 4

- 3 tbsp olive oil
- 75g (3oz) wholemeal breadcrumbs
- 1 bunch of spring onions, finely chopped
- 1 orange pepper, seeded and chopped
- 1 small green chilli, seeded and finely chopped (see Cook's Tip, page 55)
- 1 garlic clove, crushed
- 1 tsp ground turmeric (optional)
- 400g can no-added-sugar-or-salt mixed beans, drained and rinsed
- 3 tbsp mayonnaise
- a small handful of fresh basil, chopped
- salt and ground black pepper

TO SERVE
- soured cream
- freshly chopped coriander
- lime wedges (optional)

NUTRITIONAL INFORMATION
Per Serving 289 calories, 17g fat (of which 3g saturates), 27g carbohydrate, 0.5g salt

1 Heat 2 tbsp oil in a non-stick frying pan over a medium heat and fry the breadcrumbs until golden and beginning to crisp. Remove and put to one side.

2 Add the remaining oil to the pan and fry the spring onions until soft and golden. Add the orange pepper, chilli, garlic and turmeric, if using. Cook, stirring, for 5 minutes.

3 Tip in the beans, mayonnaise, two-thirds of the fried breadcrumbs and the basil. Season with salt and pepper, mash roughly with a fork, then press the mixture down to flatten and sprinkle with the remaining breadcrumbs. Fry the bean cake over a medium heat for 4–5 minutes until the base is golden. Remove from the heat, cut into wedges and serve with soured cream, coriander and the lime wedges, if you like.

Smoked Sesame Tofu

Preparation Time
20 minutes, plus marinating
Cooking Time
12 minutes

- 2 tbsp toasted sesame seeds
- 2 tbsp tamari (wheat-free Japanese soy sauce)
- 1 tsp light muscovado sugar
- 1 tsp rice wine vinegar
- 1 tbsp sesame oil
- 225g (8oz) smoked tofu, cubed
- ½ small white or green cabbage, shredded
- 2 carrots, peeled and cut into strips
- 200g (7oz) bean sprouts
- 4 roasted red peppers, roughly chopped
- 2 spring onions, shredded
- brown rice to serve

NUTRITIONAL INFORMATION
Per Serving 208 calories, 11g fat (of which 2g saturates), 19g carbohydrate, 1.4g salt

1 Put the sesame seeds into a bowl, add the tamari, sugar, vinegar and ½ tbsp sesame oil. Mix together, then add the smoked tofu and stir to coat. Leave to marinate for 10 minutes.

2 Heat a large wok or non-stick frying pan. Add the marinated tofu, reserving the marinade, and fry for 5 minutes or until golden all over. Remove from the wok with a slotted spoon and put to one side.

3 Heat the remaining oil in the wok. Add the cabbage and carrots and stir-fry for 5 minutes. Stir in the bean sprouts, peppers, spring onions, cooked tofu and reserved marinade and cook for a further 2 minutes. Serve with brown rice.

Mushroom & Bean Hotpot

Preparation Time
15 minutes
Cooking Time
30 minutes

Serves 6

- 3 tbsp olive oil
- 700g (1½lb) chestnut mushrooms, roughly chopped
- 1 large onion, finely chopped
- 2 tbsp plain flour
- 2 tbsp mild curry paste (see Cook's Tip)
- 150ml (¼ pint) dry white wine
- 400g can chopped tomatoes
- 2 tbsp sun-dried tomato paste
- 2 × 400g cans mixed beans, drained and rinsed
- 3 tbsp mango chutney
- 3 tbsp roughly chopped fresh coriander and mint

NUTRITIONAL INFORMATION
Per Serving 280 calories, 10g fat (of which 1g saturates), 34g carbohydrate, 1.3g salt

Healthy Tip
Beans are rich in protein, fibre and many vitamins and minerals. They have been linked with a reduced risk of cancers of the breast, prostate, and colon, as well as heart disease and Type 2 diabetes.

Cook's Tip
Check the ingredients in the curry paste: some may not be suitable for vegetarians.

1 Heat the oil in a large pan over a low heat. Add the mushrooms and onion and fry until the onion is soft and dark golden. Stir in the flour and curry paste and cook for 1–2 minutes.

2 Add the wine, tomatoes, sun-dried tomato paste and beans and bring to the boil, then reduce the heat and simmer gently for 30 minutes or until most of the liquid has reduced. Stir in the chutney and herbs before serving.

Chickpea & Chilli Stir-fry

Preparation Time
10 minutes
Cooking Time
15–20 minutes

Serves 4

- 2 tbsp olive oil
- 1 tsp ground cumin
- 1 red onion, sliced
- 2 garlic cloves, finely chopped
- 1 red chilli, seeded and finely chopped (see Cook's Tip, page 55)
- 2 × 400g cans chickpeas, drained and rinsed
- 400g (14oz) cherry tomatoes
- 125g (4oz) baby spinach leaves
- salt and ground black pepper
- rice or pasta to serve

NUTRITIONAL INFORMATION

Per Serving 258 calories, 11g fat (of which 1g saturates), 30g carbohydrate, 1g salt

Healthy Tip

Chickpeas are an excellent low-fat source of protein and complex carbohydrate. Being high in both soluble and insoluble fibre and with a low GI (see page 12), chickpeas can help you to feel fuller for longer, thereby helping to control appetite and manage weight. Eaten regularly they can also help to reduce the risk of chronic diseases such as obesity, diabetes, heart disease and also certain cancers.

1 Heat the oil in a wok or large frying pan. Add the cumin and fry for 1–2 minutes. Add the onion and stir-fry for 5–7 minutes.

2 Add the garlic and chilli and stir-fry for 2 minutes.

3 Add the chickpeas to the wok with the tomatoes. Reduce the heat and simmer until the chickpeas are hot. Season with salt and pepper. Add the spinach and cook for 1–2 minutes until the leaves have wilted. Serve with rice or pasta.

Pumpkin with Chickpeas

Preparation Time
15 minutes
Cooking Time
25–30 minutes

- 900g (2lb) pumpkin or squash, such as butternut, crown prince or kabocha (see Cook's Tip), peeled, seeded and chopped into roughly 2cm (¾in) cubes
- 1 garlic clove, crushed
- 2 tbsp olive oil
- 2 × 400g cans chickpeas, drained
- ½ red onion, thinly sliced
- 1 large bunch coriander, roughly chopped
- salt and ground black pepper
- steamed spinach to serve

FOR THE TAHINI SAUCE
- 1 large garlic clove, crushed
- 3 tbsp tahini paste
- juice of 1 lemon

NUTRITIONAL INFORMATION
Per Serving 228 calories, 12g fat (of which 2g saturates), 22g carbohydrate, 0.6g salt

1 Preheat the oven to 220°C (200°C fan oven) mark 7. Toss the squash or pumpkin in the garlic and oil and season. Put into a roasting tin and roast for 25 minutes or until soft.

2 Meanwhile, put the chickpeas into a pan with 150ml (¼ pint) water over a medium heat, to warm through.

3 To make the tahini sauce, put the garlic into a bowl, add a pinch of salt, then whisk in the tahini paste. Add the lemon juice and 4–5 tbsp cold water – enough to make a consistency somewhere between single and double cream – and season to taste.

4 Drain the chickpeas, put into a large bowl, then add the pumpkin, onion and coriander. Pour on the tahini sauce and toss carefully. Adjust the seasoning and serve while warm, with spinach.

Cook's Tip
Kabocha is a Japanese variety of winter squash and has a dull-coloured deep green skin with whitish stripes. Its flesh is a yellow-orange colour.

Serves 6

Lentil Chilli

Preparation Time
10 minutes
Cooking Time
30 minutes

Serves 6

- oil-water spray (see Cook's Tip, page 106)
- 2 red onions, chopped
- 1½ tsp each ground coriander and ground cumin
- ½ tsp ground paprika
- 2 garlic cloves, crushed
- 2 sun-dried tomatoes, chopped
- ¼ tsp crushed dried chilli flakes
- 125ml (4fl oz) red wine
- 300ml (½ pint) hot vegetable stock
- 2 × 400g cans brown or green lentils, drained and rinsed
- 2 × 400g cans chopped tomatoes
- sugar to taste
- salt and ground black pepper
- natural low-fat yogurt and rice to serve

NUTRITIONAL INFORMATION

Per Serving 195 calories, 2g fat (of which trace saturates), 32g carbohydrate, 0.1g salt

1 Spray a pan with the oil-water spray and cook the onions for 5 minutes or until softened. Add the coriander, cumin and paprika. Combine the garlic, sun-dried tomatoes, chilli, wine and hot stock and add to the pan. Cover and simmer for 5–7 minutes. Uncover and simmer until the onions are very tender and the liquid has almost gone.

2 Stir in the lentils and tomatoes and season with salt and pepper. Simmer, uncovered, for 15 minutes or until thick. Stir in sugar to taste. Remove from the heat.

3 Ladle out a quarter of the mixture and whiz in a food processor or blender, then combine the puréed and unpuréed portions. Serve with yogurt and rice.

Lentil Casserole

Preparation Time
20 minutes
Cooking Time
1 hour

- 2 tbsp olive oil
- 2 onions, sliced
- 4 carrots, sliced
- 3 leeks, trimmed and sliced
- 450g (1lb) button mushrooms
- 2 garlic cloves, crushed
- 2.5cm (1in) piece fresh root ginger, peeled and grated
- 1 tbsp ground coriander
- 225g (8oz) split red lentils, rinsed and drained
- 750ml (1¼ pints) hot vegetable stock
- 4 tbsp freshly chopped coriander
- salt and ground black pepper

NUTRITIONAL INFORMATION
Per Serving 239 calories, 6g fat (of which 1g saturates), 36g carbohydrate, 0.4g salt

Serves 6

Healthy Tip
Lentils have a low GI (see page 12), meaning their carbohydrate is absorbed slowly, thus giving you sustained energy. They are a good source of protein, iron, zinc, B vitamins and fibre. Their high content of fibre increases the amount of friendly bacteria in the gut that aid digestion.

1 Preheat the oven to 180°C (160°C fan oven) mark 4. Heat the oil in a flameproof casserole. Add the onions, carrots and leeks and fry, stirring, for 5 minutes. Add the mushrooms, garlic, ginger and ground coriander and fry for a further 2–3 minutes.

2 Stir the lentils into the casserole with the hot stock. Season with salt and pepper and bring back to the boil. Cover and cook in the oven for 45–50 minutes or until the vegetables and lentils are tender. Stir in the chopped coriander before serving.

Mixed Beans with Lemon Vinaigrette

Preparation Time
15 minutes

- 400g can mixed beans, drained and rinsed
- 400g can chickpeas, drained and rinsed
- 2 shallots, finely chopped
- fresh mint sprigs and lemon zest to garnish

FOR THE VINAIGRETTE
- 2 tbsp lemon juice
- 2 tsp clear honey
- 8 tbsp extra virgin olive oil
- 3 tbsp freshly chopped mint
- 4 tbsp freshly chopped flat-leafed parsley
- salt and ground black pepper

NUTRITIONAL INFORMATION
Per Serving 285 calories, 19g fat (of which 3g saturates), 22g carbohydrate, 1g salt

Serves 6

Get Ahead

To prepare ahead Complete the recipe to the end of step 2 but don't add the herbs to the vinaigrette. Cover and chill for up to two days.
To use Remove from the fridge up to 1 hour before serving, stir in the herbs. Complete the recipe.

1 Put the beans and chickpeas into a bowl and add the shallots.

2 To make the vinaigrette, whisk together the lemon juice, honey and salt and pepper to taste. Gradually whisk in the oil and stir in the chopped herbs. Just before serving, pour the dressing over the bean mixture and toss well.

3 Transfer the salad to a serving dish, garnish with mint sprigs and lemon zest and serve immediately.

Veggie Pitta

Preparation Time
8 minutes

- 1 wholemeal pitta bread
- 1 tbsp hummus, plus extra to serve (optional)
- 15g (½oz) unsalted cashew nuts
- 2 closed-cup mushrooms, finely sliced
- ¼ cucumber, chopped
- fresh watercress or mixed salad leaves
- ground black pepper

NUTRITIONAL INFORMATION
Per Serving 322 calories, 11g fat (of which 2g saturates), 47g carbohydrate, 1.2g salt

Serves 1

Healthy Tip
Hummus is made from chickpeas, which are packed with fibre, protein and iron. They also contain fructo-oligosaccharides, a type of soluble fibre that boosts the friendly bacteria in the gut and increases immunity. The cashews add extra protein, iron and zinc.

Try Something Different
Add a diced ripe avocado. It is rich in omega fats and good for your skin.

1 Split the pitta bread and spread with the hummus.

2 Fill the pitta with the cashew nuts, mushrooms, cucumber and a generous helping of fresh watercress or salad leaves. Serve with extra hummus, if you like, and season with pepper.

Summer Couscous

Preparation Time
10 minutes
Cooking Time
20 minutes

- 175g (6oz) baby plum tomatoes, halved
- 2 small aubergines, thickly sliced
- 2 large yellow peppers, seeded and roughly chopped
- 2 red onions, cut into thin wedges
- 2 fat garlic cloves, crushed
- 5 tbsp olive oil
- 250g (9oz) couscous
- 400g can chopped tomatoes
- 2 tbsp harissa paste
- 25g (1oz) toasted pumpkin seeds (optional)
- 1 large bunch of coriander, roughly chopped
- salt and ground black pepper

NUTRITIONAL INFORMATION
Per Serving 405 calories, 21g fat (of which 3g saturates), 49g carbohydrate, 0g salt

Serves 4

Healthy Tip

This tasty dish provides lots of vitamins. The tomatoes are full of vitamin C, which is a powerful antioxidant and anti-viral nutrient crucial for a healthy immune system. The yellow peppers also supply vitamin C as well as betacarotene and flavanoids that enhance vitamin C's antioxidant action.

1 Preheat the oven to 230°C (210°C fan oven) mark 8. Put the vegetables and garlic into a large roasting tin, drizzle 3 tbsp oil over them and season with salt and pepper. Toss to coat. Roast for 20 minutes or until tender.

2 Meanwhile, put the couscous into a separate roasting tin and add 300ml (½ pint) cold water. Leave to soak for 5 minutes. Stir in the tomatoes and harissa and drizzle with the remaining oil. Put in the oven next to the vegetables for 4–5 minutes to warm through.

3 Stir the pumpkin seeds, if you like, and the coriander into the couscous and season. Add the vegetables and stir through.

Curried Tofu Burgers

Preparation Time
20 minutes
Cooking Time
6–8 minutes

- 1 tbsp sunflower oil, plus extra to fry
- 1 large carrot, finely grated
- 1 large onion, finely grated
- 2 tsp coriander seeds, finely crushed (optional)
- 1 garlic clove, crushed
- 1 tsp curry paste (see Cook's Tip, page 230)
- 1 tsp tomato purée
- 225g pack firm tofu
- 25g (1oz) fresh wholemeal breadcrumbs
- 25g (1oz) mixed nuts, finely chopped
- plain flour to dust
- salt and ground black pepper
- rice and green vegetables to serve

NUTRITIONAL INFORMATION
Per Serving 253 calories, 18g fat (of which 3g saturates), 15g carbohydrate, 0.2g salt

1 Heat the oil in a large frying pan. Add the carrot and onion and fry for 3–4 minutes until the vegetables are softened, stirring all the time. Add the coriander seeds, if using, the garlic, curry paste and tomato purée. Increase the heat and cook for 2 minutes, stirring all the time.

2 Put the tofu into a bowl and mash with a potato masher. Stir in the vegetables, breadcrumbs and nuts and season with salt and pepper. Beat thoroughly until the mixture starts to stick together. With floured hands, shape the mixture into eight burgers.

3 Heat some oil in a frying pan and fry the burgers for 3–4 minutes on each side until golden brown. Alternatively, brush lightly with oil and cook under a hot grill for 3 minutes on each side or until golden brown. Drain on kitchen paper and serve hot, with rice and green vegetables.

Sweet Chilli Tofu Stir-fry

Preparation Time
5 minutes, plus marinating
Cooking Time
12 minutes

- 200g (7oz) firm tofu
- 4 tbsp sweet chilli sauce
- 2 tbsp light soy sauce
- 1 tbsp sesame seeds
- 2 tbsp toasted sesame oil
- 600g (1lb 5oz) ready-prepared mixed stir-fry vegetables, such as carrots, broccoli, mangetouts and bean sprouts
- a handful of pea shoots or young salad leaves to garnish
- rice to serve

NUTRITIONAL INFORMATION
Per Serving 167 calories, 11g fat (of which 2g saturates), 5g carbohydrate, 1.6g salt

Healthy Tip
Tofu is an excellent low fat source of protein and calcium. It is made from soy beans, which contain phytoestrogens called isoflavones, helpful for controlling menopausal symptoms such as hot flushes. Studies have shown that isoflavones can help protect against cancers of the breast and prostrate.

1 Drain the tofu, pat it dry and cut it into large cubes. Put the tofu into a shallow container and pour 1 tbsp sweet chilli sauce and 1 tbsp light soy sauce over it. Cover and marinate for 10 minutes.

2 Meanwhile, toast the sesame seeds in a hot wok or large frying pan until golden. Tip on to a plate.

3 Put the wok or frying pan on to the heat and add 1 tbsp sesame oil. Add the marinated tofu and stir-fry for 5 minutes until golden. Remove and put to one side.

4 Heat the remaining 1 tbsp oil in the pan. Add the vegetables and stir-fry for 3–4 minutes until just tender. Stir in the cooked tofu.

5 Pour the remaining sweet chilli sauce and soy sauce into the pan, toss well and cook for a further minute until heated through. Sprinkle with the toasted sesame seeds and pea shoots or salad leaves, and serve immediately, with rice.

Thai Vegetable Curry

Preparation Time
10 minutes
Cooking Time
15 minutes

- 2–3 tbsp red Thai curry paste (see Cook's Tip)
- 2.5cm (1in) piece fresh root ginger, peeled and finely chopped
- 50g (2oz) cashew nuts
- 400ml can coconut milk
- 3 carrots, cut into thin batons
- 1 broccoli head, cut into florets
- 20g (¾oz) fresh coriander, roughly chopped
- zest and juice of 1 lime
- 2 large handfuls of spinach leaves
- basmati rice to serve

NUTRITIONAL INFORMATION
Per Serving 200 calories, 10g fat (of which 2g saturates), 19g carbohydrate, 0.7g salt

Serves 4

Cook's Tip

Check the ingredients in the Thai curry paste: some contain shrimp and are therefore not suitable for vegetarians.

Try Something Different

Replace carrots and/or broccoli with alternative vegetables – try baby sweetcorn, sugarsnap peas or mangetouts and simmer for only 5 minutes until tender.

1 Put the curry paste into a large pan, add the ginger and cashew nuts and stir-fry over a medium heat for about 2–3 minutes.

2 Add the coconut milk, cover and bring to the boil. Stir the carrots into the pan, then reduce the heat and simmer for 5 minutes. Add the broccoli florets and simmer for a further 5 minutes until tender.

3 Stir the coriander and lime zest into the pan with the spinach. Squeeze the lime juice over and serve with basmati rice.

Serves 4

Aubergine & Lentil Curry

Preparation Time
15 minutes
Cooking Time
30 minutes

- 3 tbsp olive oil
- 2 aubergines, cut into 2.5cm (1in) chunks
- 1 onion, chopped
- 2 tbsp mild curry paste
- 3 × 400g cans chopped tomatoes
- 200ml (7fl oz) hot vegetable stock
- 150g (5oz) red lentils, rinsed
- 100g (31/2oz) spinach leaves
- 25g (1oz) fresh coriander, roughly chopped, plus extra leaves to garnish
- 2 tbsp fat-free Greek yogurt
- rice to serve

NUTRITIONAL INFORMATION
Per Serving 184 calories, 11g fat (of which 1g saturates), 18g carbohydrate, 0.6g salt

1 Heat 2 tbsp oil in a large pan over a low heat. Add the aubergine chunks and fry until golden. Remove from the pan and put to one side.

2 Heat the remaining oil in the same pan. Add the onion and fry for about 8–10 minutes until soft. Add the curry paste and stir-fry for a further 2 minutes.

3 Add the tomatoes, hot vegetable stock, lentils and reserved aubergines to the pan. Bring to the boil, then reduce the heat to a low simmer, half-cover with a lid and simmer for 25 minutes or according to the lentils' pack instructions.

4 At the end of cooking, stir the spinach, coriander and yogurt through the curry. Garnish with extra coriander leaves and serve with rice.

Healthy Tip

Aubergines are low in fat and have many health benefits. They contain flavanoids, which are potent antioxidants that help block the formation of harmful free radicals. This helps protect cell membranes from damage. Some studies suggest aubergines may help reduce blood cholesterol levels.

Chickpea Curry

Preparation Time
20 minutes
Cooking Time
40–45 minutes

Serves 6

- 2 tbsp vegetable oil
- 2 onions, finely sliced
- 2 garlic cloves, crushed
- 1 tbsp ground coriander
- 1 tsp mild chilli powder
- 1 tbsp black mustard seeds
- 2 tbsp tamarind paste
- 2 tbsp sun-dried tomato paste
- 750g (1lb 10oz) new potatoes, quartered
- 400g can chopped tomatoes
- 1 litre ($1\frac{3}{4}$pints) hot vegetable stock
- 250g (9oz) green beans, trimmed
- 2 × 400g cans chickpeas, drained and rinsed
- 2 tsp garam masala
- salt and ground black pepper
- basmati rice to serve

NUTRITIONAL INFORMATION

Per Serving 291 calories, 8g fat (of which 1g saturates), 46g carbohydrate, 1.3g salt

1 Heat the oil in a pan. Add the onions and fry for 10–15 minutes until golden – when they have a good colour they will add depth of flavour. Add the garlic, coriander, chilli, mustard seeds, tamarind paste and sun-dried tomato paste. Cook for 1–2 minutes until the aroma from the spices is released.

2 Add the potatoes and toss in the spices for 1–2 minutes. Add the tomatoes and hot stock and season with salt and pepper, then cover and bring to the boil. Reduce the heat and simmer, half covered, for 20 minutes or until the potatoes are just cooked.

3 Add the beans and chickpeas and continue to cook for 5 minutes or until the beans are tender and the chickpeas are warmed through. Stir in the garam masala and serve with basmati rice.

Mauritian Vegetable Curry

Preparation Time
15 minutes
Cooking Time
30 minutes

Serves 4

- 3 tbsp vegetable oil
- 1 onion, finely sliced
- 4 garlic cloves, crushed
- 2.5cm (1in) piece fresh root ginger, peeled and grated
- 3 tbsp medium curry powder
- 6 fresh curry leaves
- 150g (5oz) potato, cut into 1cm (½in) cubes
- 125g (4oz) aubergine, cut into 2.5cm (1in) sticks, 5mm (¼in) wide
- 150g (5oz) carrots, cut into 5mm (¼in) dice
- 900ml (1½ pints) hot vegetable stock
- a pinch of saffron threads
- ½ tsp salt
- 150g (5oz) green beans, trimmed
- 75g (3oz) frozen peas
- ground black pepper
- 3 tbsp freshly chopped coriander to garnish
- naan bread to serve

NUTRITIONAL INFORMATION
Per Serving 184 calories, 11g fat (of which 1g saturates), 18g carbohydrate, 0.6g salt

1 Heat the oil in a large heavy-based pan over a low heat. Add the onion and fry for 5–10 minutes until golden. Add the garlic, ginger, curry powder and curry leaves and fry for a further minute.

2 Add the potato and aubergine to the pan and fry, stirring, for 2 minutes. Add the carrots, hot stock, saffron and salt and season with plenty of pepper. Cover and cook for 10 minutes or until the vegetables are almost tender.

3 Add the beans and peas to the pan and cook for a further 4 minutes. Sprinkle with the chopped coriander and serve with naan bread.

Cook's Tip

To prepare ahead Complete the recipe, without the garnish, and chill quickly. It will keep, in the fridge, for up to two days.
To use Put into a pan, cover and bring to the boil, then reduce the heat and simmer for 10–15 minutes. Complete the recipe.

Vegetables

Lemon & Orange Carrots

Preparation Time
10 minutes
Cooking Time
10–15 minutes

- 900g (2lb) carrots, cut into long batons
- 150ml (¼ pint) orange juice
- juice of 2 lemons
- 150ml (¼ pint) dry white wine
- 50g (2oz) butter
- 3 tbsp light muscovado sugar
- 4 tbsp freshly chopped
- coriander to garnish

NUTRITIONAL INFORMATION
Per Serving 127 calories, 6g fat (of which 3g saturates), 17g carbohydrate, 0.2g salt

Serves 8

Freezing Tip
To freeze Cook the carrots for only 5 minutes, then put to one to side to cool and freeze with the remaining liquid.
To use Thaw for 5 hours, then reheat in a pan for 5–6 minutes, or cook on full power in a 900W microwave for 7–8 minutes.

1 Put the carrots, orange and lemon juices, wine, butter and sugar into a pan. Cover and bring to the boil.

2 Remove the lid and cook for about 10 minutes or until almost all the liquid has evaporated. Serve sprinkled with the coriander.

Spinach with Tomatoes

Preparation Time
10 minutes
Cooking Time
15 minutes

- 50g (2oz) butter
- 2 garlic cloves, crushed
- 450g (1lb) baby plum tomatoes, halved
- 250g (9oz) baby spinach leaves
- a large pinch of freshly grated nutmeg
- salt and ground black pepper

NUTRITIONAL INFORMATION
Per Serving 85 calories, 7g fat (of which 5g saturates), 3g carbohydrate, 0.3g salt

Healthy Tip

Spinach contains the phytochemical lutein, which helps protect against age-related deterioration of vision, as well as carotenoids, which help reduce the risk of colon cancer. It also supplies high levels of vitamin C and vitamin A.

1 Heat half the butter in a large pan, add the garlic and cook until just soft. Add the tomatoes and cook for 4–5 minutes or until just beginning to soften.

2 Put the spinach and a little water into a clean pan, cover and cook for 2–3 minutes until the spinach has just wilted. Drain well, chop roughly and stir into the tomatoes.

3 Add the remaining butter and heat through gently. Season well with salt and pepper, stir in the nutmeg and serve immediately.

Spicy Roasted Roots

Preparation Time
25 minutes
Cooking Time
about 1½ hours

- 3 carrots, sliced lengthways
- 3 parsnips, sliced lengthways
- 3 tbsp olive oil
- 1 butternut squash, chopped
- 2 red onions, cut into wedges
- 2 leeks, sliced
- 3 garlic cloves, roughly chopped
- 2 tbsp mild curry paste (see Cook's Tip, page 230)
- salt and ground black pepper

NUTRITIONAL INFORMATION
Per Serving 134 calories, 8g fat (of which 1g saturates), 14g carbohydrate, 0.1g salt

Healthy Tip

This dish is full of betacarotene – both carrots and butternut squash are rich sources of this nutrient, which strengthens the immune system and protects against colds and flu. Butternut squash also contains good amounts of vitamins C and E.

Freezing Tip

To freeze Complete the recipe, then cool, wrap and freeze for up to one month.
To use Thaw overnight at room temperature, then reheat at 200°C (180°C fan oven) mark 6 for 20 minutes with 200ml (7fl oz) hot vegetable stock.

1 Preheat the oven to 200°C (180°C fan oven) mark 6. Put the carrots and parsnips into a large roasting tin, drizzle with 1 tbsp oil and cook for 40 minutes.

2 Add the butternut squash, onions, leeks and garlic to the roasting tin. Season with salt and pepper, then drizzle with the remaining 2 tbsp oil.

3 Roast for 45 minutes until the vegetables are tender and golden. Stir in the curry paste and roast for a further 10 minutes. Serve immediately.

Charred Courgettes

Preparation Time
5 minutes
Cooking Time
10 minutes

- 4 courgettes, halved lengthways
- olive oil to brush
- coarse sea salt to sprinkle

NUTRITIONAL INFORMATION
Per Serving 36 calories, 2g fat (of which trace saturates), 2g carbohydrate, 0g salt

Serves 4

Try Something Different
- Mix the olive oil with a good pinch of dried chilli flakes and a small handful of freshly chopped rosemary leaves.
- Use a mixture of yellow and green courgettes, if you like.

1 Preheat the barbecue or a griddle pan. Score a criss-cross pattern on the fleshy side of the courgettes. Brush lightly with oil and sprinkle with sea salt.

2 Cook the courgettes on the barbecue or griddle for 10 minutes or until just tender, turning occasionally.

Braised Red Cabbage

Preparation Time
15 minutes
Cooking Time
about 50 minutes

- 1 tbsp olive oil
- 1 red onion, halved and sliced
- 2 garlic cloves, crushed
- 1 large red cabbage, about 1kg (2¼lb), shredded
- 2 tbsp light muscovado sugar
- 2 tbsp red wine vinegar
- 8 juniper berries
- ¼ tsp ground allspice
- 300ml (½ pint) vegetable stock
- 2 pears, cored and sliced
- salt and ground black pepper
- fresh thyme sprigs to garnish

NUTRITIONAL INFORMATION
Per Serving 63 calories, 1g fat (of which 0g saturates), 12g carbohydrate, 0.9g salt

Serves 6

Get Ahead
To prepare ahead Red cabbage improves if made a day ahead. Complete step 1, cover and leave to chill.
To use Reheat the red cabbage gently in a pan, then add the pears. Complete the recipe.

1 Heat the oil in a large pan. Add the onion and fry for 5 minutes. Add the remaining ingredients, except the pears, and season with salt and pepper. Bring to the boil, then reduce the heat, cover and simmer for 30 minutes.

2 Add the pears and cook for a further 15 minutes or until nearly all the liquid has evaporated and the cabbage is tender. Serve hot, garnished with thyme sprigs.

Baked Tomatoes & Fennel

Preparation Time
10 minutes
Cooking Time
1¼ hours

Serves 6

- 900g (2lb) fennel, trimmed and cut into quarters
- 75ml (2½fl oz) white wine
- 5 thyme sprigs
- 75ml (2½fl oz) olive oil
- 900g (2lb) ripe beef or plum tomatoes

NUTRITIONAL INFORMATION
Per Serving 127 calories, 9g fat (of which 1g saturates), 7g carbohydrate, 0.1g salt

Healthy Tip
Tomatoes are rich in vitamin C, vitamin E and betacarotene. Roasting them in olive oil increases the absorption of the latter two nutrients. The fennel is a good source of cancer-fighting antioxidants, fibre, and numerous vitamins including vitamin C, folate and betacarotene.

Cook's Tip
This dish is an ideal accompaniment to a vegetarian frittata.

1 Preheat the oven to 200°C (180°C fan oven) mark 6. Put the fennel into a roasting tin and pour the white wine over it. Snip the thyme sprigs over the fennel, drizzle with the oil and roast for 45 minutes.

2 Halve the tomatoes, add to the roasting tin and roast for a further 30 minutes or until tender, basting with the juices halfway through.

Spicy Squash Quarters

Preparation Time
10 minutes
Cooking Time
20–30 minutes

- 2 small butternut squash, quartered and seeded
- coarse sea salt to sprinkle
- 75g (3oz) butter, melted
- 4 tsp peppered steak seasoning
- wild rocket to serve

NUTRITIONAL INFORMATION
Per Serving 97 calories, 8g fat (of which 5g saturates), 4g carbohydrate, 0.1g salt

Serves 8

Healthy Tip

Butternut squash contains an abundance of powerhouse nutrients known as carotenoids, known to protect against heart disease. In particular, it boasts very high levels of betacarotene, identified as a deterrent against breast cancer and age-related macular degeneration. It is also rich in vitamin C and fibre.

Try Something Different

Instead of the steak seasoning, lightly toast 2 tsp coriander seeds, roughly crush and stir into the melted butter before brushing on to the squash. When cooked, toss with fresh coriander leaves.

1 Preheat the barbecue to medium-hot. Sprinkle the squash with salt, brush with butter then sprinkle the steak seasoning over.

2 Cook for 20–30 minutes until tender, turning occasionally. Serve hot, with wild rocket.

Roasted Ratatouille

Preparation Time
15 minutes
Cooking Time
1½ hours

Serves 6

- 400g (14oz) red peppers, seeded and roughly chopped
- 700g (1½lb) aubergine, stalk removed, cut into chunks
- 450g (1lb) onions, cut into wedges
- 4 or 5 garlic cloves, unpeeled and left whole
- 150ml (¼ pint) olive oil
- 1 tsp fennel seeds
- 200ml (7fl oz) passata
- sea salt and ground black pepper
- a few fresh thyme sprigs to garnish

NUTRITIONAL INFORMATION

Per Serving 224 calories, 18g fat (of which 3g saturates), 14g carbohydrate, 0g salt

Try Something Different
Replace half the aubergines with 400g (14oz) courgettes; use a mix of green and red peppers; garnish with fresh basil instead of thyme.

1 Preheat the oven to 240°C (220°C fan oven) mark 9. Put the peppers, aubergine, onions, garlic, oil and fennel seeds into a roasting tin. Season with sea salt flakes and pepper and toss together.

2 Transfer to the oven and cook for 30 minutes (tossing frequently during cooking) or until the vegetables are charred and beginning to soften.

3 Stir the passata through the vegetables and put the roasting tin back in the oven for 50–60 minutes, stirring occasionally. Garnish with the thyme sprigs and serve.

Roasted Root Vegetables

Preparation Time
15 minutes
Cooking Time
1 hour

- 1 large potato, cut into large chunks
- 1 large sweet potato, cut into large chunks
- 3 carrots, cut into large chunks
- 4 small parsnips, halved
- 1 small swede, cut into large chunks
- 3 tbsp olive oil
- 2 fresh rosemary and 2 fresh thyme sprigs
- salt and ground black pepper

NUTRITIONAL INFORMATION
Per Serving 251 calories, 10g fat (of which 1g saturates), 39g carbohydrate, 0.2g salt

Serves 4

Healthy Tip
Both potatoes and sweet potatoes provide vitamin C but the latter is also an excellent source of beta-carotene, a powerful antioxidant linked with protection against cancer. Swede and parsnips add potassium, which helps regulate fluid balance and blood pressure.

Try Something Different
Use other combinations of vegetables: try celeriac instead of parsnips, fennel instead of swede, peeled shallots instead of carrots.

1 Preheat the oven to 200°C (180°C fan oven) mark 6. Put all the vegetables into a large roasting tin and add the oil.

2 Use scissors to snip the herbs over the vegetables, then season with salt and pepper and toss everything together. Roast in the oven for 1 hour or until tender.

Sage roasted Parsnips, Apples & Prunes

Preparation Time
20 minutes
Cooking Time
45–55 minutes

- 6–8 tbsp olive oil
- 1.8kg (4lb) parsnips, peeled, quartered and cored
- 6 apples, peeled, cored and quartered
- 16 ready-to-eat prunes
- 50g (2oz) butter
- 1–2 tbsp freshly chopped sage leaves
- 1–2 tbsp clear honey (optional)
- salt and ground black pepper

NUTRITIONAL INFORMATION

Per Serving 313 calories, 16g fat (of which 5g saturates), 40g carbohydrate, 0.2g salt

Get Ahead

To prepare ahead Fry the parsnips and apples, then put to one side to cool, cover and chill for up to one day.
To use Complete the recipe.

1 Heat 3–4 tbsp oil in a large flameproof roasting tin over a medium heat. Add the parsnips in batches and fry until a rich golden brown all over. Remove from the tin and put to one side. Add 3–4 tbsp oil to the same tin. Fry the apples until golden brown. Remove from the tin and put to one side.

2 Preheat the oven to 200°C (180°C fan oven) mark 6. Put the parsnips back into the tin, season with salt and pepper and roast in the oven for 15 minutes.

3 Add the apples and roast for a further 10 minutes. Put the prunes in the tin and continue to roast for 5 minutes. At the end of this time, test the apples: if they're still firm, roast everything for a further 5–10 minutes until the apples are soft and fluffy.

4 Put the tin on the hob over a very low heat. Add the butter and sage, drizzle with honey if you like, and spoon into a hot serving dish

Roasted Mediterranean Vegetables

Preparation Time
10 minutes
Cooking Time
35–40 minutes

- 4 plum tomatoes, halved
- 2 onions, quartered
- 4 red peppers, seeded and cut into strips
- 2 courgettes, cut into thick slices
- 4 garlic cloves, unpeeled
- 6 tbsp olive oil
- 1 tbsp freshly chopped thyme leaves
- sea salt flakes and ground black pepper

NUTRITIONAL INFORMATION
Per Serving 252 calories, 18g fat (of which 3g saturates), 19g carbohydrate, 0.4g salt

Cook's Tip

- To make a nutritionally complete meal, sprinkle with toasted sesame seeds and serve with hummus.
- Use oregano instead of thyme.

Healthy Tip

This dish is packed with vitamins. The tomatoes are rich in betacarotene and vitamin C as well as the phytochemical lycopene linked to a reduced risk of prostate cancer. Studies indicate that people with low levels of lycopene in their bodies may be more likely to suffer from heart disease. The red peppers add high levels of vitamin C to the dish and the olive oil is rich in heart-healthy monounsaturated fats and vitamin E.

1 Preheat the oven to 220°C (200°C fan oven) mark 7. Put the tomatoes into a large roasting tin with the onions, peppers, courgettes and garlic. Drizzle with the oil and sprinkle with thyme, sea salt flakes and black pepper.

2 Roast, turning the vegetables occasionally, for 35–40 minutes until tender.

Sweet Roasted Fennel

Preparation Time
10 minutes
Cooking Time
about 1 hour

Serves 4

- 700g (1½lb) fennel (about 3 bulbs)
- 3 tbsp olive oil
- 50g (2oz) butter, melted
- 1 lemon, halved
- 1 tsp caster sugar
- 2 large thyme sprigs
- salt and ground black pepper

NUTRITIONAL INFORMATION
Per Serving 192 calories, 19g fat (of which 8g saturates), 4g carbohydrate, 0.2g salt

Healthy Tip
Fennel contains betacarotene, folate, vitamin C, fibre, iron and potassium. It is packed with phytochemicals, including anethole, anisic acid, fenchone and limonine, which produce the unique flavour of the vegetable and help protect the body from certain cancers. Fennel is a good digestive aid, helping to reduce gas and bloating.

1 Preheat the oven to 200°C (180°C fan oven) mark 6. Trim and quarter the fennel and put into a large roasting tin.

2 Drizzle the fennel with the oil and melted butter and squeeze the lemon juice over. Add the lemon halves to the roasting tin. Sprinkle with sugar and season generously with salt and pepper. Add the thyme and cover with a damp piece of non-stick baking parchment.

3 Roast in the oven for 30 minutes, then remove the baking parchment and roast for a further 20–30 minutes or until lightly charred and tender.

Roasted Rosemary Potatoes

Preparation Time
10 minutes
Cooking Time
20–25 minutes, plus cooling

- 750g (1lb 11oz) new potatoes, unpeeled
- 3 tbsp olive oil
- 8 rosemary stalks, each about 18cm (7in) long
- salt and ground black pepper

NUTRITIONAL INFORMATION
Per Serving 102 calories, 4g fat (of which 1g saturates), 15g carbohydrate, trace salt

Healthy Tip
All types of potatoes are a useful source of vitamin C but new potatoes are richer in this nutrient than older ones. They are also a source of hydroxycinnamic acids, which have antioxidant properties, as well as fibre, iron and B vitamins. Roasting instead of boiling the potatoes helps retain the vitamins.

Cook's Tip
Skewering the potatoes makes them easier to handle . Using rosemary stalks adds a wonderful flavour.

1 Preheat the barbecue or grill. Cook the potatoes in a pan of lightly salted boiling water for 10 minutes or until nearly tender. Drain, cool a little, then toss in the oil. Season well. Strip most of the leaves from the rosemary stalks, leaving a few at the tip; put the stripped leaves to one side.

2 Thread the potatoes on to the rosemary stalks, place on the barbecue or grill and scatter with the leaves. Cook for 10–15 minutes, turning from time to time, until tender and lightly charred.

Roasted Parma Potatoes

Preparation Time
25 minutes
Cooking Time
45–50 minutes

- about 50 fresh sage leaves
- 900g (2lb) new potatoes (around 25), scrubbed
- 200g (7oz) thinly sliced Parma ham, torn into strips
- 4 tbsp olive oil
- salt and ground black pepper

NUTRITIONAL INFORMATION
Per Serving 201 calories, 9g fat (of which 2g saturates), 24g carbohydrate, 0.9g salt

Serves 4

1 Preheat the oven to 200°C (180°C fan oven) mark 6. Put two sage leaves on each potato and wrap a strip of Parma ham around. Repeat until all the potatoes are wrapped.

2 Put half the oil in an ovenproof dish. Add the potatoes, drizzle with the remaining oil and season well with salt and pepper. Roast in the oven for 45–50 minutes or until tender.

Breads, Biscuits & Cakes

Oatmeal Soda Bread

Preparation Time
15 minutes
Cooking Time
25 minutes, plus cooling

- 25g (1oz) butter, plus extra to grease
- 275g (10oz) plain wholemeal flour
- 175g (6oz) coarse oatmeal
- 2 tsp cream of tartar
- 1 tsp salt
- about 300ml (10fl oz) milk and water, mixed
- butter to serve

NUTRITIONAL INFORMATION
Per Serving 175 calories, 4g fat (of which 1g saturates), 30g carbohydrate, 0.5g salt

Healthy Tip

This bread contains oatmeal, which is rich in betaglucan, a soluble fibre that helps lower levels of cholesterol in the bloodstream. It also helps makes you feel full longer and control blood sugar levels. Oats are also a good source of B vitamins and vitamin E.

1 Preheat the oven to 220°C (200°C fan oven) mark 7. Grease a 900g (2lb) loaf tin and baseline with baking parchment.

2 Mix together all the dry ingredients in a bowl. Rub in the butter.

3 Add the milk and water to bind to a soft dough. Spoon into the prepared tin.

4 Bake in the oven for 25 minutes or until golden brown and well risen. Turn out and leave to cool slightly on a wire rack. Serve with butter. It is best eaten on the day of making.

Corn Bread

Preparation Time
5 minutes
Cooking Time
25–30 minutes

Serves 8

- oil to oil
- 125g (4oz) plain flour
- 175g (6oz) polenta or cornmeal
- 1 tbsp baking powder
- 1 tbsp caster sugar
- ½ tsp salt
- 300ml (½ pint) buttermilk, or equal quantities of natural yogurt and milk, mixed together
- 2 medium eggs
- 4 tbsp extra virgin olive oil
- butter to serve

NUTRITIONAL INFORMATION
Per Serving 229 calories, 8g fat (of which 1g saturates), 33g carbohydrate, 1.3g salt

Cook's Tip
Serve warm with a bowl of soup for a substantial meal.

1 Preheat the oven to 200°C (180°C fan oven) mark 6. Generously oil a shallow 20.5cm (8in) square tin.

2 Put the flour into a large bowl, then add the polenta or cornmeal, the baking powder, sugar and salt. Make a well in the centre and pour in the buttermilk or yogurt and milk mixture. Add the eggs and olive oil, then stir together until evenly mixed.

3 Pour into the prepared tin and bake for 25–30 minutes until firm to the touch. Insert a skewer into the centre – if it comes out clean, the bread is done.

4 Leave the cornbread to rest in the tin for 5 minutes, then turn out and cut into chunky triangles. Serve warm with butter (see Cook's Tip).

Healthy Tip
Cornmeal is a good source of fibre, containing similar levels to wholemeal flour, as well as iron, important for making healthy red blood cells. Buttermilk has a similar nutritional profile to skimmed milk, containing good levels of protein and calcium yet is very low in fat.

Makes 2 loaves

Apricot & Hazelnut Bread

Preparation Time
25 minutes, plus rising
Cooking Time
30–35 minutes, plus cooling

- 75g (3oz) hazelnuts
- 450g (1lb) strong Granary bread flour, plus extra to dust
- 1 tsp salt
- 25g (1oz) unsalted butter, diced, plus extra to grease
- 75g (3oz) ready-to-eat dried apricots, chopped
- 2 tsp fast-action dried yeast
- 2 tbsp molasses
- milk to glaze

NUTRITIONAL INFORMATION

Per Serving 94 calories, 3g fat (of which 1g saturates), 14g carbohydrate, 0g salt

1 Preheat the grill. Spread the hazelnuts on a baking sheet. Toast under the hot grill until golden brown, turning frequently. Put the hazelnuts in a clean teatowel and rub off the skins. Cool, then chop and put to one side.

2 Put the flour into a large bowl. Add the salt, then rub in the butter. Stir in the hazelnuts, apricots and yeast. Make a well in the middle and gradually work in the molasses and about 225ml (8fl oz) hand-hot water to form a soft dough, adding a little more water if the dough feels dry. Knead for 8–10 minutes until smooth, then transfer the dough to a greased bowl. Cover and leave to rise in a warm place for 1–1¼ hours or until doubled in size.

3 Punch the dough to knock back, then divide in half. Shape each portion into a small, flattish round and put on a well-floured baking sheet. Cover loosely and leave to rise for a further 30 minutes.

4 Preheat the oven to 220°C (200°C fan oven) mark 7 and put a large baking sheet on the top shelf to heat up.

5 Using a sharp knife, cut several slashes on each round, brush with a little milk and transfer to the heated baking sheet. Bake for 15 minutes, then reduce the oven temperature to 190°C (170°C fan oven) mark 5 and bake for a further 15–20 minutes until the bread is risen and sounds hollow when tapped underneath. Turn out of the tin on to a wire rack to cool.

To Store

Store in an airtight container. It will keep for up to two days.

Try Something Different

Replace the hazelnuts with walnuts or pecan nuts and use sultanas instead of apricots.

Coconut Cake

Preparation Time
20 minutes
Cooking Time
About 40 minutes

- 150g (5oz) dairy-free sunflower spread, plus extra to grease
- Finely grated zest and juice (about 3 tbsp) of 1 orange
- 100ml (3½fl oz) coconut milk
- 75g (3oz) ground almonds
- 1 large egg
- 1 tsp gluten-free baking powder
- 125g (4oz) caster sugar
- 125g (4oz) gluten-free plain flour blend
- 50g (2oz) desiccated coconut, (optional)

FOR THE ICING

- 40g (1½oz) caster sugar
- 1 tsp cream of tartar
- 1 tbsp egg white
- A few drops of vanilla extract
- Toasted coconut flakes (optional), to decorate

NUTRITIONAL INFORMATION

Per Serving 428 calories, 25g fat (of which 8g saturates), 35g carbohydrate, 0.4g salt

1 Preheat the oven to 180°C (160°C fan oven) mark 4. Grease and line an 18cm (7 in) round cake tin with baking parchment.

2 To make the cake, put all the cake ingredients into a food processor and pulse to combine (alternatively beat by hand in a large bowl). Scrape the mixture into the lined cake tin and bake for 35–40 minutes or until golden on top and a skewer inserted into the centre comes out clean. Leave the cake to cool in the tin for 10 minutes, then remove from the tin and cool completely on a wire rack.

3 For the icing, put the sugar and cream of tartar into a small bowl and add 2 tbsp of boiling water. Stir to dissolve completely. Put the egg white into a separate medium bowl and start whisking with handheld electric beaters. With the motor running, gradually add the sugar mixture. Continue beating until the icing holds stiff peaks – for about 5 minutes. Beat in the vanilla extract.

4 Spread the meringue icing on the top of the cooled cake and decorate with coconut flakes, if you like. Serve in slices.

Serves 8

Ginger & Fruit Teabread

Preparation Time
15 minutes, plus soaking
Cooking Time
1 hour, plus cooling

- 125g (4oz) each dried apricots, apples and pitted prunes, chopped
- 300ml (½ pint) strong fruit tea
- a little butter to grease
- 25g (1oz) preserved stem ginger in syrup, chopped
- 225g (8oz) wholemeal flour
- 2 tsp baking powder
- 125g (4oz) dark muscovado sugar
- 1 medium egg, beaten

NUTRITIONAL INFORMATION
Per Slice 145 calories, 1g fat (of which trace saturates), 33g carbohydrate, 0g salt

To Store
Wrap the teabread in clingfilm and store in an airtight container. It will keep for up to three days.

Cuts into 12 slices

Healthy Tip
This teabread is very low in fat and can therefore be considered a healthier alternative to traditional cakes. The dried fruit in this recipe adds lots of fibre as well as iron and betacarotene. Ginger is a good digestive aid and useful for alleviating and preventing travel sickness.

1 Put the dried fruit into a large bowl, add the fruit tea and leave to soak for 2 hours.

2 Preheat the oven to 180°C (160°C fan oven) mark 4. Grease a 900g (2lb) loaf tin and baseline with baking parchment.

3 Add the remaining ingredients to the soaked fruit and mix thoroughly. Spoon into the prepared tin and brush with 2 tbsp cold water. Bake for 1 hour or until cooked through.

4 Leave to cool in the tin for 10–15 minutes, then turn out on to a wire rack to cool completely.

Honey & Yoghurt Muffins

Preparation Time
15 minutes
Cooking Time
17–20 minutes, plus cooling

- 225g (8oz) plain flour
- 1½ tsp baking powder
- 1 tsp bicarbonate of soda
- ½ tsp each ground mixed spice and ground nutmeg
- pinch of salt
- 50g (2oz) ground oatmeal
- 50g (2oz) light muscovado sugar
- 225g (8oz) Greek-style yoghurt
- 125ml (4fl oz) milk
- 1 medium egg
- 50g (2oz) butter, melted and cooled
- 4 tbsp runny honey

NUTRITIONAL INFORMATION

Per Cookie 180 calories, 6g fat (of which 4g saturates), 27g carbohydrate, 0.1g salt

1 Preheat the oven to 200°C (180°C fan oven) mark 6. Line a 12-hole bun tin or muffin tin with paper muffin cases.

2 Sift the flour, baking powder, bicarbonate of soda, mixed spice, nutmeg and salt into a bowl. Stir in the oatmeal and sugar.

3 Mix the yogurt with the milk in a bowl, then beat in the egg, butter and honey. Pour on to the dry ingredients and stir in quickly until just blended – don't overmix. Divide the mixture equally between the paper cases.

4 Bake for 17–20 minutes until the muffins are well risen and just firm. Cool in the tin for 5 minutes, then transfer to a wire rack. Serve warm or cold. These are best eaten on the day they are made.

Almond Macaroons

Preparation Time
10 minutes
Cooking Time
12–15 minutes, plus cooling

Makes 22

- 2 medium egg whites
- 125g (4oz) caster sugar
- 125g (4oz) ground almonds
- ¼ tsp almond extract
- 22 blanched almonds

NUTRITIONAL INFORMATION

Per Macaroon 86 calories, 6g fat (of which 1g saturates), 7g carbohydrate, 0g salt

To Store

Store in airtight containers. The macaroons will keep for up to one week.

Healthy Tip

These cookies don't contain margarine or butter. Instead, they are made from almonds, which are a source of protein, fibre, vitamin E, calcium, iron, zinc and B vitamins. Studies have shown that almonds help lower 'bad' cholesterol levels and heart disease risk, stave off hunger and also control the appetite.

1 Preheat the oven to 180°C (fan oven 160°C) mark 4. Line baking trays with baking parchment. Whisk the egg whites in a clean, grease-free bowl until stiff peaks form. Gradually whisk in the caster sugar, a little at a time, until thick and glossy. Stir in the ground almonds and almond extract.

2 Spoon teaspoonfuls of the mixture on to the prepared baking trays, spacing them slightly apart. Press an almond into the centre of each one and bake for 12–15 minutes until just golden and firm to the touch.

3 Leave on the baking sheets for 10 minutes, then transfer to wire racks to cool completely. On cooling, these biscuits have a soft, chewy centre; they harden up after a few days.

Hazelnut & Chocolate Biscotti

Preparation Time
10 minutes
Cooking Time
35–40 minutes, plus cooling

Makes about 28

- 125g (4oz) plain flour, sifted, plus extra to dust
- 75g (3oz) golden caster sugar
- ¼ tsp baking powder
- a pinch of ground cinnamon
- a pinch of salt
- 1 large egg, beaten
- 1 tbsp milk
- ¼ tsp vanilla extract
- 25g (1oz) hazelnuts
- 25g (1oz) plain chocolate chips

NUTRITIONAL INFORMATION

Per Biscuit 50 calories, 1g fat (of which trace saturates), 9g carbohydrate, 0g salt

To Store

Store in an airtight container. The biscotti will keep for up to one month.

Cook's Tip

- To enjoy Italian-style, dunk in coffee or dessert wine.
- To make as gifts, divide the biscuits among four large squares of cellophane, then draw up the edges and tie with ribbon. Label the packages with storage information and also an eat-by date.

1 Preheat the oven to 200°C (180°C fan oven) mark 6. Put the flour into a large bowl. Stir in the sugar, baking powder, cinnamon and salt. Make a well in the centre and, using a fork, stir in the beaten egg, milk, vanilla, hazelnuts and chocolate chips to form a sticky dough.

2 Turn out the dough on to a lightly floured worksurface and gently knead into a ball. Roll into a 28cm (11in) log shape. Put on a non-stick baking sheet and flatten slightly. Bake for 20–25 minutes until pale golden.

3 Reduce the oven temperature to 150°C (130°C fan oven) mark 2. Transfer the biscotti log to a chopping board and slice diagonally with a bread knife at 1cm (½ in) intervals. Arrange the slices on the baking sheet and bake for 15 minutes or until golden and dry. Cool on a wire rack.

30-minute Fruit Cake

Preparation Time
15 minutes
Cooking Time
30 minutes, plus cooling

Cuts into 18 slices

- 125g (4oz) unsalted butter, softened, plus extra to grease
- 125g (4oz) light muscovado sugar
- grated zest of 1 lemon
- 2 medium eggs
- a few drops of vanilla extract
- 150g (5oz) self-raising flour, sifted
- 1 tsp baking powder
- a little lemon juice, as needed
- 50g (2oz) glacé cherries, chopped
- 175g (6oz) mixed dried fruit
- 25g (1oz) desiccated coconut
- 25g (1oz) demerara sugar
- 50g (2oz) flaked almonds

NUTRITIONAL INFORMATION
Per Slice 180 calories, 9g fat (of which 5g saturates), 24g carbohydrate, 0.2g salt

To Store
Store in an airtight container. It will keep for up to one week.

Healthy Tip
This fruit-packed cake is a healthier choice than conventional cakes. It contains high levels of fibre, iron and antioxidant nutrients thanks to the dried fruit, while the almonds supply extra protein and vitamin E.

1 Preheat the oven to 190°C (170°C fan oven) mark 5. Grease a 28 × 18cm (11 × 7in) shallow baking tin and baseline with baking parchment.

2 Beat the butter, muscovado sugar, lemon zest, eggs, vanilla extract, flour and baking powder together. Add a little lemon juice, if necessary, to form a soft, dropping consistency. Stir in the glacé cherries, dried fruit and coconut.

3 Spoon the mixture into the prepared tin, level the surface and sprinkle with demerara sugar and almonds. Bake for 30 minutes or until golden.

4 Cool in the tin for a few minutes, then turn out on to a wire rack to cool completely.

Lemon Tart

Preparation Time
30 minutes, plus chilling and cooling
Cooking Time
about 40 minutes

- 75g (3oz) butter
- 50g (2oz) caster sugar
- finely grated zest of 1 lemon
- 125g (4oz) rice flour, plus extra to dust
- 1 large egg

FOR THE FILLING

- 3 large eggs
- 3 large egg yolks
- zest and juice of 3 lemons
- 200g (7oz) caster sugar
- 1tbsp cornflour
- 40g (1½ oz) butter
- icing sugar, to dust

NUTRITIONAL INFORMATION
Per Serving 360 calories, 17g fat (of which 9g saturates), 47g carbohydrate, 0.3g salt

To Store
Store covered in the fridge for up to three days.

1 To make the pastry, put the butter, sugar, lemon zest and rice flour into a food processor and pulse until the mixture resembles fine breadcrumbs. Add the egg and pulse again until the mixture just comes together. Shape into a disc (it will be fairly soft), wrap in clingfilm and chill for 30 minutes.

2 Preheat the oven to 200°C (180°C fan oven) mark 6. Knead the pastry to soften it slightly and bring it together. Lightly dust a work surface with rice flour and roll out the pastry. Use the pastry to line a 20.5cm (8in) round, 4cm (1½ in) deep loose-bottomed sandwich tin. Chill for 15 minutes.

3 Line the pastry with a large sheet of baking parchment, then fill with baking beans. Bake the pastry for 15 minutes, and then carefully remove the beans and parchment. Return the pastry case to the oven and cook for a further 8-10 minutes until golden. Take the pastry case out of the oven and set aside.

4 To make the filling, put the whole eggs and yolks, the lemon zest and juice, caster sugar and cornflour into a pan. Heat the mixture over a medium heat, whisking constantly, until it thickens (it will need to boil and bubble a bit) and is the consistency of lemon curd. Take it off the heat, stir in the butter until melted and combined, then spoon the mixture into the baked pastry case. Leave to cool then chill until set – for at least 4 hours.

5 To serve, dust the top of the tart with icing sugar.

Cuts into 10 slices

Banana Cake

Preparation Time
20 minutes
Cooking Time
about 1 hour

- 125g (4oz) unsalted butter, softened, plus extra to grease
- 125g (4oz) light muscovado sugar
- 2 large eggs, lightly beaten
- 50g (2oz) smooth apple sauce
- 3 very ripe bananas, about 375g (13oz) peeled weight, mashed
- 1½ tsp mixed spice
- 150g (5oz) gluten-free plain flour blend
- 1 tsp gluten-free baking powder
- a pinch of salt

ICING

- 75g (3oz) unsalted butter, softened
- 100g (3½oz) icing sugar, sifted
- 50g (2oz) light muscovado sugar
- ½ tbsp milk (optional)
- dried banana chips to decorate (optional)

NUTRITIONAL INFORMATION

Per slice (for 10) 363 cals; 18g fat (of which 11g saturates); 50g carbohydrate; 0.4g salt

1 Preheat the oven to 180°C (160°C fan oven) mark 4. Grease the base and sides of a 900g (2lb) loaf tin and line with baking parchment.

2 Using a hand-held electric whisk, beat the butter and muscovado sugar in a large bowl until pale and creamy. Gradually whisk in the eggs, then the apple sauce. Stir in the bananas.

3 Sift the spice, flour, baking powder and salt into the bowl, then use a large metal spoon to fold in (the mixture may look a little curdled). Spoon the mixture into the prepared tin and bake for 50 minutes–1 hour until risen and a skewer inserted into centre comes out clean. Cool in the tin for 10 minutes, then turn out on to a wire rack and leave to cool completely.

4 Peel off the lining paper and put the cake on a serving plate. To make the icing, whisk together the butter and both sugars until smooth. If needed, add a little milk to loosen. Spread over the top of the cooled cake. Decorate with banana chips, if you like. Slice the loaf to serve.5 Roll out the topping to 3mm (⅛in) thick. Using a small holly cutter, cut and arrange two leaves on each pie. Mark the leaves with veins. Decorate each with two cranberries. Sprinkle with caster sugar. Bake in the oven for about 12–15 minutes or until golden. Cool in the tins for 15 minutes, then cool completely on a wire rack. Store in an airtight container for up to two days.

Bran & Apple Muffins

Preparation Time
20 minutes
Cooking Time
30 minutes, plus cooling

- 250ml (9fl oz) semi-skimmed milk
- 2 tbsp orange juice
- 50g (2oz) All Bran
- 9 ready-to-eat dried prunes
- 100g (3½oz) light muscovado sugar
- 2 medium egg whites
- 1 tbsp golden syrup
- 150g (5oz) plain flour, sifted
- 1 tsp baking powder
- 1 tsp ground cinnamon
- 1 eating apple, peeled and grated
- demerara sugar to sprinkle

NUTRITIONAL INFORMATION

Per Muffin 137 calories, 1g fat (of which trace saturates), 31g carbohydrate, 0.3g salt

1 Preheat the oven to 190°C (170°C fan oven) mark 5. Line a bun tin or muffin tin with 10 paper muffin cases.

2 Mix the milk and orange juice with the All Bran in a bowl. Put to one side for 10 minutes.

3 Put the prunes into a food processor or blender with 100ml (3½fl oz) water and whiz for 2–3 minutes to make a purée, then add the muscovado sugar and whiz briefly to mix.

4 Put the egg whites into a clean, grease-free bowl and whisk until soft peaks form. Add the whites to the milk mixture with the golden syrup, flour, baking powder, cinnamon, grated apple and prune mixture. Fold all the ingredients together gently – don't over-mix or the muffins will be tough.

5 Spoon the mixture into the paper cases and bake for 30 minutes or until well risen and golden brown. Transfer to a wire rack to cool. Sprinkle with demerara sugar just before serving. These are best eaten on the day they are made.

Healthy Tip

These muffins are very low in fat and high in fibre. They contain no margarine or butter; instead they are made with prunes, which provide sweetness and a moist texture. Prunes are also a concentrated source of fibre and a number of antioxidant nutrients. All Bran in this recipe supplies high levels of fibre, as well as iron and B vitamins.

Freezing Tip

To freeze Complete the recipe, but don't sprinkle with the sugar topping. Once the muffins are cold, pack, seal and freeze.
To use Thaw at cool room temperature. Sprinkle with the demerara sugar to serve.

Makes 10

Low-Fat Brownies

Preparation Time
10 minutes
Cooking Time
20 minutes, plus cooling

- 50ml (2fl oz) sunflower oil, plus extra to grease
- 250g (9oz) plain chocolate (at least 50% cocoa solids)
- 4 medium eggs
- 150g (5oz) light muscovado sugar
- 1 tsp vanilla extract
- 75g (3oz) plain flour
- ¼ tsp baking powder
- 1 tsp cocoa powder

NUTRITIONAL INFORMATION
Per Muffin 172 calories, 8g fat (of which 3g saturates), 24g carbohydrate, 0.1g salt

Makes 16

1 Preheat the oven to 200°C (180°C fan oven) mark 6. Line a 12-hole bun tin or muffin tin with 12 paper muffin cases.

2 Sift the flour, baking powder, bicarbonate of soda, mixed spice, nutmeg and salt into a bowl. Stir in the oatmeal and sugar.

3 Mix the yogurt with the milk in a bowl, then beat in the egg, butter and honey. Pour on to the dry ingredients and stir in quickly until just blended – don't overmix. Divide the mixture equally between the paper cases.

4 Bake for 17–20 minutes until the muffins are well risen and just firm. Cool in the tin for 5 minutes, then transfer to a wire rack. Serve warm or cold. These are best eaten on the day they are made.

Apple Shorties

Preparation Time
20 minutes
Cooking Time
30 minutes, plus cooling

- 75g (3oz) unsalted butter, softened, plus extra to grease
- 40g (1½oz) caster sugar
- 75g (3oz) plain flour, sifted
- 40g (1½oz) fine semolina
- 1 cooking apple, about 175g (6oz), peeled and grated
- 125g (4oz) sultanas
- ½ tsp mixed spice
- 2 tbsp light muscovado sugar
- 1 tsp lemon juice

NUTRITIONAL INFORMATION
Per Square 100 calories, 4g fat (of which 3g saturates), 17g carbohydrate, 0.1g salt

To Store
Store in an airtight container. The shortbreads will keep for up to three days.

1 Preheat the oven to 190°C (170°C fan oven) mark 5. Grease an 18cm (7in) square shallow cake tin.

2 Beat the butter, caster sugar, flour and semolina together in a bowl until the mixture is blended. Press the mixture into the prepared tin and level the surface. Bake in the oven for 15 minutes.

3 Meanwhile, mix the apple with the remaining ingredients. Spoon evenly over the shortbread and put back in the oven for a further 15 minutes.

4 Leave to cool in the tin for a few minutes, then cut into 16 squares. Leave to cool completely, then remove from the tin.

Serves 8

Egg-free Chocolate Fudge Cake

Preparation Time
25 minutes, plus cooling
Cooking Time
about 40 minutes

- 75ml (3fl oz) vegetable oil, plus extra to grease
- 125g (4oz) caster sugar
- 175g (6oz) plain flour
- 25g (1oz) cocoa powder
- ¾ tsp bicarbonate of soda
- ¾ tsp baking powder
- 1 tsp vanilla extract
- 2 tsp cider vinegar
- 200ml (7fl oz) milk

FOR THE ICING

- 300g (10oz) full-fat cream cheese
- 2 tbsp cocoa powder
- 125g (4oz) icing sugar, sifted
- 2 tbsp maple syrup

NUTRITIONAL INFORMATION

Per Brownie 473 calories, 27g fat (of which 13g saturates), 56g carbohydrate, 0.7g salt

To Store

Store in an airtight container. in the fridge for up to three days.

1 Preheat the oven to 180°C (160°C fan oven) mark 4. Grease and line an 18cm (7in) round cake tin with baking parchment. Sift the sugar, flour, cocoa, bicarbonate of soda and baking powder into a large bowl.

2 In a separate jug, mix the oil, vanilla extract, vinegar and milk. Pour the wet ingredients on to the dry ones. Quickly whisk together to mix (the mixture will be quite liquid). Pour into the prepared tin and bake for 40 minutes or until risen and a skewer inserted into the centre comes out clean. Leave the cake to cool for 5 minutes in the tin. Lift out and cool completely on a wire rack.

3 To ice, split the cake in half horizontally. In a large bowl, beat the cream cheese to soften. Sift over the cocoa and icing sugar, then add the syrup. Whisk until smooth. Use some of the icing to sandwich the cake layers back together. Spread the remaining icing over the top of the cake.

Desserts & Puddings

Baked Apples

Preparation Time
10 minutes, plus soaking
Cooking Time
15–20 minutes

- 125g (4oz) hazelnuts
- 125g (4oz) sultanas
- 2 tbsp brandy
- 6 large Bramley apples, cored
- 4 tbsp soft brown sugar
- 100ml (3½fl oz) apple juice
- plain low-fat yogurt to serve

NUTRITIONAL INFORMATION
Per Serving 280 calories, 13g fat (of which 1g saturates), 36g carbohydrate, 0g salt

Healthy Tip
Bramley apples are a good source of vitamin C, containing about twice as much as eating apples. This low fat dessert is also a good source of fibre while the hazelnuts provide useful amounts of vitamin E, iron and zinc.

1 Preheat the oven to 190°C (170°C fan oven) mark 5 and preheat the grill. Spread the hazelnuts over a baking sheet and toast under a hot grill until golden brown, turning them frequently. Put the hazelnuts in a clean teatowel and rub off the skins, then chop the nuts. Put to one side.

2 Soak the sultanas in the brandy and put to one side for 10 minutes. Using a small sharp knife, score around the middle of the apples to stop them from bursting, then stuff each apple with equal amounts of brandy-soaked sultanas. Put the apples in a roasting tin and sprinkle with the brown sugar and apple juice. Bake in the oven for 15–20 minutes until soft.

3 Serve the apples with the toasted hazelnuts and some yogurt.

Apple & Blueberry Strudel

Preparation Time
15 minutes
Cooking Time
40 minutes

Serves 6

- 700g (1½lb) red apples, quartered, cored and thickly sliced
- 1 tbsp lemon juice
- 2 tbsp golden caster sugar
- 100g (3½oz) dried blueberries
- 1 tbsp olive oil
- 6 sheets of filo pastry, thawed if frozen
- plain low-fat yogurt to serve

NUTRITIONAL INFORMATION
Per Serving 178 calories, 2g fat (of which trace saturates), 40g carbohydrate, 0g salt

Healthy Tip
This dessert is low in fat as it is made with filo pastry (which contains virtually no fat) instead of shortcrust pastry (around 30g at per 100g). The blueberries are rich in anthocyanins – the pigment that gives berries their intense colour – which help prevent cancer and heart disease. Apples provide good levels of vitamin C and fibre.

1 Preheat the oven to 190°C (170°C fan oven) mark 5. Put the apples into a bowl and mix with the lemon juice, 1 tbsp sugar and the blueberries.

2 Warm the oil. Lay three sheets of filo pastry side by side, overlapping the long edges. Brush with the oil. Cover with three more sheets of filo and brush again.

3 Tip the apple mixture on to the pastry and roll up from a long edge. Put on to a non-stick baking sheet. Brush with the remaining oil and sprinkle with the remaining caster sugar. Bake for 40 minutes or until the pastry is golden and the apples soft. Serve with yogurt.

Serves 4

Rum & Raisin Rice Pudding

Preparation Time
15 minutes
Cooking Time
about 25 minutes

- 75g (3oz) raisins
- 50ml (2fl oz) rum
- 1 litre (1¾ pint) skimmed milk
- 150g (5oz) basmati rice
- 1 large cinnamon stick, broken into pieces
- 3 tbsp Sweet Freedom Natural Sweetener
- 1 tsp vanilla extract
- ground cinnamon, optional, to sprinkle

NUTRITIONAL INFORMATION
Per Meringue 328 calories, 1g fat (of which 0.3g saturates), 63g carbohydrate, 0.3g salt

1 Put the raisins into a bowl and pour over the rum. Set aside.

2 Put the milk, raw rice and cinnamon stick pieces into a heavy-based saucepan and bring to the boil. Cover, reduce the heat to a gentle simmer and cook for 20 minutes, stirring frequently, or until the rice is tender.

3 Lift out and discard the cinnamon pieces and stir in the sweetener and vanilla. Spoon into bowls, and top with the rum-soaked raisins and sprinkle over a little extra ground cinnamon, if you like.

Cook's Tip

Prepare to the end of step 2 a day ahead. Transfer to a bowl, cool completely, then cover and chill. To serve, reheat gently in a pan, adding more milk as mecessary. Then complete the recipe.

Rhubarb & Raspberry Meringue

Preparation Time
15 minutes
Cooking Time
15–20 minutes

- 450g (1lb) rhubarb, cut into 2.5cm (1in) pieces
- 75g (3oz) caster sugar
- 2.5cm (1in) piece preserved stem ginger (optional), finely chopped
- finely grated zest and juice of 1 orange
- 75g (3oz) frozen raspberries
- 1 large egg white

NUTRITIONAL INFORMATION
Per Serving 94 calories, trace fat, 22g carbohydrate, 0.1g salt

Serves 4
A little effort

1 Preheat the oven to 180°C (160°C fan) mark 4. Place the rhubarb in a large pan with 25g (1oz) caster sugar, the chopped stem ginger, if using, and the orange zest. Cover and cook gently for 2–3 minutes, adding a little orange juice if necessary.

2 Add the raspberries. Spoon the mixture into four 150ml (5fl oz) ramekins or ovenproof teacups.

3 Whisk the egg white and remaining sugar together until foamy. Place the bowl over a pan of simmering water and continue to whisk for 5 minutes or until stiff and shiny.

4 Place a spoonful of meringue mixture on top of each ramekin and bake in the oven for 5–10 minutes until lightly golden.

Baked Apricots with Almonds

Preparation Time
5 minutes
Cooking Time
20-25 minutes

Serves 6

- 12 apricots, halved and stoned
- 3 tbsp golden caster sugar
- 2 tbsp amaretto liqueur
- 25g (1oz) flaked almonds

NUTRITIONAL INFORMATION

Per Serving 124 calories, 6g fat (of which 2g saturates), 16g carbohydrate, 0.1g salt

1 Preheat the oven to 200°C (180°C fan oven) mark 6. Put the apricot halves, cut-side up, in an ovenproof dish. Sprinkle with the sugar, drizzle with the liqueur, then dot each apricot half with a little butter. Scatter the flaked almonds over them.

2 Bake in the oven for 20–25 minutes until the apricots are soft and the juices are syrupy. Serve warm.

Tropical Fruit Pots

Preparation Time
15 minutes
Cooking Time
5 minutes

- 400g can apricots in fruit juice
- 2 balls of preserved stem ginger in syrup, finely chopped, plus 2 tbsp syrup from the jar
- ½ tsp ground cinnamon
- juice of 1 orange
- 3 oranges, cut into segments
- 1 mango, peeled, stoned and chopped
- 1 pineapple, peeled, core removed, and chopped
- 450g (1lb) coconut yogurt
- 3 tbsp lemon curd
- 3–4 tbsp light muscovado sugar

NUTRITIONAL INFORMATION

Per Serving 192 calories, 1g fat (of which trace saturates), 45g carbohydrate, 0.1g salt

Get Ahead

To prepare ahead Complete the recipe to the end of step 2 up to 2 hours before you plan to eat – no need to chill.

To use Complete the recipe.

Serves 8

Healthy Tip

This dessert is brimming with betacarotene, vitamin C and cancer-protective nutrients. Mango is a good source of the phytochemical beta-cryptoxanthin, which has antioxidant properties. Pineapple is a useful source of potassium and vitamin C.

1 Drain the juice from the apricots into a pan and stir in the syrup from the ginger. Add the chopped preserved stem ginger, the cinnamon and orange juice. Put over a low heat and stir gently. Bring to the boil, then reduce the heat and simmer for 2–3 minutes to make a thick syrup.

2 Roughly chop the apricots and put into a bowl with the segmented oranges, the mango and pineapple. Pour the syrup over the fruit. Divide among eight 300ml (½ pint) glasses or dessert bowls.

3 Beat the yogurt and lemon curd together in a bowl until smooth. Spoon a generous dollop over the fruit and sprinkle with muscovado sugar. Chill if not serving immediately.

Oranges with Caramel Sauce

Preparation Time
15 minutes
Cooking Time
30–40 minutes

- 6 oranges
- 25g (1oz) butter
- 2 tbsp golden caster sugar
- 2 tbsp Grand Marnier
- 2 tbsp marmalade
- grated zest and juice of 1 large orange
- plain yogurt or crème fraîche to serve

NUTRITIONAL INFORMATION
Per Serving 139 calories, 4g fat (of which 2g saturates), 24g carbohydrate, 0.1g salt

Serves 6

Healthy Tip

Oranges are rich in vitamin C – one fruit supplies more than 100% of your daily vitamin C, which helps keep blood vessels healthy and defend the body against bacteria and viruses. They also contain bioflavanoids, which help lower blood cholesterol levels and protect your eyesight from age-related damage.

Cook's Tip

Use thick-skinned oranges, such as navel oranges, as they are much easier to peel.

1 Preheat the oven to 200°C (180°C fan oven) mark 6. Cut away the peel and pith from the oranges, then put them in a roasting tin just big enough to hold them.

2 Melt the butter in a pan and add the sugar, Grand Marnier, marmalade, orange zest and juice. Heat gently until the sugar dissolves. Pour the mixture over the oranges in the tin, then bake for 30–40 minutes until the oranges are caramelised. Serve warm with yogurt or crème fraîche.

Summer Pudding

Preparation Time
10 minutes, plus chilling
Cooking Time
10 minutes

- 800g (1lb 12oz) mixed summer berries, such as 250g (9oz) each redcurrants and blackcurrants and 300g (11oz) raspberries
- 125g (4oz) golden caster sugar
- 3 tbsp crème de cassis
- 9 thick slices slightly stale white bread, crusts removed
- crème fraîche to serve

NUTRITIONAL INFORMATION
Per Serving 173 calories, 1g fat (of which trace saturates), 38g carbohydrate, 0.4g salt

1 Put the redcurrants and blackcurrants into a medium pan. Add the sugar and cassis. Bring to a simmer and cook for 3–5 minutes until the sugar has dissolved. Add the raspberries and cook for 2 minutes. Once the fruit is cooked, taste it – there should be a good balance between tart and sweet.

2 Meanwhile, line a 1 litre (1¾ pint) bowl with clingfilm. Put the base of the bowl on one piece of bread and cut around it. Put the circle of bread in the base of the bowl.

3 Line the inside of the bowl with more slices of bread, slightly overlapping them to prevent any gaps. Spoon in the fruit, making sure the juice soaks into the bread. Keep back a few spoonfuls of the juice in case the bread is unevenly soaked when you turn out the pudding.

4 Cut the remaining bread to fit the top of the pudding neatly, using a sharp knife to trim any excess bread from around the edges. Wrap in clingfilm, weigh down with a saucer and a can and chill overnight.

5 To serve, unwrap the outer clingfilm, upturn the pudding on to a plate and remove the inner clingfilm. Drizzle with the reserved juice and serve with crème fraîche.

Serves 8

Strawberry Compôte

Preparation Time
15 minutes, plus chilling
Cooking Time
10 minutes, plus cooling

Serves 4

- 175g (6oz) raspberry conserve
- juice of 1 orange
- juice of 1 lemon
- 1 tsp rosewater
- 350g (12oz) strawberries, hulled and thickly sliced
- 150g (5oz) blueberries

NUTRITIONAL INFORMATION
Per Serving 156 calories, 0g fat, 40g carbohydrate, 0g salt

Healthy Tip

Berries are densely packed with vitamins, antioxidants and other phytonutrients. They contain compounds called anthocyanins – the pigment that gives berries their intense colour, mops up damaging free radicals and helps prevent cancer and heart disease. They are also are rich in vitamin C, which, together with the anthocyanins, helps strengthen blood capillaries and improve blood flow around the body.

1 Put the raspberry conserve into a pan with the orange and lemon juices. Add 75ml (2½fl oz) boiling water. Stir over a low heat to melt the conserve, then leave to cool.

2 Stir in the rosewater and taste – you may want to add a squeeze more lemon juice if it's too sweet. Put the strawberries and blueberries into a large serving bowl, then strain the raspberry conserve mixture over them. Cover and chill overnight. Remove the bowl from the fridge 30 minutes before serving.

Exotic Fruit Salad

Preparation Time
10 minutes

- 2 oranges
- 1 mango, peeled, stoned and chopped
- 450g (1lb) peeled and diced fresh pineapple
- 200g (7oz) blueberries
- ½ Charentais melon, cubed
- grated zest and juice of 1 lime

NUTRITIONAL INFORMATION
Per Serving 187 calories, 1g fat (of which 0g saturates), 47g carbohydrate, 0.1g salt

Serves 4

Healthy Tip
This dessert is packed with vitamins C and betacarotene. Fresh pineapple contains the enzyme bromelain, which aids digestion and is beneficial for inflammatory conditions such as sinusitis and rheumatoid arthritis.

Try Something Different
- Use 2 papayas, peeled, seeded and chopped, instead of the pineapple.
- Mix the seeds of 2 passion fruit with the lime juice before adding to the salad.

1 Using a sharp knife, peel the oranges, remove the pith and cut the flesh into segments. Put into a bowl.

2 Add the mango, pineapple, blueberries and melon to the bowl, then add the lime zest and juice. Gently mix together and serve immediately.

Fruit Kebabs with Spiced Pear Dip

Preparation Time
20 minutes, plus soaking
Cooking Time
8 minutes

Serves 6

- 3 large fresh figs, cut into quarters
- 1 large ripe mango, peeled, stoned and cut into cubes
- 1 baby pineapple or 2 thick slices, peeled and cut into cubes
- 1 tbsp clear honey

FOR THE SPICED PEAR DIP

- 150g (5oz) ready-to-eat dried pears, soaked in hot water for 30 minutes
- juice of 1 orange
- 1 tsp finely chopped fresh root ginger
- ½ tsp vanilla extract
- 50g (2oz) very low-fat plain yogurt
- ½ tsp ground cinnamon, plus extra to dust
- 1 tsp clear honey
- 25g (1oz) hazelnuts, toasted (see step 1, page 267) and roughly chopped

NUTRITIONAL INFORMATION

Per Serving 122 calories, 3g fat (of which trace saturates), 23g carbohydrate, 0g salt

Get Ahead

To prepare ahead Make the dip as in step 1 and spoon the dip into a bowl. Cover and chill for up to two days. Thread the fruit on to the skewers as in step 2. Cover and chill for up to one day.

To use Drizzle the dip with honey, sprinkle with toasted nuts and dust with cinnamon. Allow the chilled kebabs to come to room temperature. Complete step 2.

1 Soak six 20.5cm (8in) wooden skewers in water for 30 minutes. To make the dip, drain the pears and put into a food processor or blender with the orange juice, ginger, vanilla extract, yogurt, cinnamon and 50ml (2fl oz) water. Whiz until smooth. Spoon the dip into a bowl. Drizzle with the honey, sprinkle with the toasted hazelnuts and dust with a little ground cinnamon. Cover and put to one side in a cool place until ready to serve.

2 Preheat the grill to its highest setting. To make the kebabs, thread pieces of fruit on to the skewers, using at least two pieces of each type of fruit per skewer. Put the skewers on a foil-covered tray. Drizzle with honey and grill for about 4 minutes on each side, close to the heat, until lightly charred. Serve warm or at room temperature with the spiced pear dip.

Rice Pudding

Preparation Time
5 minutes
Cooking Time
1½ hours

- butter to grease
- 125g (4oz) short-grain pudding rice
- 1.1 litres (2 pints) full-fat milk
- 4 tbsp golden caster sugar
- grated zest of 1 small orange
- 2 tsp vanilla extract
- whole nutmeg to grate

NUTRITIONAL INFORMATION
Per Serving 235 calories, 7g fat (of which 5g saturates), 35g carbohydrate, 0.2g salt

Serves 6

Healthy Tip
This comfort pud is a good source of protein and calcium, needed for maintaining strong bones. You can use semi-skimmed milk to reduce the fat content further.

1 Preheat the oven to 180°C (160°C fan oven) mark 4. Lightly grease a 900ml (1½ pint) ovenproof dish. Add the pudding rice, milk, sugar, orange zest and vanilla extract and stir everything together. Grate a little nutmeg all over the top of the mixture.

2 Bake the pudding in the oven for 1½ hours or until the top is golden brown, then serve.

Serves 6

Chocolate & Prune Pudding

Preparation Time
10 minutes
Cooking Time
30–40 minutes

- 600ml (1 pint) skimmed milk
- 50g (2oz) plain chocolate, broken into tiny pieces (at least 70% cocoa solids), or chocolate chips
- 2 large eggs
- 2 large egg yolks
- 40g (1½oz) light brown sugar
- ½ tsp cornflour
- 2 tbsp unsweetened cocoa powder, plus extra to dust
- 100g (3½oz) ready-to-eat prunes, chopped

NUTRITIONAL INFORMATION
Per Serving 195 calories, 8g fat (of which 4g saturates), 24g carbohydrate, 0.3g salt

1 Preheat the oven to 170°C (150°C fan oven) mark 3. Heat the milk to simmering point, then remove from the heat. Add the broken chocolate and stir until it has melted completely.

2 In a heatproof bowl, whisk together the eggs, egg yolks, sugar, cornflour and cocoa until smooth. Gradually pour in the hot chocolate milk, stirring until it is combined.

3 Put the prunes into the base of a serving dish or individual dishes, then strain in the milk mixture through a sieve. Put the dish(es) in a roasting tin and carefully fill the tin with boiling water so it comes halfway up the sides of the dish(es). Bake in the oven for about 30–40 minutes until just set.

4 Remove the dish(es) from the roasting tin and serve warm. Alternatively, leave to cool, then chill until ready to serve. Dust with cocoa before serving.

Healthy Tip
This dish is made with skimmed milk, which supplies high levels of protein and calcium but very little fat. Cocoa powder and plain chocolate are rich in flavanols, which may help lower blood pressure, blood cholesterol, and heart disease risk. They also contain useful amounts of magnesium and iron.

Mocha Soufflés

Preparation Time
15 minutes
Cooking Time
12 minutes, plus cooling

- 50g (2oz) plain chocolate (at least 70% cocoa solids), roughly chopped
- 1 tbsp cornflour
- 1 tbsp cocoa powder
- 1–1½ tsp instant coffee granules
- 4 tbsp golden caster sugar
- 150ml (¼ pint) skimmed milk
- 2 medium egg yolks
- 3 medium egg whites
- icing sugar or cocoa powder to dust

NUTRITIONAL INFORMATION
Per Serving 132 calories, 5g fat (of which 2g saturates), 20g carbohydrate, 0.2g salt

1 Preheat the oven to 190°C (170°C fan oven) mark 5 and put a baking sheet inside to heat up.

2 Put the chocolate into a non-stick pan with the cornflour, cocoa powder, coffee granules, 1 tbsp caster sugar and the milk. Warm gently, stirring over a low heat, until the chocolate has melted. Increase the heat and cook, stirring continuously, until the mixture just thickens. Leave to cool a little, then stir in the egg yolks. Cover the surface with a piece of damp greaseproof paper and leave to cool.

3 Put the egg whites into a clean, grease-free bowl and whisk until soft peaks form. Gradually whisk in the remaining caster sugar, a spoonful at a time, until the meringue is stiff but not dry.

4 Stir one-third of the meringue into the cooled chocolate mixture to lighten it, then gently fold in the remainder, using a large metal spoon. Divide the mixture among six 150ml (¼ pint) ramekins or ovenproof tea or coffee cups. Stand them on the hot baking sheet and bake for about 12 minutes or until puffed up.

5 Dust the soufflés with a little sifted icing sugar or cocoa powder and serve immediately.

Serves 6

Serves 6

Dark Chocolate Soufflés

Preparation Time
20 minutes
Cooking Time
20 minutes, plus cooling

- 50g (2oz) plain chocolate (at least 70% cocoa solids), broken into pieces
- 2 tbsp cornflour
- 1 tbsp cocoa powder
- 1 tsp instant coffee granules
- 4 tbsp golden caster sugar
- 150ml (¼ pint) skimmed milk
- 2 medium eggs, separated, plus 1 egg white

NUTRITIONAL INFORMATION

Per Serving 134 calories, 4g fat (of which 2g saturates), 22g carbohydrate, 0.1g salt

1 Preheat the oven to 190°C (170°C fan oven) mark 5 and put a baking sheet inside to heat up. Put the chocolate into a pan with the cornflour, cocoa powder, coffee, 1 tbsp sugar and the milk. Warm gently to melt the chocolate. Increase the heat and stir until the mixture thickens. Leave to cool a little, then stir in the egg yolks. Cover with a piece of damp greaseproof paper.

2 Whisk the egg whites in a clean, grease-free bowl until soft peaks form. Gradually whisk in the remaining sugar until the mixture is stiff.

3 Stir one-third of the egg whites into the chocolate mixture. Fold in the remaining whites and divide among six 150ml (¼ pint) ramekins. Put the ramekins on a baking sheet and bake for 12 minutes or until well risen. Serve immediately.

Try Something Different

Use flavoured plain chocolate for an unusual twist, such as ginger, mint or even chilli.

Chocolate Cherry Roll

Preparation Time
30 minutes
Cooking Time
30 minutes, plus cooling

- 4 tbsp cocoa powder, plus extra to dust
- 100ml (3½fl oz) milk, plus 3 tbsp extra
- 5 medium eggs, separated
- 125g (4oz) golden caster sugar
- 1–2 tbsp cherry jam
- 400g can pitted cherries, drained and chopped
- icing sugar to dust

NUTRITIONAL INFORMATION
Per Serving 185 calories, 5g fat (of which 2g saturates), 30g carbohydrate, 0.3g salt

Serves 8
A Little Effort

1 Preheat the oven to 180°C (160°C fan oven) mark 4. Line a 30.5 × 20.5cm (12 × 8in) Swiss roll tin with baking parchment. Mix the cocoa and 3 tbsp milk together in a bowl. Heat 100ml (3½fl oz) milk in a pan until almost boiling, then add to the bowl, stirring. Leave to cool for 10 minutes.

2 Whisk the egg whites in a clean grease-free bowl until soft peaks form. In a separate bowl, whisk together the egg yolks and caster sugar until pale and thick. Gradually whisk in the cooled milk, then fold in the egg whites. Spoon the mixture into the prepared tin and smooth the surface. Bake in the oven for 25 minutes or until just firm.

3 Turn out on to a board lined with baking parchment and peel off the lining parchment. Cover with a damp teatowel.

4 Spread the jam over the sponge and top with the cherries. Roll up from the shortest end, dust with cocoa and icing sugar, then cut into slices and serve.

Elderflower & Fruit Jelly

Preparation Time 15 minutes, plus chilling
Cooking Time 10 minutes, plus cooling

- 2–3 tbsp elderflower cordial
- 200g (7oz) caster sugar
- 4 gelatine leaves (see Cook's Tip)
- 150g (5oz) raspberries
- 150g (5oz) seedless grapes, halved

NUTRITIONAL INFORMATION

Per Serving 189 calories, 0g fat, 42g carbohydrate, 0g salt

Serves 6

Cook's Tip

- Gelatine is available in leaf and powdered forms. Both must be soaked in liquid to soften before being dissolved in a warm liquid. Always add dissolved gelatine to a mixture that is warm or at room temperature – if added to a cold liquid, it will set in fine threads and spoil the final texture of the dish.
- Gelatine is derived from meat bones, but there are also several vegetarian alternatives, such as agar agar and gelazone.

1 Put the elderflower cordial into a large pan and add 750ml (1¼ pints) water and the sugar. Heat gently, stirring to dissolve the sugar.

2 Soak the gelatine leaves in cold water for 5 minutes. Lift out the gelatine, squeeze out the excess water, then add to the liquid in the pan. Stir to dissolve, then strain into a jug.

3 Divide the raspberries and grapes among six 200ml (7fl oz) glass dishes. Pour the liquid over the fruit, then cool and chill in the fridge for at least 4 hours or overnight.

Lemon Sorbet

Preparation Time
10 minutes, plus chilling and freezing
Cooking Time
15 minutes, plus cooling

- 3 juicy lemons
- 125g (4oz) golden caster sugar
- 1 large egg white

NUTRITIONAL INFORMATION
Per Serving 130 calories, 0g fat, 33g carbohydrate, 0g salt,

1 Finely pare the lemon zest, using a zester, then squeeze the juice. Put the zest into a pan with the sugar and 350ml (12fl oz) water and heat gently until the sugar has dissolved. Increase the heat and boil for 10 minutes. Leave to cool.

2 Stir the lemon juice into the cooled sugar syrup. Cover and chill in the fridge for 30 minutes.

3 Strain the syrup through a fine sieve into a bowl. In another bowl, beat the egg white until just frothy, then whisk into the lemon mixture.

4 For best results, freeze in an ice-cream maker. (Alternatively, pour into a shallow freezerproof container and freeze until almost frozen; mash well with a fork and freeze until solid.) Transfer the sorbet to the fridge 30 minutes before serving to soften slightly.

Healthy Tip
This dessert contains virtually no fat so is a good option if you are on a low fat diet. The lemon juice is rich in vitamin C, as well as phytochemicals called limonoids and limonene, which have recognised cancer-fighting actions.

Try Something Different
Orange Sorbet Replace two of the lemons with oranges.
Lime Sorbet Replace two of the lemons with four limes.

Serves 4

Chocolate Cinnamon Sorbet

Preparation Time
5 minutes, plus chilling and freezing
Cooking Time
15 minutes, plus cooling

Serves 8

- 200g (7oz) golden granulated sugar
- 50g (2oz) unsweetened cocoa powder
- 1 tsp instant espresso coffee powder
- 1 cinnamon stick
- 8 tsp crème de cacao (chocolate liqueur) to serve (optional)

NUTRITIONAL INFORMATION

Per Serving 118 calories, 1g fat (of which 1g saturates), 27g carbohydrate, 0.2g salt

1 Put the sugar into a large pan and add the cocoa powder, coffee and cinnamon stick with 600ml (1 pint) water. Bring to the boil, stirring until the sugar has completely dissolved. Boil for 5 minutes, then remove from the heat. Leave to cool. Discard the cinnamon stick, then chill in the fridge.

2 If you have an ice-cream maker, put the mixture into it and churn for about 30 minutes until firm. (Alternatively, pour into a shallow freezerproof container and freeze until almost frozen; mash well with a fork and freeze for at least 1 hour or until solid.)

3 To serve, scoop the sorbet into individual cups and, if you like, drizzle 1 tsp chocolate liqueur over each portion. Serve immediately.

Instant Banana Ice Cream

Preparation Time
5 minutes, plus freezing

Serves 4

- 6 ripe bananas, about 700g (1½lb), peeled, cut into thin slices and frozen (see Cook's Tip)
- 1–2 tbsp virtually fat-free fromage frais
- 1–2 tbsp orange juice
- 1 tsp vanilla extract
- splash of rum or Cointreau (optional)
- a few drops of lime juice to taste

NUTRITIONAL INFORMATION
Per Serving 173 calories, 1g fat (of which 0g saturates), 42g carbohydrate, 0g salt

Cook's Tip
To freeze bananas, peel them and slice thinly, then put the banana slices on a large non-stick baking tray and put into the freezer for 30 minutes or until frozen. Transfer to a plastic bag and store in the freezer until needed.

1 Leave the frozen banana slices to stand at room temperature for 2–3 minutes. Put the still frozen pieces in a food processor or blender with 1 tbsp fromage frais, 1 tbsp orange juice, the vanilla extract and the liqueur, if using.

2 Whiz until smooth, scraping down the sides of the bowl and adding more fromage frais and orange juice as necessary to give a creamy consistency. Add lime juice to taste and serve at once or turn into a freezerproof container and freeze for up to one month.

Serves 8

Frozen Yogurt Sorbet

Preparation Time
15 minutes, plus freezing

- 450g (1lb) frozen mixed fruit, thawed, plus extra to serve
- 100g (3½oz) clear honey
- 3 medium egg whites
- 450g (1lb) low-fat Greek yogurt

NUTRITIONAL INFORMATION
Per Serving 120 calories, 6g fat (of which 3g saturates), 14g carbohydrate, 0.2g salt

1 Line a 750ml (1¼ pint) loaf tin with clingfilm. Whiz the thawed fruit in a food processor or blender to make a purée. Strain through a fine nylon sieve into a bowl, pressing all the juice through with the back of a spoon. Stir the honey into the juice.

2 Put the egg whites into a clean, grease-free bowl and whisk until soft peaks form, then fold into the fruit with the yogurt. Pour the mixture into the prepared tin and freeze for 4 hours. Stir to break up the ice crystals, then freeze again for 4 hours. Stir again, then freeze for a further 4 hours or until firm.

3 Transfer the sorbet to the fridge 20 minutes before serving. Turn out on to a serving plate and remove the clingfilm. Slice and serve with a spoonful of thawed fruit.

Healthy Tip

This is a low fat dessert that is also a good source of protein and calcium. Greek yogurt contains 10% fat but low fat varieties containing just 2% fat and fat-free varieties are also available. Frozen mixed fruit contains similar levels of vitamin C as fresh fruit.

Cook's Tip

Use any selection of frozen mixed fruit. Summer berries and forest fruits work well.

Zabaglione

Preparation Time
5 minutes
Cooking Time
20 minutes

- 4 medium egg yolks
- 100g (3½oz) caster sugar
- 100ml (3½fl oz) sweet Marsala wine

NUTRITIONAL INFORMATION

Per Serving 193 calories, 6g fat (of which 2g saturates), 28g carbohydrate, 0g salt

Serves 4

1 Heat a pan of water to boiling point. Put the egg yolks and sugar into a heatproof bowl large enough to rest over the pan without its base touching the water. With the bowl in place, reduce the heat so that the water is just simmering.

2 Using a hand-held electric whisk, whisk the yolks and sugar for 15 minutes until pale, thick and foaming. With the bowl still over the heat, gradually pour in the Marsala, whisking all the time.

3 Pour the zabaglione into four glasses or small coffee cups and serve immediately.

Cinnamon Pancakes

Preparation Time
5 minutes, plus standing
Cooking Time
20 minutes

- 150g (5oz) plain flour
- ½ tsp ground cinnamon
- 1 medium egg
- 300ml (½ pint) skimmed milk
- olive oil to fry
- fruit compote or sugar and Greek yogurt to serve

NUTRITIONAL INFORMATION
Per Serving 141 calories, 5g fat (of which 1g saturates), 20g carbohydrate, 0.1g salt

Try Something Different
Serve with sliced bananas and vanilla ice cream instead of the fruit compote and Greek yogurt.

1 Whisk the flour, cinnamon, egg and milk together in a large bowl to make a smooth batter. Leave to stand for 20 minutes.

2 Heat a heavy-based frying pan over a medium heat. When the pan is really hot, add 1 tsp oil, pour in a ladleful of batter and tilt the pan to coat the base with an even layer. Cook for 1 minute or until golden. Flip over and cook for 1 minute. Repeat with the remaining batter, adding more oil if necessary, to make six pancakes. Serve with a fruit compote or a sprinkling of sugar, and a dollop of yogurt.

Vitality Drinks

Banana Vitality Shake

Preparation Time
10 minutes

Serves 2, makes 600ml (1 pint)

- 25g (1oz) whole shelled almonds
- 1 large ripe banana
- 150ml (¼ pint) low-fat milk
- 150ml (¼ pint) low-fat plain yogurt
- 8g sachet powdered egg white
- 2 tsp wheatgerm
- 1–2 tsp maple syrup
- a pinch of freshly grated nutmeg

NUTRITIONAL INFORMATION

Per Serving 246 calories, 9g fat (of which 1 g saturates), 32g carbohydrate, 0.4g salt

Healthy Tip

A good source of protein, calcium, carbohydrates and B vitamins, this shake makes a highly nutritious supplement for regular exercisers. Almonds add healthy monounsaturated fats as well as vitamin E and iron.

1 Grind the almonds in a spice grinder or food processor – the mixture needs to be very fine to get a good blend.

2 Peel and roughly chop the banana, then put into a blender with the ground almonds. Add the milk, yogurt, powdered egg white and wheatgerm to the blender and whiz for a few seconds until smooth.

3 Add maple syrup to taste, then pour into two glasses and serve immediately, sprinkled with nutmeg.

Mega Vitamin C Tonic

Preparation Time
10 minutes

- 1 large orange
- 1 lemon
- 1 lime
- ½ pink grapefruit
- 1–2 tsp clear honey
- crushed ice
- slices of citrus fruit to decorate

NUTRITIONAL INFORMATION
Per Serving 144 calories, trace fat, 35g carbohydrate, 0g salt

Serves 1, makes 200ml (7fl oz)

Healthy Tip
As the name implies this drink is rich in antioxidant vitamin C, which helps maintain the immune system and promote healthy skin, blood vessels and gums. It's also rich in potassium and folate.

Try Something Different
For a refreshing, longer and less concentrated drink, divide this smoothie between two glasses and top up with sparkling mineral water.

1 Using a sharp knife, cut off the peel from all the citrus fruit, removing as much of the white pith as possible. Chop the flesh roughly, discarding any pips, and put into a blender.

2 Add the honey to taste and whiz for a few seconds until smooth.

3 Pour over crushed ice in a glass and decorate with citrus fruit to serve.

Busy Bee's Comforter

Preparation Time
5 minutes

- 2 lemons
- 150ml (¼ pint) full-fat plain or soya yogurt, at room temperature
- 1–2 tsp thick honey
- 2–3 tsp bee pollen grains or equivalent in capsule form (see Health Tip)

NUTRITIONAL INFORMATION

Per Serving 130 calories, 2g fat (of which 1g saturates), 24g carbohydrate, 0.3g salt

Healthy Tip

You can buy bee pollen grains at specialist food health shops and online. This drink is a very good source of protein and calcium. It contains honey, which is a source of slow-releasing sugars, and a powerful antibacterial and anti-viral ingredient.

Cook's Tip

Not suitable for those with an allergy to pollen, such as hayfever sufferers.

Try Something Different

Use oranges instead of lemons.

1 Using a sharp knife, cut off the peel from one lemon, removing as much of the white pith as possible. Chop the flesh roughly, discarding any pips, and put into a blender. Squeeze the juice from the remaining lemon and add to the blender.

2 Spoon in the yogurt and whiz until smooth. Taste and sweeten with honey as necessary. Stir in the bee pollen, then pour into a glass and serve immediately.

Strawberry & Camomile Calmer

Preparation Time
5 minutes, plus infusing and cooling

- 2 camomile teabags
- 5cm (2in) piece cinnamon stick
- 175g (6oz) strawberries
- 150ml (¼ pint) freshly pressed apple juice or 2 large dessert apples, juiced

NUTRITIONAL INFORMATION
Per Serving 52 calories, trace fat, 13g carbohydrate, 0g salt

Serves 2, Makes 600ml (1 pint)

Try Something Different
Camomile teabags are very convenient and easy to use, but freshly dried flowers will give a stronger flavour.

1 Put the teabags and cinnamon stick into a small heatproof jug and pour in 150ml (¼ pint) boiling water. Leave to infuse for 5 minutes, then discard the bags and cinnamon stick. Leave to cool.

2 When ready to serve, remove the hulls from the strawberries, then wash and pat the fruit dry with kitchen paper. Put into a blender.

3 Pour in the apple juice and cold camomile tea. Whiz for a few seconds until smooth. Pour into two tall glasses and serve.

Green Tea Pick-me-up

Preparation Time
10 minutes, plus infusing and cooling

- 1 tsp, or 1 teabag, Japanese green tea
- 1 ripe kiwi fruit
- 8 fresh lychees
- a few ice cubes

NUTRITIONAL INFORMATION
Per Serving 99 calories, trace fat, 24g carbohydrate, 0g salt

Serves 1, makes 300ml (½ pint)

Healthy Tip

Green tea is a powerhouse of polyphenols, which help counteract cancer-causing agents and lower the risk of heart disease. It may also help lower blood pressure and blood cholesterol. Kiwi fruit and lychees both add vitamin C.

Try Something Different

For extra zing, add a 5cm (2in) piece fresh root ginger, peeled and chopped, to the blender in step 2.

1 Put the tea or teabag into a heatproof jug and pour in 200ml (7fl oz) boiling water. Leave to infuse for 3 minutes, then strain to remove the tea leaves, or discard the teabag. Leave to cool.

2 When ready to serve, peel and roughly chop the kiwi fruit. Put into a blender. Peel the lychees, then cut in half and remove the stones.

3 Add to the blender with the cold tea. Whiz until smooth, then pour over ice in a glass to serve.

Raspberry Rascal Booster

Preparation Time
5 minutes

- 225g (8oz) raspberries, thawed if frozen, juices reserved
- 1 medium orange
- 2 tsp thick honey

NUTRITIONAL INFORMATION
Per Serving 147 calories, 1g fat (of which trace saturates), 33g carbohydrate, 0g salt

Serves 1, makes 300ml (½ pint)

Healthy Tip
This drink is bursting with vitamin C and anthocyanins, which help strengthen blood vessels and boost your immune system.

Cook's Tip
If you find this smoothie too thick, water it down a little.

1 If using fresh raspberries, remove the hulls, then wash and pat the fruit dry with kitchen paper. Put two raspberries to one side for decoration and put the rest into a blender. If the fruit has been frozen, add the juices as well.

2 Peel the orange, removing as much of the white pith as possible. Chop the flesh roughly, discarding any pips, and put into blender. Add the honey. Whiz until smooth, then pour into a glass, decorate with the raspberries and serve immediately.

Serves 1, makes 200ml (7fl oz)

Wheatgrass Juice

Preparation Time
10 minutes

- 25g (1oz) fresh parsley
- 25g (1oz) fresh coriander
- 75g (3oz) watercress
- 75g (3oz) cucumber
- 5cm (2in) round wheatgrass (see Cook's Tip)

NUTRITIONAL INFORMATION

Per Serving 43 calories, 2g fat (of which trace saturates), 3g carbohydrate, 0.1g salt

1 Wash and shake dry the herbs and watercress, then put into a blender.

2 Wash and pat the cucumber dry with kitchen paper. Peel if you like, then roughly chop and put into the blender.

3 Wash and shake the wheatgrass dry, then juice in a slow-turning or wheatgrass juicer. Add the juice to the cucumber and herbs. Whiz for a few seconds until well blended, then serve immediately, topped up with chilled water, if you like.

Healthy Tip

Wheatgrass is a concentrated source of vitamins A and C, calcium, potassium, zinc, magnesium and iron. The watercress, parsley and coriander also add folate and iron.

Cook's Tip

Wheatgrass deteriorates quickly, so to ensure that you are getting the freshest drink possible it should be juiced once everything else has been prepared. You can buy wheatgrass from a health-food shop and online; it is sold sprouting, in cartons like mustard and cress. Using scissors, snip the wheatgrass as close to the base as possible and measure it tightly bunched in 'rounds' like spaghetti – a 5cm (2in) round will yield about 50ml (2fl oz) juice.

Creamy Dairy-free Banana

Preparation Time
5 minutes

- 1 large ripe banana
- 125g (4oz) silken tofu, well chilled (see Cook's Tip)
- 175ml (6fl oz) unsweetened soya milk, well chilled
- 2 tsp thick honey
- a few drops of vanilla extract

NUTRITIONAL INFORMATION

Per Serving 238 calories, 8g fat (of which 1g saturates), 25g carbohydrate, 0.2g salt

Cook's Tip
Silken tofu is very smooth and is the best for blending in drinks. It is available fresh or vacuum-packed in cartons. Firmer types can be used but give a grainier texture when blended.

1 Peel the banana and slice thickly. Put into a blender.

2 Drain the tofu, mash lightly with a fork and add to the blender.

3 Pour in the milk and add the honey with a few drops of vanilla extract. Whiz for a few seconds until thick and smooth. Pour into a large glass and serve.

Apricot & Orange Smoothie

Preparation Time
5 minutes, plus chilling

- 400g (14oz) canned apricots in natural juice
- 150g (5oz) apricot yogurt
- 200–250ml (7–9fl oz) unsweetened orange juice

NUTRITIONAL INFORMATION
Per Serving 172 calories, 1g fat (of which trace saturates), 39g carbohydrate, 0.2g salt

Serves 2, makes about 450ml (¾ pint)

1 Put the apricots, yogurt and orange juice into a blender or food processor and whiz for 1 minute or until smooth.

2 Chill well, then pour into two glasses and serve.

Fruity Carrot with Ginger

Preparation Time
10 minutes

Serves 2, makes 400ml (14fl oz)

- 2 medium oranges
- 1cm (½in) piece fresh root ginger, peeled and roughly chopped
- 150ml (¼ pint) freshly pressed apple juice or 2 dessert apples, juiced
- 150ml (¼ pint) freshly pressed carrot juice or 3 medium carrots, 250g (9oz), juiced
- mint leaves to decorate

NUTRITIONAL INFORMATION
Per Serving 128 calories, 1g fat (of which trace saturates), 30g carbohydrate, 0.1g salt

Healthy Tip

This drink is full of vitamin C and betacarotene, making it a great immunity-boosting supplement. Fresh ginger is good for calming an upset stomach and providing relief from bloating and gas.

1 Using a sharp knife, cut a slice of orange and put to one side for the decoration. Cut off the peel from the oranges, removing as much of the white pith as possible. Chop the flesh roughly, discarding any pips, and put into a blender. Add the chopped ginger.

2 Pour in the apple and carrot juice and blend until smooth. Divide between two glasses, decorate with quartered orange slices and a mint leaf and serve.

Apple Crush

Preparation Time
5 minutes, plus freezing

- 175g (6oz) strawberries
- 150ml (¼ pint) freshly pressed apple juice or 2 dessert apples, juiced
- strawberry leaves or mint leaves to decorate

NUTRITIONAL INFORMATION
Per Serving 100 calories, trace fat, 24g carbohydrate, 0g salt

Serves 1, makes 300ml (½ pint)

Try Something Different
Use raspberries instead of strawberries.

1 Remove the hulls from the strawberries, then wash and pat the fruit dry with kitchen paper. Put on a tray and freeze for 40 minutes or until firm.

2 When ready to serve, put the frozen strawberries into a blender and pour in the juice. Blend until smooth and slushy. Pile into a serving glass and decorate with strawberry or mint leaves.

Cranberry Cooler

Preparation Time
2 minutes

- 75ml (3fl oz) cranberry juice
- ice cubes
- lemonade
- slice of lemon (optional)

NUTRITIONAL INFORMATION

Per Serving 51 calories, trace fat, 13g carbohydrate, 0g salt

1 Pour the cranberry juice into a tall glass half-filled with ice. Top up with lemonade, mix together quickly and finish with a slice of lemon, if you like. Serve immediately.

Healthy Tip

Cranberry juice is rich in vitamin C and anthocyanins, which help mop up harmful free radicals that damage cells and lead to heart disease. It also has unique 'anti-stick' properties that help ward off urinary tract infections, ulcers and gum disease.

Try Something Different

For a less sweet drink, double the amount of juice and top up with sparkling water.

Serves 1

Mango & Oat Smoothie

Preparation Time
5 minutes

- 150g (5oz) natural yogurt
- 1 small mango, peeled, stoned and chopped
- 2 tbsp oats
- 4 ice cubes

NUTRITIONAL INFORMATION

Per Serving 145 calories, 2g fat (of which 1g saturates), 27g carbohydrate, 0.2g salt

Serves 2

Healthy Tip

This oaty drink will help satisfy hunger for relatively few calories. The fibre in oats helps stabilise blood sugar levels, lower cholesterol and control the appetite. Mangoes add lots of betacarotene.

Try Something Different

Instead of mango, use 2 nectarines or peaches, or 175g (6oz) soft seasonal fruits such as raspberries, strawberries or blueberries.

1 Put the yogurt into a blender. Put a little chopped mango to one side for the decoration, if you like, and add the remaining mango, oats and ice cubes to the yogurt. Whiz until smooth. Serve immediately, decorated with chopped mango.

Summer Berry Smoothie

Preparation Time
10 minutes

Serves 6, Makes 900ml (1½ pints)

- 2 large ripe bananas, about 450g (1lb)
- 150g (5oz) plain yogurt
- 500g (1lb 2oz) fresh or frozen summer berries

NUTRITIONAL INFORMATION
Per Serving 108 calories, 1g fat (of which trace saturates), 24g carbohydrate, 0.1g salt

Try Something Different
Six ripe apricots or 16 ready-to-eat dried apricots or 400g (14oz) canned apricots in natural juice can be used instead of the berries.

1 Peel and chop the bananas, then put into a blender. Add the yogurt and 150ml (¼ pint) water, then whiz until smooth. Add the berries and whiz to a purée.

2 Strain the mixture through a fine nylon sieve into a large jug, using the back of a ladle to press it through the sieve. Pour into six glasses and serve immediately.

Index